MW00748851

ESSENTIAL EXERCISES
YEAR 5
MATHS

Authors

Jomary Roble B.Sc. Ed.

Warwick Marlin B.Sc. Dip.Ed.

Editors / Authors:
Warwick Marlin B.Sc. Dip.Ed.
Jomary Roble B.Sc. Ed.

Publisher:
Five Senses Education
ABN: 16 001 414437
2/195 Prospect Highway
Seven Hills NSW Australia 2147
sevenhills@fivesenseseducation.com.au
www.fivesenseseducation.com.au

Trade Enquiries:
Phone (02) 9838 9265
Fax (02) 9838 8982
Email: fsonline@fivesenseseducation.com.au

ISBN: 978-1-74130-784-9
1st Edition: November 2012
Copyright: Five Senses Education Pty. Ltd. © Warwick Marlin

All rights reserved: Except under the conditions described in the Copyright Act 1968 of Australia and subsequent amendments, no part of this book may be reproduced, stored in a retrieval system or transmitted in any form or by any means electronic, mechanical, photocopying, recording or otherwise, without the prior permission of the copyright owners.

AUTHOR'S ACKNOWLEDGEMENTS

To **Jomary Roble** my co-author

Jomary has a very sharp and analytical mind, and she has done a wonderful job in formulating the majority of these original and interesting mathematical questions. She is a person of many diverse talents, and she is a perfectionist in many of the varied tasks that she decides to undertake. It has been a pleasure and a privilege working with her on this project of 6 mathematics exercise work books, and I hope that we can work together on many more other titles in the future.

To **Jones** my typesetter

I have been working with Jones for almost a year now on the "Understanding Maths Series" of books. He has done so much excellent and brilliant work in translating our thoughts and ideas, and sometimes our messy hand written pages, into the final high standard of overall presentation shown in this new series of books. A patient and very professional man, he aims for, and achieves excellence in his work at all times. We hope Jones and his team will work with us on many more projects in the future.

To **Roger Furniss** my publisher

I have had an association with Roger for well over 15 years now, and I thank him most sincerely for publishing, distributing and recommending my books to teachers, parents and other educators. He has been in the publishing and retail industry for many years, and he knows much more about educational books than any other person that I know. Also a very special thanks to all the staff at **Five Senses Education** who have always proved over the years to be so cooperative, friendly and supportive.

To **Parents and Teachers**

I started writing the original "Understanding Maths Series" of books over 20 years ago, and during that time many hundreds of parents have either phoned us, or written into us, to tell us how these summary guides have helped their children in terms of better understanding and improved examination results. This is a special thanks for all those positive comments, and also to the many Mathematics teachers and other educators who are recommending our books to their students. I hope you will embrace our two new series (Essential Exercises and Understanding Maths) with the same positivity and enthusiasm.

AVAILABILITY OF BOOKS IN AUSTRALIA.....by the same Author/or Editor

All of the books below incorporate the same high presentation, format and philosophy. They can be purchased directly from Five Senses Education, but they are also available in many educational bookshops throughout NSW and Australia (and also some selected bookshops in New Zealand).

Understanding Maths Series

Understanding Year 1 Maths
Understanding Year 2 Maths
Understanding Year 3 Maths
Understanding Year 3 Maths (Advanced Edition)
Understanding Year 4 Maths
Understanding Year 4 Maths (Advanced Edition)
Understanding Year 5 Maths
Understanding Year 5 Maths (Advanced Edition)
Understanding Year 6 Maths
Understanding Year 6 Maths (Advanced Edition)
Understanding Year 7 Maths
Understanding Year 8 Maths
Understanding Year 9 Maths (Advanced Edition)
Understanding Year 9 & 10 Intermediate Maths
Understanding Year 9 & 10 Advanced Maths
Understanding Year 11 & 12 General Maths
Understanding Year 11 3 Units Maths
Understanding Year 12 3 Units Maths

Essential Exercises Series

Essential Exercises Year 1 Maths
Essential Exercises Year 2 Maths
Essential Exercises Year 3 Maths
Essential Exercises Year 4 Maths
Essential Exercises Year 5 Maths
Essential Exercises Year 6 Maths
Year 5 & 6 Scholarship Tests

Important Facts and Formulas Series

Important Facts and Formulas Year 7
Important Facts and Formulas Year 8
Important Facts and Formulas Year 9&10 Intermediate
Important Facts and Formulas Year 9&10 Advanced
Important Facts and Formulas Year 11 2/3 unit
Important Facts and Formulas Year 12 2/3 unit

Understanding Comprehension Series

Understanding Year 3 Comprehension
Understanding Year 4 Comprehension
Understanding Year 5 Comprehension
Understanding Year 6 Comprehension
Understanding Year 7 Comprehension
Understanding Year 8 Comprehension

For all educational needs, Five Senses Education is probably the largest supplier of educational books and learning aids in Australia.

For availability and all other information regarding the above titles:

Five Senses Education
2/195 Prospect Highway
Seven Hills Sydney NSW 2147

www.fivesenseseducation.com.au

www.understandingmaths.com

CONTENTS

NOTE: The New Australian National Curriculum has been split into 3 major strands:

Ⓐ Number & Algebra   Ⓑ Measurement & Geometry   Ⓒ Statistics & Probability

In the Year 5 content descriptions, these 3 major strands have been further subdivided into the sub-strands shown above.

Essential Exercises – Year 5 Maths
Warwick Marlin © Five Senses Education

THE NEW NATIONAL AUSTRALIAN CURRICULUM

The authors acknowledge the dedicated work of the Australian Curriculum Assessment and Reporting Authority (ACARA), and the many who have contributed to the development of the Australian curriculum in response to the aims of the 2008 Melbourne declaration on Educational Goals for Young Australians.

This book provides a summary and interpretation of their guidelines for those interested in developing mathematical understanding in Year 5 students.

The Australian National Curriculum, developed by ACARA, states that, by the end of Year 5, students should be able to do the following:

- identify and describe factors and multiples.
- use estimation and rounding to check if answers look reasonable.
- solve multiplication and division problems.
- compare, order and represent decimals.
- perform addition and subtraction of fractions with the same denominator.
- continue patterns with fractions and decimals.
- plan simple budgets.
- list the outcomes of chance experiments as fractions.
- pose questions to gather data.
- construct, describe and interpret different data sets.
- calculate perimeter and area of rectangles.
- connect and construct different angles.
- describe transformations of 2 dimensional shapes.
- describe the enlargement transformation.
- identify line and rotational symmetry.

THE MATHEMATICS CURRICULUM OPERATES ON ANOTHER LEVEL, THE SO CALLED PROFICIENCY LEVEL.

The Proficiency strands at this level include:

1. **Understanding:** the connecting of number calculations with counting sequences, partitioning and counting numbers flexibly, identifying and describing the relationship between addition and subtraction and between multiplication and division.
2. **Fluency:** the counting of numbers in sequences readily, using units iteratively to compare measurements, listing possible outcomes of chance events, describing and comparing time durations.
3. **Problem solving:** this includes formulating problems from authentic situations, making models and using number sentences that represent problem situations, planning routes on maps, and matching transformations with their original shape.
4. **Reasoning:** using known facts to derive strategies for unfamiliar calculations, comparing and contrasting related models of operations, describing connections between 2-D and 3-D representations, and creating and interpreting simple representations of data.

Understanding, Fluency, Problem Solving and Reasoning are a central part of Mathematics content across the three major strands as mentioned earlier (Number and Algebra, Measurement and Geometry, and Statistics and Probability).

SOME FEATURES AND BENEFITS OF THIS EXERCISE BOOK

The book has been divided into the 9 sub-strands as proposed by ACARA (Australian Curriculum Assessment and Reporting Authority) for the new National Curriculum. These sub-strands are listed on page v of the "Contents" page. Each of the sub-strands starts off by giving the ACARA references, and explains what the student is expected to know by the end of Year 5 in that particular sub-strand. This information is very useful to both teachers and parents to ensure that children are following and understanding the key points of the curriculum.

This is followed by a brief two page summary of some of the key ideas, words and important points that are covered in the exercises to follow. This is a two page synopsis of the sub-strand only, in order to quickly refresh the minds of parents and students on the most important words and ideas that will follow. Please remember that this book is primarily a book of graded exercises to help students of all ability groups practice their understanding and skills. For a more in-depth explanation of each sub-strand, parents are advised to look at the thicker and more comprehensive "Understanding Maths Series" by the same publisher and editor.

This two page summary for every sub-strand is then followed by:

LEVEL 1: 2 pages of easier questions

LEVEL 2: 2 pages of average questions

All students should try to complete at least the first 3 levels. The last 2 levels are aimed at keener and more gifted students.

LEVEL 3: 2 pages of average problem solving questions

LEVEL 4: 2 pages of difficult questions (to test and challenge the more talented students)

LEVEL 5: 2 pages of difficult problem solving questions (to test and extend the more talented students)

Note: Problem solving questions are playing an increasingly important role in the study of mathematics. These sentence type questions are not straight forward, and they usually require the student to interpret the information given, and then use several different thinking skills to solve the problem. Most testing and examination procedures now have a section of questions relating to problem solving skills.

As you can see from above, the comprehensive range of graded exercises are intended to benefit and challenge the majority of ability groups to be found throughout Australia. All students should try to complete the first three levels of each sub-strand, because completion of these levels will show a good overall grasp and understanding of the concepts involved. The last two levels are primarily aimed at the students who are keener and more talented in mathematics. If a student completes all the exercises relatively quickly, then it is recommended that they wait for a few months and then practice on them again, or alternatively go onto the next more challenging book in this series.

Essential Exercises – Year 5 Maths
Warwick Marlin © Five Senses Education

CALCULATORS AND COMPUTERS

CALCULATORS are useful tools, giving opportunities, for example, to check whether or not an answer is correct, to explore number patterns and place value, to develop problem solving skills, etc.

* Calculators can be used to check if an answer is correct or reasonable.
* They allow children to take risks and experiment with numbers privately.
* Playing with calculators gives opportunities for discovery, often stimulating learning and interest in mathcmatical processes.
* Calculators quickly provide answers allowing children to work through a problem involving large numbers which would otherwise require unnecessarily time-consuming and unwieldy pencil and paper calculations. The most important part of problem solving is understanding which operation or process is used to get the answer.
* Calculators empower children who have difficulty manipulating numbers but who, nevertheless, understand which operations are required to solve a problem.

There are however four points which must be made.

1. With simpler problems, the brain is often quicker than the calculator.
2. It is easy to press a wrong key, so it is essential to estimate the answer to ensure the calculator's answer is a reasonable one to a particular problem.
3. If a child does not know which operation, or series of operations, is needed, a calculator is useless. It does as it's told!
4. Calculators do not eliminate the need to thoroughly know addition / subtraction facts or times tables!

COMPUTERS provide access to many websites, thus giving unlimited practice with a particular mathematical concept, and allowing children to explore Mathematics at a greater depth and to develop problems solving skills and special awareness.

Many programs allow children to take risks and explore alternative strategies. They involve decision making and interpretation of information, often involving analysis and evaluation.
Word processing and design programs can be used effectively to improve presentation. Graphing, data bases and spread sheets provide links with other curriculum areas.

In summary, the author fully acknowledges that, if used correctly, internet technology can enhance learning and complement basic learning skills. However, due to the very large range and diversity of calculators and computers in the market place, each with their own different function keys, it is almost impossible in this type of summary book to incorporate them into the exercises. Also the author feels strongly, particularly in these early years of schooling, that a thorough understanding of the fundamentals of mathematics is far more important than knowing which buttons to press. Consequently there is very little mention of calculators and computers in this book, and most exercises are meant to be completed WITHOUT THE AID OF CALCULATORS.

YEAR 5
ESSENTIAL EXERCISES

NUMBER AND PLACE VALUE

The "Australian Curriculum Mathematics" (ACM) references for this sub-strand of "Number and Algebra" (NA) are below:

 Identify and describe factors and multiples of whole numbers and use them to solve problems (ACMNA 098).

 Use estimation and rounding to check the reasonableness of answers to calculations (ACMNA 099).

 Solve problems involving multiplication of large numbers by one or two-digit numbers using efficient mental or written strategies, and appropriate digital technologies (ACMNA 100).

 Solve problems involving division by a one digit number, including those that result in a remainder (ACMNA 101).

 Use efficient mental or written strategies and appropriate digital technologies to solve problems (ACMNA 291).

❖ PLACE VALUE

Our number system today is based on the Hindu-Arabic system where the **VALUE** of a number is determined by its **PLACE** in a particular column.

Example: What does 34 972 really mean?

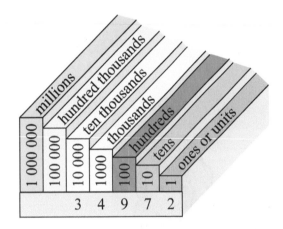

The place value of 3 is $3 \times 10\ 000$ or 30 000.

The place value of 4 is $4 \times 1\ 000$ or 4 000.

The place value of 9 is 9×100 or 900.

The place value of 10 is 7×10 or 70.

The place value of 2 is 2×1 or 2.

It can be seen that each column has a different PLACE VALUE.

❖ 3 MAIN WAYS OF DESCRIBING A NUMBER

1. As an ordinary numeral: 34 972.

2. In words: Thirty Four thousand, nine hundred and seventy two.

3. In expanded notation: $(3 \times 10\ 000) + (4 \times 1\ 000) + (9 \times 100) + (7 \times 10) + (2 \times 1)$.

Note: We can also describe numbers using Base Ten blocks, the abacus, and numeral expanders.

FACTORS

A factor is a number which leaves no remainder after division.

The factors of 12 are { 1, 2, 3, 4, 6, 12}.

 HIGHEST COMMON FACTOR (HCF)

This is the highest factor which is common to 2 or more numbers.

Example: Find the highest common factor of 12 and 20.
          Factors of 12 are {1, 2, 3, 4, 6, 12}.
          Factors of 20 are {1, 2, 4, 5, 10, 20}.
          ∴ The HCF of 12 and 20 is 4.

 MULTIPLES

To find the multiples of a particular counting number, simply multiply it by the counting numbers.

Say we wished to find the first 5 multiples of 7.

$1 \times 7 = 7$
$2 \times 7 = 14$
$3 \times 7 = 21$
$4 \times 7 = 28$
$5 \times 7 = 35$

OR
We can draw a WEB:

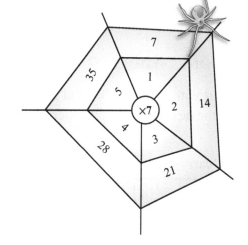

The first 5 multiples of 7 are {7, 14, 21, 28, 35}.

 LOWEST COMMON MULTIPLE (LCM)

This is the lowest multiple which is common to 2 or more numbers.

Example: Find the LCM of 8 and 10.
          Multiples of 8 are {8, 16, 24, 32, 40, 48,....}.
          Multiples of 10 are {10, 20, 30, 40, 50,....}.
          ∴ The LCM of 8 and 10 is 40.

 AVERAGE

The average of a set of scores is obtained by finding the total, and dividing by the number of scores.

The average of 7, 11 and 15 $= \dfrac{7 + 11 + 15}{3} = \dfrac{33}{3} = 11.$

Please refer to page 124 for a more detailed explanation.

Year 5 Essential Exercises
Warwick Marlin © Five Senses Education

ROUNDING OFF

In some situations in Maths, particularly when using a calculator, we do not require the exact answer, but an approximate answer only. The question will then ask you to ROUND OFF the given number to the nearest ten, nearest hundred or nearest thousand.

Example:
If we round off 73 to the nearest ten, then the answer is 70, because 73 is closer to 70 than it is to 80.
If we round off 659 to the nearest hundred, then the answer is 700, because 659 is closer to 700 than it is to 600.

 ESTIMATING

When using a calculator, you will be surprised how easy it is to press the wrong button and then get a ridiculous answer which is way out from the correct answer. If we quickly and mentally estimate an approximate answer to begin with, then this will prevent us from making careless blunders.
Estimate the answer to 469 + 1 728
469 rounds off to 500.
1 728 rounds off to 1 700.
Therefore ESTIMATE = 500 + 1 700
= 2 200

 ADDING WHOLE NUMBERS (+ SIGN)

Start with the far right hand column of digits. Add them up and place the 'carry over' at the top of the next column in smaller print, as shown in the example below.

'carry over numbers'

$$
\begin{array}{r}
^1\,^1\,^2\,^1\quad\ \\
7\,6\,8\,3 \\
5\,9\,4 \\
+\,8\,6\,3\,7\,5 \\
\hline
9\,4\,6\,5\,2
\end{array}
$$

Step 1 : 3 + 4 + 5 = 12. Write down the number 2 and place the carry over ① at the top of the next column.

Step 2 : 1 + 8 + 9 + 7 = 25. Write down the number 5 and place the carry over ② at the top of the next column.

Repeat these steps for the next 3 columns as shown.

SUBTRACTING WHOLE NUMBERS (– SIGN)

The most popular and widely used method is called "TRADING" or "DECOMPOSITION".

$$
\begin{array}{c}
\text{H T U} \\
^4\ ^1\quad \\
\not{5}\,2\,9 \\
-\,3\,8\,4 \\
\hline
1\,4\,5
\end{array}
$$

In the first unit column, 9 subtract 4 = 5
In the second tens column, 2 cannot subtract 8.
We trade one hundred from the hundreds column and change the 5 into a 4 as shown. We now have 12 in the tens column. 12 subtract 8 = 4, and finally in the hundreds column, 4 – 3 = 1.

MULTIPLYING WHOLE NUMBERS (× SIGN)

When multiplying whole numbers by 10 or 100 or 1 000 simple add on one, two or three zeros onto the end of the whole number. For other multiplications, follow the steps shown in the example below.

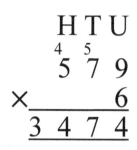

STEPS:

(i)   6 × 9 = 54.
(ii) Write down 4 and carry over 5.
(iii) 6 × 7 = 42 plus 5 = 47.
(iv) Write down 7 and carry over 4.
(v)   6 × 5 = 30 plus 4 = 34.
(vi) Write down 34.

 DIVIDING WHOLE NUMBERS ($\overline{)}$ or ÷ SIGN)

Divisor $\overline{)\text{Dividend}}$ = Quotient + Remainder

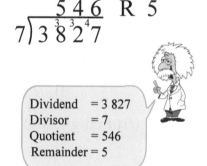

Dividend = 3 827
Divisor   = 7
Quotient = 546
Remainder = 5

STEPS:

(i)   7 will not divide into 3.
(ii) Carry the 3 over to make 38.
(iii) 7 divides into 38 five times, plus remainder 3
(iv) Carry the 3 over to make 32.
(v)   7 divides into 32 four times, plus remainder 4.
(vi) Carry the 4 over to make 47.
(vii) 7 divides into 47 six times, plus remainder 5.

 PROBLEM SOLVING (See "Appendix" for some strategies)

Problem solving questions are becoming an increasingly important part of the Mathematics syllabus. These sentence type questions are not straight forward, and they usually require the student to interpret the information given, and then to use one or more thinking skills to solve the problem. It will also often involve 2 or more operations (+, −, ×, ÷) to find the solutions. Some important strategies for 'Problem Solving' are to be found in chapter 1 of the 'Understanding Year 5 Maths'. Students should also have an understanding of the meaning of some important words given below:

Sum, difference, product, quotient, descending, ascending, average (see page 123)

 For further reference, see 'Understanding Year 5 Maths' by W. Marlin

Year 5 Essential Exercises
Warwick Marlin © Five Senses Education

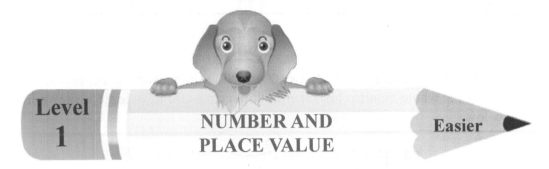

Q1. Write the number shown on each abacus below:

a)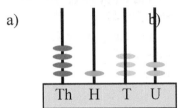

b)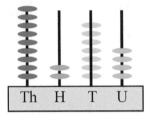

c)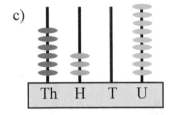

Q2. Write the following numbers on the place value chart shown:

a) 7 531   b) 6 284

c) 5 076   d) 4 309

Thousands	Hundreds	Tens	Units

Q3. What is the place value of 3 in the following:

a) 432   b) 73   c) 3 168   d) 7 391

Q4. Write the following numbers in descending order (from highest to lowest):

a) 7 312, 7 132, 7 321, 7 231, 7 123

b) 4 609, 4 690, 4 096, 4 906, 4 069

Q5. Write the following numbers in words:

a) 1 097   b) 3 592   c) 6 803   d) 2 560

Q6. Write the following numbers as ordinary numerals:
a) Four thousand, six hundred and forty eight
b) Two thousand, seven hundred and five

Q7. Write the following numbers as ordinary numerals:
a) $(4 \times 1\,000) + (8 \times 100) + (6 \times 10) + (3 \times 1)$
b) $(7 \times 1\,000) + (4 \times 100) + (9 \times 10) + (8 \times 1)$

Q8. Write the following numbers in expanded notation (this is the reverse of Q7. above):

a) 2 498   b) 5 365   c) 6 803   d) 9 760

Q9. List all the factors of the following:

a) 8   b) 10   c) 20   d) 17

Q10. The listings you did in Q9. should help you to find the highest common factor (HCF) of the following pairs of numbers:

a) 8 and 10   b) 8 and 20   c) 10 and 20   d) 10 and 15

Q11. a) List the first four multiples of 10.
     b) List the first six multiples of 4.
     c) List the first five multiples of 6.

Q12. The listings you did in Q9. should help you to find the lowest common multiple (LCM) of the following pairs of numbers:

a) 4 and 10   b) 4 and 6   c) 6 and 10

Q13. a) Is 67 closer to 60 or 70? Now round off 67 to the nearest 10.
     b) Is 143 closer to 140 or 150? Now round off 143 to the nearest 10.
     c) Is 95 closer to 90 or 100? Now round off 95 to the nearest 10.

Q14. In this question, do not find the exact answers. Firstly in your head, round each number off, and then give an ESTIMATE of the answer.
     In a) and b) round off to the nearest hundred first, and in c) and d) round off to the nearest ten first.

a) $497 + 308$ b) $602 - 389$

c) 89×11 d) $53 \div 9$

Try not to use a calculator in the following 4 questions.

Q15. Find:

a)   387   b)   694   c)   2 483   d)   5 479
     $+ 295$ $+ 127$ $+ 3 347$ $+ 2 586$

Q16. Find:

a)   879   b)   996   c)   3 574   d)   7 692
     $- 365$ $- 546$ $- 1 239$ $- 4 468$

Q17. Find:

a)   97   b)   89   c)   363   d)   569
     $\times\ 3$ $\times\ 6$ $\times\ 8$ $\times\ 7$

Q18. Find:

a) $7\overline{)84}$ b) $3\overline{)54}$ c) $5\overline{)85}$ d) $7\overline{)30}$

Year 5 Essential Exercises
Warwick Marlin © Five Senses Education

Q1. Find the value for each underlined digit in the numbers below:

    a) 5 9<u>7</u>3   b) <u>3</u> 821   c) <u>26</u> 915   d) 39 <u>4</u>18

Q2. Write the following numbers in ascending order (lowest to highest)

    a) 4 312, 4 213, 4 123, 4 321, 4 231   b) 6 789, 6 879, 6 978, 6 897, 6 798

Q3. Write the following numerals in words:

    a) 752   b) 1 006   c) 23 789   d) 18 074

Q4. Write the following numbers as ordinary numerals:

    a) Seven thousand, two hundred and five
    b) Thirty nine thousand, eight hundred and twenty three

Q5. Write the following numbers as ordinary numerals:

    a) $(8×1\,000) + (3×100) + (5×1)$
    b) $(4×10\,000) + (9×100) + (6×10) + (7×1)$

Q6. Write the following numbers in expanded notation (the reverse of Q5. above):

    a) 7 305   b) 6 082   c) 13 049   d) 10 073

Q7. For each abacus below, write the numeral and also the numeral in expanded notation:

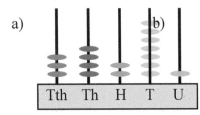 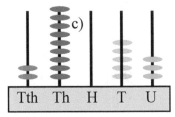 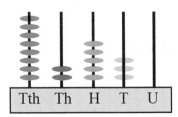

Q8. List all the factors of the following numbers:

    a) 12   b) 20   c) 29   d) 24

Q9. a) List the first four multiples of 9.
    b) List the first five multiples of 8.
    c) List all the multiples of 3 between 20 and 31.

Q10 a) List all the factors of 18.
    b) List all the factors of 27.
    c) What is the highest common factor (HCF) of 18 and 27?

Q11. Find the highest common factor (HCF) of the following pairs of numbers. (**Hint:** Some of your listings from Q8. will be useful.)

    a) 12 and 20   b) 20 and 24   c) 36 and 48

Q12. Find the lowest common multiple (LCM) of the following pairs of numbers:

    a) 5 and 8   b) 9 and 15   c) 8 and 14

Q13. Round off each number below to the nearest ten, and then ESTIMATE the final answer.

    a) $157 + 42$ b) $94 - 38$ c) $174 - 52$

    Round off ☐ + ☐   Round off ☐ – ☐   Round off ☐ – ☐

    Estimate =   Estimate =   Estimate =

Q14. Round off each number below to the nearest hundred, and then ESTIMATE the final answer.

    a) $426 + 189$ b) $853 - 248$ c) $761 + 928$

    Round off ☐ + ☐   Round off ☐ – ☐   Round off ☐ + ☐

    Estimate =   Estimate =   Estimate =

Q15. Find:

    a) $135 + 269$ b) $784 + 359$ c) $498 + 746$ d) $758 + 999$

Q16. Find:

    a) $938 - 425$ b) $327 - 145$ c) $674 - 379$ d) $427 - 358$

Q17. Find:

    a) 374×8 b) 678×9 c) 453×12 d) 692×23

Q18. Find:

    a) $7\overline{)91}$ b) $6\overline{)1158}$ c) $8\overline{)5913}$ d) $5\overline{)2453}$

Q19. Use a quick method to do the following multiplications:

    a) 10×27 b) 10×318 c) 100×48 d) $1\,000 \times 73$

Q20. Use Maths symbols to show the following (Revise page 123 first):
    a) 9 is not equal to 12   b) 6 is less than the sum of 3 and 4
    c) Therefore, the square of 5 is 25.   d) 18 is greater than the product of 3 and 5
    e) The quotient of 12 and 3 is less   f) Therefore, the letter x = 10
       than or equal to 4

Year 5 Essential Exercises
Warwick Marlin © Five Senses Education

NUMBER AND PLACE VALUE

Average

PROBLEM SOLVING

Q1. There were 135 people at the wedding. If there were 11 more ladies than men, how many men were attending?

Q2. Tom bought 3 075 paving stones to make a footpath. If he only uses 2 798 of them, how many were left over?

Q3. I am taking a slow drive from Sydney to the Sunshine Coast. I drive 389 km on the first day, 249 km on the second day and 436 km on the final third day.
a) How long was the complete trip?
b) What is the average amount of kilometres (km) that I travelled each day?

Q4. If my odometer reading showed 43 073 km at the beginning of my trip (from previous question), what would it show at the end of the three day trip?

43 073

Q5. A small lotto prize win of $13 824 has to be equally shared among the 8 members of the syndicate. How much will each person receive?

Q6. A brick layer can lay 140 bricks each hour.
a) How many bricks will he lay in a 7 hour working day?
b) If he works like this, how many bricks will he lay in a 5 day working week?

Q7. Stephanie used her cell phone 7 145 times last year. Each call costs 8 cents. By rounding off 7 145 to the nearest thousand, and rounding off 8 cents to the nearest 10, ESTIMATE how much Stephanie spent on calls last year?

Q8. Trin scored 87%, 73% and 68% in three different spelling tests. What was her average mark?

 87% 73% 68%

Q9. A machine at a factory makes bottle openers. If it makes 138 each day, how many will it make during a six day working week?

Q10. Zac loves to text his friends. If he sends out at least 7 text messages each day, how many messages will he send out in one full year (365 days)?

Q11. Mount Everest, the highest mountain in the world, has a height of 8 850 m. The climbing team managed to climb 2 731 m on the first day, and 1 846 m on the second day. How much further did they have to climb?

Q12. Jude is practicing for a cycle race. He wants to ride a total of 1 000 km every week in training. On Monday, he cycles 83 km, Tuesday 129 km and Wednesday 96 km. How many more kilometres does he have to cycle during the rest of the week to keep his goal alive?

Q13. Judy has saved $180. This is four times as much as her younger sister Sue. How much have both of them saved in total?

Q14. Using a quick and clever method, find the sum of the following numbers:

$$7 + 8 + 9 + 7 + 8 + 9 + 7 + 8 + 9 + 7 + 8 + 9 + 7 + 8 + 9 + 7 + 8 + 9$$

Q15. At the last one day cricket international 9 780 spectators attended. Each ticket cost $9.45. By rounding off the spectators to the nearest thousand, and the cost of each ticket to the nearest dollar, ESTIMATE how much the total ticket takings were?

Q16. Kate is 5 years older than Jess. Twice Kate's age plus three times Jess's age add up to 75. What are the ages of Kate and Jess?

Q17. Find two numbers that multiply to give 24, but at the same time, these two numbers must also add up to give 11.

Q18. Find: a) Product of 10 and 23   b) Sum of 1 482 and 3 976
            c) Quotient of 85 and 7   d) Difference of 3 821 and 1 963
            e) 9 squared   f) 4 cubed
            g) Average of 12 and 20   h) Decrease 3 712 by 1 584

Q19. a) Name all the ways that you can arrange the numbers 7, 8 and 9 without repeating any.
     b) Then list the numbers you found in decreasing order.
     c) What is the third largest number?

Q20. Susan earns $147 each day.
     a) How much does she earn in 5 days?
     b) If she pays $124 in tax and $28 in medicare, how much will she have left over to spend each week?

Q21. I am 36 years old now. In 4 years time, I will be twice as old as my son. How old is my son now?

Q22. A farmer sold 7 pigs at the auction for $369 each. He had to pay a stock agent $258 for selling them, and he also had to hire a special truck for $183 to take them to the market. How much did the farmer have left over after his sales and expenses?

Year 5 Essential Exercises
Warwick Marlin © Five Senses Education

Q1. Find the value for each underlined digit in the numbers below:
a) 7<u>3</u> 875   b) <u>2</u>4 359   c) <u>4</u>27 298   d) 27 <u>5</u>89

Q2. Write the following numbers as ordinary numerals:
a) $(5 \times 10\,000) + (7 \times 1\,000) + (2 \times 100) + (6 \times 10) + (9 \times 1)$
b) $(4 \times 100\,000) + (9 \times 10\,000) + (7 \times 100) + (8 \times 10) + (6 \times 1)$
c) $(7 \times 1\,000\,000) + (6 \times 100\,000) + (6 \times 1\,000) + (4 \times 100) + (3 \times 1)$
d) $(9 \times 1\,000\,000) + (6 \times 10\,000) + (7 \times 1\,000) + (4 \times 10) + (8 \times 1)$

Q3. Write the following numbers in expanded notation:
a) 7 325   b) 17 291   c) 1 034 701   d) 3 402 068

Q4. Write the following numbers in words:
a) 9 483   b) 17 291   c) 2 071 803   d) 18 306 027

Q5. Write the following as numerals:
a) Three thousand, eight hundred and five
b) Sixty eight thousand and twenty seven
c) Two million, three hundred and seventy four thousand, nine hundred and two

Numerals take up far less space, and are very much quicker to write than words.

Q6. Write the following numbers in ascending order:

25 765 389, 25 756 983, 25 657 398, 25 576 938, 25 765 398

Q7. Write the following numbers in descending order:

34 235 891, 34 325 981, 34 352 891, 34 532 198, 34 523 189

Q8. List all the factors of the following:
a) 40   b) 36   c) 45   d) 60

Q9. Find the highest common factor (HCF) of the following pairs of numbers:
a) 40 and 60   b) 40 and 36   c) 45 and 60   d) 36 and 45

Q10. a) List the first 6 multiples of 12.
b) List the first 7 multiples of 15.
c) List the first 5 multiples of 20.
d) List the multiples of 9 between 20 and 60.

Q11. Find the lowest common multiple (LCM) of the following pairs of numbers:
a) 12 and 18   b) 15 and 20   c) 14 and 21   d) 20 and 35

Q12. Round off the following numbers to the nearest 100:

a) 348   b) 728   c) 3 483   d) 7 250

Q13. Round off the following numbers to the nearest 1 000:

a) 7 349   b) 9 603   c) 4 500   d) 18 607

Q14. Firstly round off each of the following numbers to the nearest hundred, and then ESTIMATE the final answer:

a) 648 + 259   b) 739 − 452   c) 7 348 − 852   d) 641 × 78

Q15. Firstly round off each of the following numbers to the nearest ten and then ESTIMATE the final answer:

a) 792 − 203   b) 739 ÷ 8   c) 824 × 12   d) 1 618 + 783

Q16. Find: a) 931 + 8 926 + 14 039 + 27
                b) 17 821 + 987 + 3 574 + 2 589
                c) 36 + 7 832 + 19 087 + 5 369
                d) 271 + 34 712 + 16 + 2 094 + 8

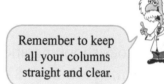

Remember to keep all your columns straight and clear.

Q17. Find:

a) 7 028 − 3 259   b) 6 734 − 4 789
c) 11 703 − 2 536   d) 14 381 − 7 426

Q18. Find:

a) 47 × 29   b) 127 × 15   c) 320 × 47   d) 639 × 78

Q19. Find:

a) 5 872 ÷ 8   b) 38 346 ÷ 7   c) 6 298 ÷ 5   d) 12 348 ÷ 9

Q20. Use a quick method to do the following:

a) 71 × 10   b) 38 × 100   c) 25 × 1 000   d) 230 ÷ 10

Q21. Find the value of the following:

a) 8 + 2 × 5   b) 16 + 10 ÷ 2
c) (8 + 2) × 5   d) 10 + 2 × 3 − 4
e) 8 × 3 − 2 × 4   f) 20 ÷ (2 + 3)
g) 10 − 4 × 2   h) 8 ÷ 2 + 3 × 4

Before doing this section please read about BODMAS on page 125.

Q22. a) Increase the product of 4 and 5 by 13
        b) What is the difference between the square of 7 and 13.
        c) Decrease the quotient of 63 and 7 by 9
        d) The sum of 8 and 12 is increased by the quotient of 40 and 5.

Year 5 Essential Exercises
Warwick Marlin © Five Senses Education

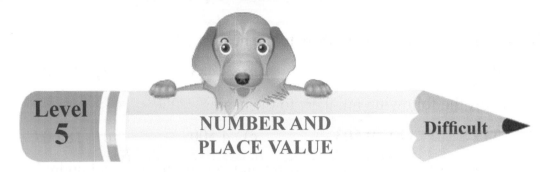

PROBLEM SOLVING

Q1. In the school library, there were 7 324 books in Room A, 4 547 books in Room B and 6 489 books in Room C.
   a) Round off each of the above quantities to the nearest thousand, and then ESTIMATE the total number of books altogether.
   b) Now find the exact total of the books in the 3 rooms.
   c) What is the average number of books in each room?
   d) The school has a goal to reach a total of 25 000 books in the library. How many more books do they still need?

Q2. Jinhi goes shopping and buys 4 mangoes at $2.85 each, a loaf of rye bread for $5.64, margarine for $3.45 and a bottle of peach jam for $6.87.
   a) Round off each amount to the nearest dollar, and ESTIMATE the total cost.
   b) Now find the exact total cost of the 4 items.
   c) What will her change be from $50.00?

Q3. Mr. & Mrs. Stanley took their 4 children to the movies. They spent a total of $60.00 for the 6 tickets. If the children were charged at one third of the adult price, what was the cost of each adult ticket?

Q4. Steve bought 3 hamburgers and 4 cokes for $18.50. The following day Malcolm went to the same shop and bought 4 hamburgers and 2 cokes for $20.50. How much is the cost of each item?

Q5. If ☐ + ☐ + △ = 73   The value of △ = ?
   and △ + △ + ☐ = 65   The value of ☐ = ?

Q6. A one-way train ticket costs $15.00. A return ticket costs $25.00. The total cash collected from the sale of 30 tickets was $530. How many return tickets were sold?

Q7. Josh and Jess took part in a multiple choice mathematics competition. Altogether there were 50 questions in the test. Each correct answer would be given 7 marks, but for each incorrect answer a 4 mark penalty would be deducted. The total score for both together was 370. If Jess made 4 extra mistakes compared to Josh, how many did Jess get correct?

Q8. After 6 cricket matches Ricky has a batting average of 21 runs per match. He wants to end the season with a batting average of 25 runs per match. How many runs will he have to score in the final 7th match to achieve his goal?

Q9. A group of bush walkers went on a 14 day hike up into the mountains. On a good sunny day they could walk 20 km in one day, but on a rainy day they could only manage 16 km. If they walked 260 km during the 2 weeks, how many days were fine and sunny.

Q10. James is 6 years older than his youngest sister Susan. Three times James's age plus 4 times Susan's age is equal to 123. What are the ages of James and Susan?

Q11. A farmer owns some cows and chickens. The legs of his animals total up to 142. However, if somehow all the cows turned into chickens, and all the chickens turned into cows, there would be a total of 176 legs. How many chickens and cows did he have?

Q12. Mr. & Mrs. Huang had five children. All five children married, and 3 of the couples had 4 children each, and two of the couples had 3 children each. How many were in the Huang family altogether?

Q13. I think of a number, multiply it by 9, then I subtract 8 and obtain a final answer of 55. What is the number I first thought of?

Q14. By using a quick method, find the sum of the first 50 odd numbers:

$1 + 3 + 5 + 7 + 9 + 11$ .... $+ 95 + 97 + 99$.

Explain how you got your answer.

Q15. $\overset{\text{Quotient + Remainder}}{\text{Divisor}\,\overline{)\text{Dividend}}}$ Find the dividend when the divisor $= 6$, quotient $= 628$ and remainder $= 2$.

Q16. If the sum of all the digits of a number can be divided by 3, the number is then divisible by 3.
By knowing this law find all the possible 1-digit numbers represented by ▢ so that the number 7 2 9 ▢ is divisible by 3.

This is a mathematical law about division.

Q17. 64 small cubes have been glued together to make one larger cube as shown below. This large cube is then painted all over. How many of the small cubes will have:

a) 3 sides painted?   b) 2 sides painted?
c) 1 side painted?   d) No sides painted?

Q18. Write the 6th smallest number using all the digits 6, 7, 8 and 9. However, no digit may be repeated.

Q19. I think a of certain number larger than 20, and when I divide it by 7 I get a remainder of 2. And when I divide the number by 4, I get a remainder of 1. What is the number?

Year 5 Essential Exercises
Warwick Marlin © Five Senses Education

FRACTIONS AND DECIMALS

The "Australian Curriculum Mathematics" (ACM) references for this sub-strand of "Number and Algebra" (NA) are below:

 Compare and order common unit fractions and locate and represent them on a number line (ACMNA 102).

 Investigate strategies to solve problems involving addition and subtraction of fractions with the same denominator (ACMNA 103).

 Recognize that the number system can be extended beyond hundredths (ACMNA 104).

 Compare, order and represent decimals (ACMNA 105).

❖ WHAT IS A FRACTION?

Everyday living doesn't only involve whole numbers. We often have to use part of whole numbers which we call FRACTIONS.

3 parts have been shaded out of 5 equal parts.
This is written in fraction form as:

$$\frac{3}{5} \quad \begin{array}{l} \leftarrow \text{numerator (is the top part)} \\ \leftarrow \text{denominator (is the bottom part)} \end{array}$$

❖ EQUIVALENT FRACTIONS

These are obtained by multiplying or dividing both numerator and denominator by the same number.

$$\frac{1}{2} \quad = \quad \frac{2}{4} \quad = \quad \frac{4}{8}$$

Shading one half is the same as shading two quarters, and this is the same as shading four eighths.

❖ LOCATING FRACTIONS ON A NUMBER LINE

For this first section of work on simple fractions, we just use the number line from 0 to 1, and split this up into even parts or shares.

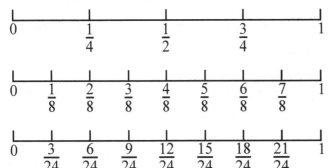

These 3 number lines show EQUIVALENT FRACTIONS.

Can you see from the number lines above that $\frac{1}{4} = \frac{2}{8} = \frac{6}{24}$?

You can also compare different fractions using the number line.

$\frac{3}{4}$ is bigger than $\frac{5}{8}$, or we can say $\frac{3}{4} > \frac{5}{8}$.

❖ **SIMPLIFYING FRACTIONS**

Both numerator and denominator must be divided by the same number - this is often called CANCELLING DOWN.

Example: $\frac{15}{18}$ simplifies to $\frac{5}{6}$ when dividing top and bottom by 3.

❖ **COMPARING FRACTIONS**

Step 1:   Firstly, make the denominators the same by using equivalent fractions.
Step 2:   Then compare the numerators.

Example: Which is larger out of $\frac{2}{5}$ and $\frac{3}{10}$?

$\frac{2}{5}$ can be written as $\frac{4}{10}$ and therefore it is the larger fraction.

❖ **TYPES OF FRACTIONS**

MIXED FRACTIONS have a whole number part and a fraction part: $2\frac{1}{4}$

IMPROPER FRACTIONS have a numerator larger than the denominator: $\frac{9}{4}$

$2\frac{1}{4}$ (two and a quarter)   = $\frac{9}{4}$ (nine quarters)

> Students must be able to convert from mixed to improper, and vice versa.

❖ **ADDING AND SUBTRACTING SIMPLE FRACTIONS**

Find $\frac{3}{10} + \frac{4}{10}$
Both fractions already have the same common denominator of 10, so the numerators can be simply added

$\frac{3}{10} + \frac{4}{10} = \frac{7}{10}$

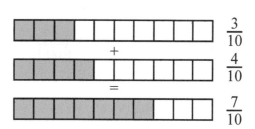

$\frac{3}{10}$

$+$

$\frac{4}{10}$

$=$

$\frac{7}{10}$

Examples: $\frac{7}{8} - \frac{1}{8} = \frac{6}{8}$ or $\frac{3}{4}$

$\frac{1}{4} + \frac{3}{8} = \frac{2}{8} + \frac{3}{8} = \frac{5}{8}$

$\frac{2}{3} - \frac{1}{2} = \frac{4}{6} - \frac{3}{6} = \frac{1}{6}$

Both fractions already have the same common denominator of 8.

First obtain a common denominator, then add numerators.

First obtain a common denominator, then subtract numerators.

❖ **FINDING THE FRACTION OF A QUANTITY**

The word 'OF' in Maths means 'Multiply'!
Examples: Find $\frac{1}{4}$ of apples means $\frac{1}{4} \times 12$ apples = 3 apples

Find $\frac{2}{3}$ of $15 means $\frac{2}{3} \times \$15 = \$10$

Year 5 Essential Exercises
Warwick Marlin © Five Senses Education

WHAT ARE DECIMALS?

Decimals are special fractions which have denominators of 10, 100, 1 000, etc.

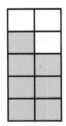

7 parts of 10 equal parts have been shaded.

As a FRACTION, we write $\frac{7}{10}$

As a DECIMAL, we write 0.7

 PLACE VALUE

What does 672.384 really mean?

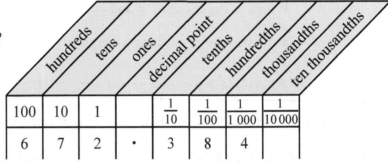

hundreds	tens	ones	decimal point	tenths	hundredths	thousandths	ten thousandths
100	10	1		$\frac{1}{10}$	$\frac{1}{100}$	$\frac{1}{1\,000}$	$\frac{1}{10\,000}$
6	7	2	•	3	8	4	

The numbers to the left of the decimal point have the same place value as reviewed in **WHOLE NUMBERS**. Each column to the right of the decimal point also has a special place value.

Place value of 3 is $3 \times \frac{1}{10} = \frac{3}{10}$

Place value of 8 is $8 \times \frac{1}{100} = \frac{8}{100}$

Place value of 4 is $4 \times \frac{1}{1\,000} = \frac{4}{1\,000}$

> The place value gets smaller as the columns go further to the right.

Therefore the decimal numbers 672.384 can be written in expanded notation as:

$$672.384 = (6 \times 100) + (7 \times 10) + (2 \times 1) + (3 \times \frac{1}{10}) + (8 \times \frac{1}{100}) + (4 \times \frac{1}{1\,000})$$

 ORDERING DECIMALS

Arranging numbers in **ASCENDING ORDER** means to place them in order from the smallest to the largest.
Arranging numbers in **DESCENDING ORDER** means to place them in order from largest to the smallest.

Example: Order the following numbers in descending order.

	15	15.1	15.01	15.101	15.11
Solution:	15.11	15.101	15.1	15.01	15

CHANGING DECIMALS TO FRACTIONS

For 1 figure after the decimal point, place the number over 10.
For 2 figures after the decimal point, place the number over 100.
For 3 figures after the decimal point, place the number over 1 000, etc.

Always end
by simplifying
where possible.

Examples: $0.6 = \dfrac{6}{10} = \dfrac{3}{5}$ $0.45 = \dfrac{45}{100} = \dfrac{9}{20}$

 CHANGING EASY FRACTIONS TO DECIMALS

Step 1:   Change the fractions to equivalent fractions with denominators of 10, 100 or 1 000.
Step 2.   Then simply convert the fraction to its equivalent decimal.

$\dfrac{2}{5}$ can be changed to an equivalent fraction of $\dfrac{4}{10} = 0.4$

$\dfrac{7}{20}$ can be changed to an equivalent fraction of $\dfrac{35}{100} = 0.35$

 THE 4 MAJOR OPERATIONS $(+ - \times \div)$

Students should know how to do these important operations with, and without, the aid of a calculator.

Examples: (i) $8.32 + 15.49 + 6.07 + 27.36$ (ii) $82.75 - 63.49$
            (iii) 6.31×2.4 (iv) $16.52 \div 4$

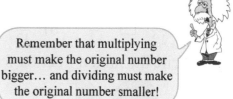 **MULTIPLYING AND DIVIDING DECIMALS BY POWERS OF 10**

When multiplying decimal by 10, 100 or 1 000 simply move the decimal point either 1, 2 or 3 places to the right.

$5.748 \times 100 = 574.8$

When dividing a decimal by 10, 100 or 1 000 simply move the decimal point 1, 2 or 3 places to the left.

Remember that multiplying
must make the original number
bigger... and dividing must make
the original number smaller!

$627.5 \div 10 = 62.75$

 DECIMAL CURRENCY

Dollars are placed in the whole numbers column.

Cents are placed in the hundredths column.

Five dollars and 14 cents is written $5.14.

All answers should be rounded off to 2 decimal places.

   For further reference, see 'Understanding Year 5 Maths' by W. Marlin

Year 5 Essential Exercises
Warwick Marlin © Five Senses Education

Q1. What fraction has been shaded in the figures below:

a)   b)   c)   d)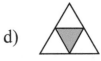

e)   f)   g)   h)

Q2. Change the following to equivalent fractions:

a) $\frac{1}{4} = \frac{\square}{8}$ b) $\frac{1}{2} = \frac{\square}{6}$ c) $\frac{2}{3} = \frac{\square}{6}$ d) $\frac{3}{4} = \frac{\square}{8}$

Q3. Simplify the following (Hint: divide the top and bottom of each fraction by 2):

a) $\frac{10}{12}$ b) $\frac{4}{6}$ c) $\frac{6}{10}$ d) $\frac{18}{20}$

Q4.

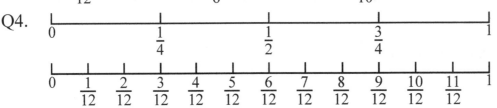

Using the number lines shown, write equivalent fractions for:

a) $\frac{1}{2}$ b) $\frac{1}{4}$ c) $\frac{3}{4}$

Q5. Using the number lines shown above, place one of the symbols (= or > or <) between each of the fractions below to make a true statement:

a) $\frac{7}{12} \square \frac{6}{12}$ b) $\frac{5}{12} \square \frac{1}{2}$ c) $\frac{10}{12} \square \frac{3}{4}$ d) $\frac{1}{4} \square \frac{3}{12}$

Q6. Write the mixed fraction for each of the shapes below:

a) 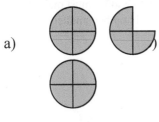   b)   c)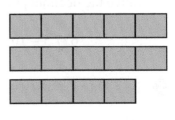

quarters   thirds   fifths

Q7. Write down the improper fraction for each of the shapes shown in Q6.

Q8. Find:

a) $\frac{1}{8} + \frac{4}{8}$ b) $\frac{9}{12} - \frac{2}{12}$ c) $\frac{3}{5} + \frac{1}{5}$ d) $\frac{6}{7} - \frac{2}{7}$

Q9. Change the mixed fractions to improper fractions (part has been done for you):

a) $1\frac{1}{4} = \frac{\square}{4}$ b) $2\frac{1}{3} = \frac{\square}{3}$ c) $3\frac{1}{2} = \frac{\square}{2}$ d) $2\frac{3}{5} = \frac{\square}{5}$

Q10. Change these improper fractions to mixed fractions (part has been done for you):

a) $\frac{7}{3} = 2\frac{\square}{3}$ b) $\frac{11}{4} = 2\frac{\square}{4}$ c) $\frac{9}{2} = 4\frac{\square}{2}$ d) $\frac{8}{5} = 1\frac{\square}{5}$

Q11. Write down the shaded area as a decimal:

a)  b)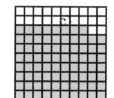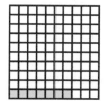

Q12. Write the decimal numeral for each abacus:

a) 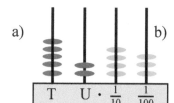 b) 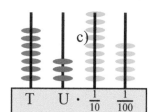 c)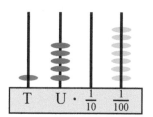

Q13. What is the place value of 8 in each of the following:

a) 67.38 b) 49.82 c) 127.318 d) 82.596

Q14. Write the following as decimals:

a) $\frac{9}{10}$ b) $\frac{41}{100}$ c) $\frac{8}{1\,000}$ d) $3\frac{17}{100}$

Q15. Write the following amounts of money as decimals:

a) 4 dollars and 18 cents b) 26 dollars and 8 cents
c) 9 dollars and 40 cents d) 27 cents

Q16. Write the following as decimals:

a) $(7 \times 100) + (8 \times 10) + (3 \times 1) + (4 \times \frac{1}{10}) + (9 \times \frac{1}{100}) + (2 \times \frac{1}{1\,000})$

b) $(8 \times 100) + (6 \times 10) + (7 \times \frac{1}{10}) + (5 \times \frac{1}{100}) + (9 \times \frac{1}{1000})$

c) $(6 \times 1\,000) + (4 \times 100) + (9 \times 1) + (8 \times \frac{1}{100}) + (3 \times \frac{1}{1\,000})$

Q17. Change the following decimals to fractions:

a) 0.7 b) 0.23 c) 0.593 d) 1.9

Year 5 Essential Exercises
Warwick Marlin © Five Senses Education

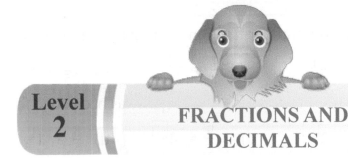

FRACTIONS AND DECIMALS

Level 2

Average

Q1. Redraw the figures below and shade in the amount shown:

a) Shade in $\frac{2}{5}$

b) Shade in $\frac{5}{8}$

c) Shade in $\frac{3}{5}$

d) Shade in $\frac{3}{4}$

Q2. Change the following to equivalent fractions:

a) $\frac{1}{4} = \frac{\square}{20}$

b) $\frac{2}{5} = \frac{\square}{15}$

c) $\frac{2}{3} = \frac{\square}{30}$

d) $\frac{3}{4} = \frac{\square}{12}$

Q3. Simplify the following fractions:

a) $\frac{8}{20}$

b) $\frac{12}{15}$

c) $\frac{15}{20}$

d) $\frac{21}{28}$

Q4.

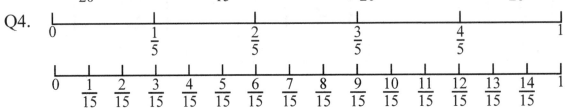

Using the number lines shown above, write equivalent fractions for the following:

a) $\frac{1}{5}$

b) $\frac{2}{5}$

c) $\frac{3}{5}$

d) $\frac{12}{15}$

Q5. Using the number lines shown in Q4. above, place one of the symbols (= or > or <) between each of the fractions below to make a true statement:

a) $\frac{2}{5} \square \frac{5}{15}$

b) $\frac{4}{5} \square \frac{12}{15}$

c) $\frac{8}{15} \square \frac{3}{5}$

d) $\frac{4}{5} \square \frac{11}{15}$

Q6. Write the improper fraction for each of the shapes below:

a) $\frac{1}{2}$ $\frac{1}{2}$ $\frac{1}{2}$ $\frac{1}{2}$ b) $\frac{1}{2}$

'halves'

'quarters'

| $\frac{1}{5}$ | $\frac{1}{5}$ | $\frac{1}{5}$ | $\frac{1}{5}$ | $\frac{1}{5}$ | $\frac{1}{5}$ |
| $\frac{1}{5}$ | $\frac{1}{5}$ | $\frac{1}{5}$ | $\frac{1}{5}$ | $\frac{1}{5}$ | $\frac{1}{5}$ |

'fifths'

Q7. Write the mixed fraction for each of the shapes in Q6.

Q8. Add the following fractions (**Hint:** Some answers will have to be changed to mixed fractions.):

a) $\frac{6}{8} + \frac{1}{8}$

b) $\frac{3}{15} + \frac{4}{15}$

c) $\frac{4}{5} + \frac{3}{5}$

d) $\frac{5}{7} + \frac{6}{7}$

Q9. Subtract the following fractions and simplify the final answers where possible:

a) $\frac{5}{9} - \frac{1}{9}$ b) $\frac{9}{10} - \frac{1}{10}$ c) $\frac{3}{4} - \frac{1}{4}$ d) $\frac{7}{12} - \frac{4}{12}$

Q10. Change the mixed fractions to improper fractions:

a) $1\frac{3}{4}$ b) $3\frac{2}{5}$ c) $2\frac{1}{2}$ d) $3\frac{4}{10}$

Q11. Change these improper fractions to mixed fractions:

a) $\frac{8}{3}$ b) $\frac{10}{5}$ c) $\frac{14}{5}$ d) $\frac{19}{4}$

Q12. Write the decimal numbers for each abacus:

a) 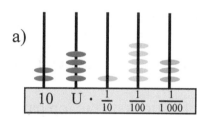 b) 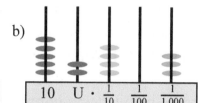 c)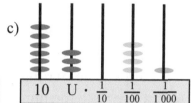

Q13. What is the place value of each underlined digit in the following:

a) 73.2<u>8</u>1 b) 645.30<u>2</u> c) <u>9</u>73.815 d) 64.<u>3</u>76

Q14. Write the following fractions as decimals:

a) $\frac{7}{10}$ b) $\frac{341}{1\,000}$ c) $3\frac{28}{100}$ d) $15\frac{6}{100}$

Q15. Write the following as decimals:

a) $(5 \times 1\,000) + (3 \times 100) + (8 \times 1) + (7 \times \frac{1}{10}) + (4 \times \frac{1}{100})$

b) $(9 \times 1\,000) + (6 \times 1) + (2 \times \frac{1}{10}) + (4 \times \frac{1}{100}) + (8 \times \frac{1}{1\,000})$

c) $(4 \times 1\,000) + (7 \times 10) + (6 \times \frac{1}{10}) + (9 \times \frac{1}{1\,000})$

Q16. Write the following decimals in expanded notation (reverse of Q15. above):

a) 5.96 b) 7.832 c) 39.604 d) 872.039

Q17. Write the following amounts of money as decimals:

a) 7 dollars and 28 cents b) 13 dollars and 6 cents

c) 59 cents d) 83 dollars

Q18. Write the following decimals in ascending order (from lowest to highest):

a) 7.813, 7.803, 7.831, 7.318, 7.138

b) 9.407, 9.417, 9.471, 9.147, 9.4

Q19. Change the following decimals to their equivalent fractions:

a) 0.9 b) 0.38 c) 1.92 d) 0.365

Year 5 Essential Exercises
Warwick Marlin © Five Senses Education

FRACTIONS AND DECIMALS

Average

PROBLEM SOLVING

Q1. James had 80 marbles. If he gave $\frac{1}{4}$ of them to his best friend, how many marbles did he give away?

Q2. Tracey went shopping and bought a dozen of eggs. If she gave $\frac{1}{3}$ of the eggs to her neighbour, how many eggs did she have left?

Q3. The spelling test was out of 24. If Annie got $\frac{7}{8}$ of the answers correct, how many did she get wrong?

Q4 Complete the number line below using improper fractions on the top part of the line, and mixed fractions on the bottom part of the line. Also where possible, simplify any mixed fractions on the bottom line.

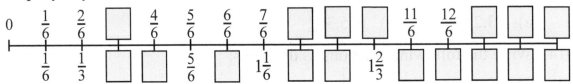

Q5. With the help of the number line in Q4. above, place one of the following signs (=, > or <) to make a true statement:

a) $\frac{1}{3}$ ☐ $\frac{3}{6}$

b) $\frac{13}{6}$ ☐ $2\frac{1}{6}$

c) $1\frac{2}{3}$ ☐ $\frac{9}{6}$

d) $\frac{14}{6}$ ☐ $2\frac{1}{3}$

Q6.

0 — $\frac{1}{12}$ — $\frac{1}{6}$ — $\frac{1}{4}$ — $\frac{1}{3}$ — $\frac{5}{12}$ — $\frac{1}{2}$ — $\frac{7}{12}$ — $\frac{2}{3}$ — $\frac{3}{4}$ — $\frac{5}{6}$ — $\frac{11}{12}$ — 1

0 — $\frac{1}{12}$ — $\frac{2}{12}$ — $\frac{3}{12}$ — $\frac{4}{12}$ — $\frac{5}{12}$ — $\frac{6}{12}$ — $\frac{7}{12}$ — $\frac{8}{12}$ — $\frac{9}{12}$ — $\frac{10}{12}$ — $\frac{11}{12}$ — 1

With the help of the 2 number lines shown above, briefly explain why

a) $\frac{1}{3} > \frac{1}{4}$

b) $\frac{5}{12} < \frac{1}{2}$

c) $\frac{3}{4} > \frac{2}{3}$

d) $\frac{5}{6} = \frac{10}{12}$

Q7. If it takes Stuart $\frac{1}{4}$ of an hour to vacuum one room, then how long will it take him to vacuum 7 rooms?

Q8. The bathroom tiler uses 30 tiles and only manages to complete two thirds of the job. How many more tiles will he have to lay down to complete the task?

Q9. One quarter of a bottle can hold 200 mL of water. How much will the bottle hold when it is full?

Q10. For the tea break, twenty one children in the class were each given one quarter of an apple for a snack. How many apples were given away?

Q11. There are 24 hours in a full day. If we sleep for $\frac{1}{3}$ of each day, how many hours do we sleep each week?

Q12. Ruby got a birthday present of $40 from her grandmother. She spends $\frac{1}{4}$ of it on lollies and $\frac{2}{5}$ of it on a T-shirt.

    a) How much does she have left?
    b) What fraction of the $40 does she have left?

Q13. a) What is $30 \div 5 = \Box$

$$\frac{2}{5} \times \frac{\Box}{\Box} = \frac{?}{30}$$

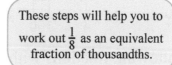

These steps will help you to work out $\frac{1}{8}$ as an equivalent fraction of thousandths.

    b) What is $1\,000 \div 8 = \Box$

$$\frac{1}{8} \times \frac{\Box}{\Box} = \frac{?}{1\,000}$$

    c) Now change $\frac{1}{8}$ to a decimal.

Q14. a)  $5 \times \frac{1}{2} =$

    b) 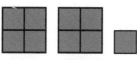 $9 \times \frac{1}{4} =$

    c) 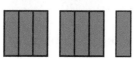 $7 \times \frac{1}{3} =$

Q15. a) How many quarters in 3?

    b) Divide 3 by $\frac{1}{4}$.

    c) $3 \div \frac{1}{4} = ?$

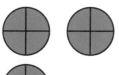

There are 3 ways of asking the same division question.

Q16. a) How many fifths ($\frac{1}{5}$) in 2?

    b) Divide 2 by $\frac{1}{5}$.

    c) $2 \div \frac{1}{5} = ?$

Q17. What fraction is exactly half way between $\frac{7}{12}$ and $\frac{2}{3}$?

Q18. Jade can sprint 100 metres in 15 seconds.

    a) If he can keep going at this rate, how many meters can he run in 1 minute?

    b) How many metres can he run in 1 hour?

    c) What is his speed in kilometres per hour?

Q19. In a 100 metres race Jim is $\frac{4}{5}$ of the way to the finish line, while Sam is $\frac{3}{4}$ of the way to the finish line. At this point, how far ahead of Sam is Jim?

Year 5 Essential Exercises
Warwick Marlin © Five Senses Education

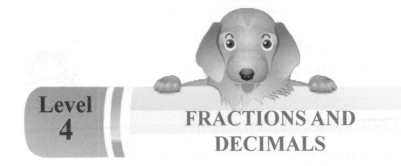

Q1. Change the following to equivalent fractions:

a) $\frac{4}{5} = \frac{\square}{100}$ b) $\frac{1}{4} = \frac{\square}{100}$ c) $\frac{13}{20} = \frac{\square}{100}$ d) $\frac{3}{8} = \frac{\square}{1000}$

Q2. Write the following fractions with the same denominators (using equivalent fractions), and then insert one of the following signs (=, > or <) to make the statement true:

a) $\frac{3}{5}$, $\frac{7}{10}$ b) $\frac{3}{4}$, $\frac{8}{12}$ c) $\frac{4}{5}$, $\frac{17}{20}$ d) $\frac{13}{20}$, $\frac{7}{10}$

e) $\frac{8}{12}$, $\frac{2}{3}$ f) $\frac{3}{4}$, $\frac{3}{5}$ g) $\frac{5}{6}$, $\frac{4}{5}$ h) $\frac{2}{3}$, $\frac{7}{10}$

Q3. Write the following fractions with the same denominator (using equivalent fractions) and then place them in ascending order:

a) $\frac{3}{4}$, $\frac{11}{12}$, $\frac{5}{6}$, $\frac{2}{3}$ b) $\frac{1}{2}$, $\frac{5}{6}$, $\frac{2}{3}$, $\frac{11}{18}$ c) $\frac{1}{4}$, $\frac{2}{5}$, $\frac{3}{10}$, $\frac{7}{20}$

Q4. Add the following fractions, and simplify final answers where possible:

a) $\frac{1}{3} + \frac{5}{12}$ b) $\frac{3}{4} + \frac{7}{20}$ c) $\frac{2}{3} + \frac{1}{4}$ d) $1\frac{1}{3} + \frac{5}{6}$

e) $2\frac{1}{5} + 1\frac{3}{10}$ f) $1\frac{1}{2} + 3\frac{7}{10}$ g) $\frac{2}{3} + \frac{2}{5}$ h) $1\frac{2}{3} + 3\frac{4}{5}$

Q5. Subtract the following fractions and simplify final answers where possible:

a) $\frac{3}{4} - \frac{5}{12}$ b) $\frac{11}{15} - \frac{2}{3}$ c) $\frac{17}{20} - \frac{3}{4}$ d) $1\frac{1}{2} - \frac{1}{6}$

e) $2\frac{3}{4} - 1\frac{5}{8}$ f) $\frac{3}{4} - \frac{2}{3}$ g) $2\frac{1}{2} - \frac{5}{6}$ h) $3\frac{1}{4} - 1\frac{4}{5}$

Q6. Change the following fractions into mixed numerals:

a) $\frac{17}{3}$ b) $\frac{29}{8}$ c) $\frac{19}{5}$ d) $\frac{25}{7}$

Q7. Change the following decimals to fractions, and write the fractions in simplest form where possible:

a) 0.8   b) 0.45   c) 0.75   d) 0.56

Q8. Change the following fractions into decimals:

a) $\frac{3}{5}$ b) $\frac{17}{1\,000}$ c) $\frac{7}{20}$ d) $\frac{39}{50}$

Q9. Find:

a)
17.21
93.75
+ 138.64

b)
29.73
183.45
+ 57.68

c)
231.6
89.73
+ 592.86

d)
62.71
385.08
+ 5 721.69

Q10. Find:

a)
385.72
− 138.64

b)
92.81
− 15.76

c)
128.32
− 47.29

d)
703.91
− 345.28

Q11. Find:

a) 3.72×10 b) $0.678 \times 1\,000$ c) 3.12×100 d) 67.831×100

e) $57.3 \div 10$ f) $137 \div 10$ g) $6321 \div 1\,000$ h) $3.2 \div 100$

Q12. Find:

a) $37.82 + 69$ cents   b) $\$1\,000 - \$372.68$

c) $\$8.42 \times 10$ d) $\$36.70 \div 10$

Q13. Find:

a) $\frac{1}{4}$ of 20   b) $\frac{2}{3}$ of 30   c) $\frac{3}{5}$ of 20   d) $\frac{3}{4}$ of 60

Q14. a) What fraction is 4 months of the year?
b) What fraction is 25 cents out of $2.00?
c) What fraction is 45 cm out of 1 metre?
d) What fraction is 200 grams out of 1 kilogram?

Write your final answer in simplest form.

Q15. Change the following units:
a) 3.21 cm to mm
b) 6.32 kg to g
c) 3 450 m to km
d) 534 mL to L
e) 6.354 m to cm
f) 3 460 g to kg

Q16. Write the following in descending order:

a) 0.253, 0.352, $\frac{1}{4}$, 0.235, $\frac{1}{5}$, 0.325

b) 6.893, 6.839, 6.389, $6\frac{4}{5}$, 6.83, $\frac{69}{10}$

c) 73.549, 73.594, $73\frac{1}{2}$, 73.495, 73.45, $73\frac{2}{5}$

Year 5 Essential Exercises
Warwick Marlin © Five Senses Education

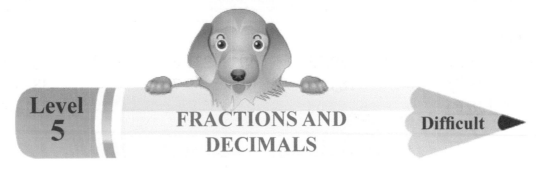

PROBLEM SOLVING

Q1. In the decimal number 7.832, the digits 8 and 3 are swapped over to create a new number. What is the difference between the original number and the new number?

Q2. My glass is $\frac{1}{3}$ full of water. I add 80 mL of water so that it is now $\frac{3}{5}$ full. How much water does the glass hold when completely full?

Q3. If 4 pizzas are shared equally between 6 people, how much does each person get?

Q4. If it takes Sven $\frac{3}{4}$ of an hour to mow one lawn, how long will it take him to mow 7 lawns?

Q5. Kim works part time and earns $275 for working 10 hours during the week. How much does she earn each hour?

Q6. Sammy decides to go on a weight loss program. She presently weighs 67.8 kg. Her goal is to lose 1.5 kg each week. If she achieves her goal, what will her weight be after 7 weeks?

Q7. Four members of the relay swimming team completed all four laps in the time of 96.74 seconds.
    a) What was the average time for each lap?
    b) Round this time off to the nearest tenth of a second.

Q8. Mrs. Stuart bought two pieces of material. The first piece was 6.8 m long and the second piece was 13.9 m long. If these two pieces were cut from a roll which has 27.3 m of material, how much will be left on the roll?

Q9. A group of ladies working at the same factory decided to each donate $\frac{1}{5}$ of their daily wage to help raise funds for a dog animal shelter. How many days pay was given, if 37 ladies contributed to the shelter.

Q10. Todd uses $7\frac{2}{3}$ pages to draw many similar sized graphs. If each graph uses $\frac{1}{3}$ of a page, how many graphs did Todd draw altogether?

Q11. It takes $\frac{3}{8}$ of a Coke bottle to fill a glass. How many glasses can be filled from 6 Coke bottles?

Q12. Steve walks 16.47 metres in 9 seconds. How far would he walk in one minute?

Q13. Tess is paid $7.40 per hour. How much will she get paid for working 50 hours?

Q14. Greta has to pay 34 cents tax for every dollar that she earned. If she earns $350 per week, how much tax will she have to pay?

Q15. Change the following times into decimals:
a) 3 hours and 15 minutes
b) 6 hours and 12 minutes

Q16. A sprinter practiced for the 100 metres and records the following times in seconds: 10.7, 10.5, 10.8, 10.9, 11.0 and 10.3. What was his average time in seconds?

Q17. Change the following to their decimal equivalent:
a) 5 cm and 3 mm
b) 4 kilograms and 75 grams
b) 3 Litres and 8 mL
d) 27 metres and 18 cm
e) 6 kilometres and 37 metres
f) 3 451 grams

Q18. Anne plays tennis for exactly the same length of time each day. During the 5 days she plays for a total of 11.8 hours.

a) How many hours and minutes does she play each day? Write the answer as a decimal.
b) Write the hours and minutes in fraction form.

Q19. The Napoli under 12 soccer team won 15 out of 21 of its matches. If $\frac{3}{5}$ of these were won by more than one goal, what fraction of all the matches were won by more than one goal? (Simplify final answer if possible.)

Q20. a) What is the sum of $\frac{1}{4}$, $\frac{2}{3}$, and $\frac{3}{5}$?
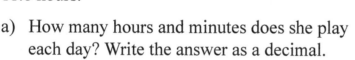

b) What is the difference between $5\frac{1}{3}$ and $2\frac{5}{12}$?

c) Increase 37.28 by 14.91 and subtract the result from 60.

d) What is the product of 11 and $\frac{2}{5}$?

e) What is the quotient of $5\frac{1}{2}$ and $\frac{1}{4}$?

Year 5 Essential Exercises
Warwick Marlin © Five Senses Education

MONEY AND FINANCIAL MATHEMATICS

The "Australian Curriculum Mathematics" (ACM) reference for this sub-strand of "Number and Algebra" (NA) is below:

☞ *Create simple financial plans (ACMNA 106).*

❖ **PROBLEMS INVOLVING MONEY**

Wendy bought 1 packet of cornflakes for $2.95, 3 tins of peaches at $1.17 each, and 6 packets of chips at 43c each. How much change does she get from $10.00?

This problem involves several steps. You must first find the total cost of all the items of food, then subtract this amount from $10.00 to find the change.

Peaches	Chips	Total	Change
$1.17	0.43	$2.95	$10.00
× 3	× 6	+ $3.51	− $9.04
$3.51	$2.58	+ $2.58	$0.96
		$9.04	

> You must know how to add, subtract, multiply and divide decimals.

She got 96c change from $10.00. As will be explained below, her actual change will be rounded down to 95c.

❖ **ROUNDING OFF MONEY**

The smallest coin denomination that we correctly use in Australia is the 5 cent piece. Therefore shop keepers and all other merchants who deal with money have to round off all amounts to the nearest 5 cents.

Example: Round off the following amounts to the nearest 5 cents.

$17.31 ⟶ rounded down to $17.30
$17.32 ⟶ rounded down to $17.30
$17.33 ⟶ rounded up to $17.35
$17.34 ⟶ rounded up to $17.35
$17.35 ⟶ stays the same $17.35
$17.36 ⟶ rounded down to $17.35
$17.37 ⟶ rounded down to $17.35
$17.38 ⟶ rounded up to $17.40
$17.39 ⟶ rounded up to $17.40

❖ **SOME BANKING TERMS**

Deposit: This is the amount of money you put into your account.

Withdrawal: This is the amount of money you take out of your account.

Balance: This is the amount of money you currently have in your account.

Payslip: This is a written or typed piece of paper given to you each payday by your employer. It shows how much you earned during the week, and how much tax has been deducted.

Statement: This is a very useful monthly document which informs you of all your deposits, withdrawals, and the balance you have in your account.

PROFIT AND EXPENSES

When operating any business, either small or large, remember the following:
Gross profit is the total amount of money obtained from the sales of the product.
Expenses are all the costs needed to make the products.
Net profit is the money you are left with after all the expenses have been paid.

Net profit = Gross profit subtract expenses

 PERSONAL BUDGETING

A budget is the most important step in controlling your money. It is as well planned, written set of goals on how to use or spend your money. It allows you to keep a close check on your income and your expenses, and it also helps you to formulate a realistic savings plan.

 GOODS AND SERVICES TAX OR GST

Goods include any visible items like: food, clothes, cars, all house holds items, etc.
Services include any non visible items like: tuition, medical, dental, chiropractic, etc.

On any invoice, you should also see a separate amount which shows the component of GST that you have paid. GST is 10% or $\frac{1}{10}$ of the value of the goods or services. This 10% GST is collected by the government as an extra means of taxing everyone.

WHITE GOODS ELECTRICAL Pty Ltd 4 JAMES ST NOOSA QLD 4566			
TAX INVOICE NUMBER: Date: 24/8/11			
Product	**Product#**	**Quantity**	**Total $**
KETTLE	3781	1	$33.00
		TOTAL $33.00	
		G.S.T CONTENT $ 3.00	
NO EXCHANGE WITHOUT RECEIPT			

The GST component of $3.00 has been clearly stated at the bottom of the invoice.

 DISCOUNT

(i) A discount is expressed as a percentage of the marked price.
(ii) The amount is then SUBTRACTED from the normal marked price.

A clothes boutique offers a discount of 25% on all dresses at a special end of summer season sale. What would you pay for a dress which normally sells at $60.00?

Find 25% of $60.00

i.e. $\frac{25}{100} \times \frac{60}{1} = 15.00

The discount is $15.00

This problem could also have been done more easily by converting 25% to a simple fraction of $\frac{1}{4}$. For table of important conversions see page 127.

The sale price is $60.00 – $15.00
= $45.00

 For further reference, see 'Understanding Year 5 Maths' by W. Marlin

 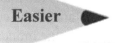
Q1. Find:
a) $8.47 + $16.98 + $32.56   b) $50.00 − $17.83
c) $9.76 × 8   d) $4.56 ÷ 3
e) $13.84 × 7   f) $138.64 ÷ 8
g) $48.71 × 10   h) $59.68 ÷ 10

Q2. Round off the following amounts of money to the nearest 5 cents:

a) $4.73   b) $29.68   c) $13.47   d) $159.72

Q3. Which is the best buy in the fruit shop. The best buy means the best value for money, or the cheapest amount for each piece of fruit.

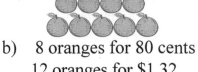

a) 5 apples for 40 cents   b) 8 oranges for 80 cents   c) 10 pears for $1.20
6 apples for 54 cents   12 oranges for $1.32   8 pears for 88 cents
10 apples for 70 cents   5 oranges for 60 cents   18 pears for $1.98

Q4. Some parents were selling hot dogs to help raise money for a new computer at the school. On one Saturday morning they sold 420 hot dogs for $2.00 each. How much profit did they make if the bread rolls, sausages, sauces and all the other expenses added up to a total of $375.00?

Q5. The balance in my bank account is $130.00. What will be my new balance if I do any of the following:

a) I deposit $40.   b) I deposit $125.   c) I withdraw $80.

Q6. Steve gets his weekly payslip. His total gross wages were $520, but he has to pay $85 in taxes. What is his net wage after he has paid his taxes?

Q7. The manager at the men's clothes shop is selling the items below at the prices shown. However, he still has to add on the GST amount. Calculate the GST amount for each item:

Remember that the GST amount is 10% of the value of the goods.

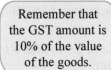

a) Shoes $60   b) Shirts $35   c) Trousers $45   d) Ties $12

Q8. Winnie gets her weekly net wages of $520. What is left after she pays the following expenses:
Food $90, rent $140, Gym $35, Bus fare $38, cafe (coffee and snacks) $45

Q9. Winnie saves what is left over after she pays all the weekly expenses shown in Q8. above. She is trying to save $2 000 for an overseas holiday to Bali.
How many full weeks will it take her to save the $2 000?

Q10. What percentage of the following squares have been shaded?

(a) 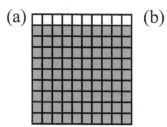 (b) 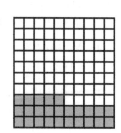 (c) 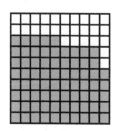 (d)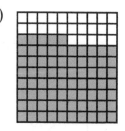

Q11. Change each of the percentages in Q10. to fractions, and write each answer in simplest form.

Q12. Find the percentages of the following amount of money. You may find it easier to do each problem by first converting each percentage to its simplified fraction.

a) 25% of $40   b) 10% of $80
c) 50% of $120   d) 75% of $20
e) 20% of $30   f) 80% of $40

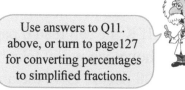

Use answers to Q11. above, or turn to page127 for converting percentages to simplified fractions.

Q13. The following items are on sale at a ladies clothing boutique.
If a 25% discount is offered on everything, calculate the discount on each the following items:

a) dress $40   b) leather jacket $120
c) blouse $60   d) jeans $80

25% DISCOUNT

Q14. The Year 5 students decided to sell t-shirts for a fund raising drive at their school to raise money for famine relief in North Africa. The students were able to purchase the t-shirts at the low cost of only $6 each, and resold them at $15 each. If they sold 230 t-shirts in total, calculate their:

a) gross profit   b) expenses   c) net profit

Year 5 Essential Exercises
Warwick Marlin © Five Senses Education

Q1.

$18.40 $16.85

$28.49 $14.53

Mrs Tan went shopping and bought the 4 items shown on the left.

a) What is the total cost of the 4 items?

b) What exact change she receive from $100.00?

c) What is the change she actually receives after rounding off to the nearest 5 cents takes place?

Q2. a) If 5 exercise books cost $12.40, how much will 7 exercise books cost?

b) If 3 hamburgers cost $13.05, how much will 5 hamburgers cost?

The trick here is to first find the cost of 1 item.

c) If Liam earns $107.52 in 7 hours, how much will he earn in 9 hours?

d) If Kylie can read 6 pages of her book in 42 minutes, how long will it take her to read a chapter containing 28 pages? Give the answer in hours and minutes.

Q3. Round off the following amounts of money to the nearest 5 cents:

a) $3.78   b) $15.34   c) $19.62   d) $8.37

Q4.

Ruler $0.74

Pencil $0.42

 Eraser $0.37

I purchase 2 rulers, 5 pencils and 2 erasers for my sister and myself before we go back to school.

a) What is the total cost of the 9 items?

b) What exact change should I receive from $10.00?

c) What is the actual change that I receive after rounding off to the nearest 5 cents has taken place?

Q5. Which is the best buy?

a) 500 g of steak at $7.80 or 2 kg at $29.40?

b) 1 kg of potatoes at $3.90 or 10 kg at $37.50?

c) 250 g of chocolate at $4.70 or 1.5 kg at $29.10?

Q6. What percentage of the following squares have been shaded?

a) 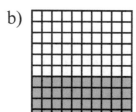   b) 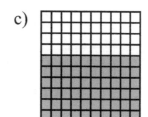   c) 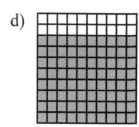   d)

Q7. Change each of the percentages in Q6. above into fractions, and write the answers in simplest form.

Q8.

The discount warehouse is offering 40% discount on the 4 items shown. How much would I pay for each item after the discount has been subtracted?

a) doll   b) toy car
c) shoes   d) t-shirt
e) How much would I save on the normal price if I bought 4 t-shirts?

Q9. The manager of a hardware store is selling the items below at the prices shown. However, he still has to add on the 10% GST amount. Calculate the price of each items AFTER the GST has been added:

a) Hose   b) Watering Can   c) Wheel barrow   d) set of screwdrivers

Q10. On the 7th April, Jenny Green gets her weekly pay. She also has to pay the following expenses:

PAYSLIP FOR 7th APRIL 2011			
Name	**Gross Wage**	**Tax**	**Net Wage**
Jenny Green	$480.00	$135.00	

hairdresser $37, birthday lunch for her friend $42, makeup $26.50, rent $128 and food $68.

a) What was Jenny's net wage after paying tax?
b) What was her total expenses?
c) How much will she have left over after paying her expenses?

Year 5 Essential Exercises
Warwick Marlin © Five Senses Education

PROBLEM SOLVING

Q1. Mr. Nguyen went shopping at the local hardware store and received the invoice shown on the right.

ABC HARDWARE		
4 MERLIN ST		
CABRAMATTA NSW		
TAX INVOICE #: 78935		Date: 17/6/12
Product	**Quantity**	**Price**
Electric drill	1	$38.00
Hammer	1	$17.00
Paint	2	$20.00
	Total	$82.50
	GST Amount	$7.50

a) What is the total he has to pay for the 4 items?

b) What is the GST amount?

c) If there was no GST, what would the total cost be?

d) What is the invoice number?

e) Calculate the GST amount on the electric drill.

Q2. Round off the following amounts of money to the nearest 5 cents:

a) $38.23   b) $16.28   c) $124.17   d) $69.42

Q3. Jill Stanton receives the following statement from her bank at the end of April.

JILL STANTON		STATEMENT END APRIL 2012	
16 HILL ST			
PARRAMATTA NSW			
Date	**Deposit ($)**	**Withdrawal ($)**	**Balance ($)**
Carried Forward			380.00
2.4.12	200.00		580.00
8.4.12		75.00	505.00
16.4.12	230.00		735.00
21.4.12		180.00	555.00
30.4.12	245.00		800.00

a) How much did she already have 'carried forward' in her account from the previous month?

b) On what date did she withdraw $75.00?

c) What was the amount that she deposited on the 16th April?

d) What was the total of her withdrawals during the month of April?

e) What was the total of her deposits during the month of April?

f) What was the balance in her account on the 21st April?

g) By looking at the statement, on what day of the week do you think Jill gets paid?

h) Do you think that she is paid weekly or fortnightly?

On the 14th May, Jill receives another payslip from her work. But she has to pay the following expenses first: rent $130, food $85, beautician $35, telecom $48, electricity $64 .

PAYSLIP FOR 14th MAY 2012				
Name	**Gross Wage**	**Tax**	**Medicare levy**	**Net Wage**
Jill Stanton	$560.00	$145.00	$38.00	

i) What was her net wage after tax and medicare levy was deducted?

j) After paying all her expenses (rent, food, etc.) how much will she have left from her weekly wages?

k) She decided to deposit this into her bank. What will her new balance be?

Q4. Stephanie is saving for a holiday to the Gold Coast. She has a job, but she is living with her parents, and she doesn't have to pay any rent. However, she still has to pay for other expenses like her train fares, clothes, entertainment, make up, coffee shop and other extras. She has made up a monthly BUDGET to help her save more.

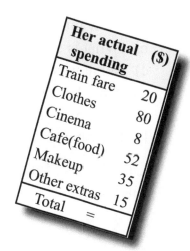

a) What is her total budget?

b) What does she actually spend during the month?

c) On which item did she over spend the most from her budget?

d) Name an item on which she spent $10 more than her budget plan?

e) What item did she spend $5 less than her budget plan?

f) What do you think Stephanie must try to do in the following month to keep closer to her budget goals?

Year 5 Essential Exercises
Warwick Marlin © Five Senses Education

Q1. A fifth grade class was set a project to raise funds for a new computer at the school. They needed exactly $867 to buy this computer, and the class decided to organise a BBQ and sell hamburgers for the day outside one of the busy shopping centres. One of the parents offered the loan of BBQ, and many of the other parents offered to help with the overall supervision.

During the Saturday of the BBQ, they sold 380 hamburgers at $3 each. They used most of the gas in the cylinder, which cost $35, and there were also many other expenses shown below.

- 400 bread rolls at 15 cents each
- 6 large containers of BBQ sauce at $5 per container
- 4 jars of mustard at $2.50 per jar
- 5 litres of cooking oil at $7 per litre
- 13 kilograms of minced meat at $9 per kilogram
- 8 kilograms of onions at $1.50 per kilogram
- 8 packets of serviettes at 50 cents per packet

a) How much money (gross profit) do they make by selling the hamburgers?
b) What is the total of all expenses, including the gas for the cylinder?
c) What was their net profit, after paying for all the expenses?
d) How far ahead or short were they of achieving their goal?
e) What was the highest expense?
f) How many more hamburgers did they need to sell to achieve their goal?

Q2. Calculate the final prices of the articles below AFTER the discounts have been calculated:

a)  Dress
Normally $45
10% discount

b) Handbag
Normally $35
20% discount

c)  Jeans
Normally $70
30% discount

Q3. Thaliah went shopping on the Gold Coast for souvenirs and presents. At one shop she bought 3 t-shirts at $8.34 each, 5 key rings at $3.72 each, and 4 basketball caps at $8.34 each. How much change (rounded to the nearest 5 cents) does she receive from $100 ?

Q4. The following items are getting sold at a newsagency, but the prices do not yet include the 10% GST. Calculate the price of each item AFTER the GST has been added:

a) birthday card $4.30   b) diary $15.60
c) pen $3.40   d) eraser 30 cents

Q5. At a sports store the GST has already been added to the items below. Calculate the price of each item BEFORE the GST was added.

a) cricket bat $88   b) tennis jacket $110
c) fishing rod $16.50   e) golf club $49.50

This is a tricky question, so be careful. You cannot simply subtract 10% from the item!

Q6. Which is the best buy in the following at the local supermarket:

a) **Minced meat**
   2 kg for $15.00
   3 kg for $22.80
   5 kg for $36.00

b) **Basmati rice**
   500 g for $1.35
   2 kg for $4.90
   5 kg for $11.00

c) **Washing detergent**
   500 g for $2.10
   1.5 kg for $5.85
   3 kg for $12.42

Q7. Raina has a balance of $756.47 in her bank account. During the next 2 weeks she makes a deposit of $325.48 and two withdrawals. What is her balance now if the first withdrawal was for $238.46 and the second withdrawal was for $190.88?

Q8. Alessandro bought an old used computer for $85 and a Hi-Fi set for $67. He then spent a further $47.30 on repairing them. If he sold both items on eBay for $260.00, how much profit did he make?

Q9. Liang and Juan decided to go to a chinese restaurant to celebrate Liang's birthday.
The dishes they liked were:
Honey King Prawns ($27.50) , Sweet & Sour pork ($22.40) and Peking Duck with Broccoli ($34.80). The coconut cake was $6.80 per serving, and the green tea was $3.45 per person. Liang chose the Peking Duck and Juan chose the Sweet & Sour Pork, and they both had tea and desserts. If they gave a $5 tip to the waitress for her good service, how much change did they get from $100?

Year 5 Essential Exercises
Warwick Marlin © Five Senses Education

PROBLEM SOLVING

Q1. Gloria is trying to save money for her annual holiday. She has decided to try and keep to a strict weekly budget as shown on the left. Her actual expenses for the first week are shown on the right hand side.

Gloria's estimated budget

WEEK 1

Wages	$300
Expenses:	
Taxes	$40
Bus fares	$22
Coffee/Snacks	$25
Cellphone	$30
Clothes	$45
Makeup	$18
Presents	$20
Savings	?

Gloria's actual income and expenses   WEEK 1

Wages	$340
Expenses:	
Taxes	
Bus fares	$50
Coffee/Snacks	$22
Cellphone	$32
Clothes	$35
Makeup	$57
Hair dresser	$18
Presents	$35
Savings	$40
	?

a) What was the total of Gloria's estimated expenses?

b) How much is left over for her to save on her estimated budget?

c) What was the total of Gloria's actual expenses?

d) How much was left over for her to save?

e) Which expense was $12 higher than she budgeted for?

f) She was lucky in WEEK 1 that she earned $40 more than she expected. If she hadn't earned the extra money, how much would she have left over to save?

g) Which expense was double what she budgeted for?

h) Comment on whether you think Gloria was close to her budget or not.

Q2. Calculate the following prices after the GST has been added:

a) Bicycle $185
   plus 10% GST

b) Helmet $38.50
   plus 10% GST

c) Sunglasses $19.80
   plus 10% GST

Q3. Anna, Giovanni and Carmela go out to an Italian restaurant.
Anna orders the garlic bread, fettuccine carbonara and a lemonade.
Giovanni orders the Caesar salad, Spaghetti bolognese, cheeses and coffee.
Carmela orders the Orecchiette with broccoli, plus ice cream and coffee.
Giovanni is paying for the meal and he only has $100 in his pocket.

Bon Appetito Menu	
Starters:	
Garlic bread	$5.00
Calamari rings	$6.80
Caesar salad	$12.40
Mains:	
Spaghetti bolognese	$17.80
Fettucine carbonara	$18.50
Orecchiette with broccoli	$16.40
Pizza Margarita	$22.30
Desserts:	
Mixed cheeses	$11.00
Cassata ice cream	$6.00
Lemonade	$3.50
Coffee	$4.80

a) So he decides to do a quick estimate of what the bill will come to.
   He does that by rounding off all the amounts to the nearest $5. What is his estimate?

b) The waiter then tells him that these prices do not yet include GST.
   So Giovanni cancels his order for Caesar salad. What is the exact total amount of the bill without GST?

c) What is the total of the bill when GST is added?

d) How much change does Giovanni get from his $100?

Q4. Amy has a balance of $380.40 in her bank account. She added a deposit of $320.75 and made a withdrawal. After the withdrawal the balance in her account is $512.45. How much did she withdraw?

Q5. Calculate the following sale prices at a hardware store, once the discount has been calculated and subtracte

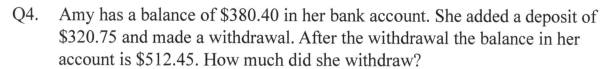

a)

Paint
Normally $35
10% discount

b
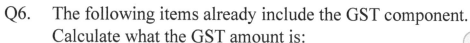
Tool set
Normally $75
25% discount

c)
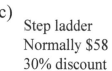
Step ladder
Normally $58
30% discount

Q6. The following items already include the GST component.
Calculate what the GST amount is:

This is a very difficult question!!

a)

Computer $792

b)

Monitor $132

c)

Keyboard $165

41

PATTERNS AND ALGEBRA

The "Australian Curriculum Mathematics" (ACM) references for this sub-strand of "Number and Algebra" (NA) are below:

☞ Describe, continue and create patterns with fractions, decimals and whole numbers resulting from addition and subtraction (ACMNA 107).

☞ Use equivalent number sentences involving multiplication and division to find unknown quantities (ACMNA 121).

❖ **SOME SPECIAL NUMBER PATTERNS**

Even numbers	2, 4, 6, 8, 10…
Odd numbers	1, 3, 5, 7, 9….
Square numbers	1, 4, 9, 16, 25….1^2, 2^2, 3^2, 4^2, etc.
Triangular numbers	1, 1+2, 1+2+3, 1+2+3+4, etc.

In streets, you will usually see the even numbered houses on one side of the road, and odd numbered houses on the other side.

NOTE: Triangular numbers can also be obtained from building up triangles from dots. This is how they got their name, because the pictures look like triangles.

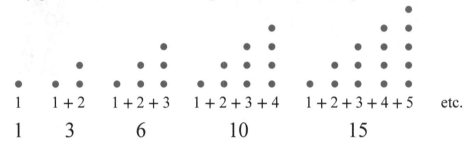

1	1 + 2	1 + 2 + 3	1 + 2 + 3 + 4	1 + 2 + 3 + 4 + 5	etc.
1	3	6	10	15	

❖ **RECOGNISING PATTERNS**

(1) 3, 6, 12, ☐, ☐   ⇒ Double the previous number

(2) 14, 21, 28, ☐, ☐   ⇒ Add 7 to the previous number

(3) 10.1, 11.2, 12.3, ☐, ☐   ⇒ Add 1.1 to the previous number

(4) $1\frac{1}{2}$, 3, $4\frac{1}{2}$, 6, ☐, ☐   ⇒ Add $1\frac{1}{2}$ to the previous number

(5) 1, 4, 9, 16, ☐, ☐   ⇒ Square numbers

(6) 1, 3, 6, 10, ☐, ☐   ⇒ Triangular numbers

(7) 78, 70, 62, 54, ☐, ☐   ⇒ Subtract 8 from the previous number

Discover the rule and then write down the next 2 numbers in the pattern. The pattern could involve whole numbers, fractions or decimals.

COMPLETING TABLES

Sometimes you will be given part of a table with one set of numbers on the top line and a second set of numbers on the bottom line. You will then be asked to find a rule that connects each pair of numbers on the top line to the bottom. You will then also be asked to complete the missing numbers in the table.

Example: Write the rule for the following table, and then complete the table.

Top number	3	4	5	6	7	8
Bottom number	12	16	20	24	?	?

The same rule must work for every pair of numbers on the table.

 USING RULES TO COMPLETE A TABLE

This is the opposite or reverse idea from above. Here, we are given a rule connecting the top numbers to the bottom numbers, and we are asked to complete the table.

Example: Complete the table using the rule: $\triangle = \square + 5$

$\square$	1	3	5	10
$\triangle$				

I am sure you can see that this rule says "add 5 to the top number each time".

 GEOMETRIC PATTERNS

Many patterns can be found by using geometrical shapes, or matchsticks or dots. Some of the patterns are quite simple, but there are also some more difficult ones.

Example: Triangles are formed using match sticks as shown below.

Number of triangles	1	2	3	4
Number of matches	3	6	9	12

 NUMBER SENTENCES

In number sentences, you will be required to work out the value of the symbol ($\square$, $\triangle$, $\hexagon$) which makes the sentence true.

$\square$ + 7 = 10   What number plus 7 is equal to 10? $\square$ = 3

$\triangle$ × 3 = 15   What number multiplied by 3 is equal to 15? $\triangle$ = 5

$\hexagon$ ÷ 4 = 5   What number divided by 4 is equal to 5? $\hexagon$ = 20

 For further reference, see 'Understanding Year 5 Maths' by W. Marlin

Year 5 Essential Exercises
Warwick Marlin © Five Senses Education

Q1. a) List the odd numbers between 30 and 40.
b) List the even numbers between 51 and 59.
c) List the first five triangular numbers.
d) List the square numbers between 20 and 60.
e) List the multiples of 4 between 10 and 30.

Look at page 42 as a reminder, if you are having any difficulty.

Q2. Briefly explain the rule in each of the following number patterns, and then write down the next two numbers in the pattern:

a) 18, 16, 14, 12, ☐ , ☐   Rule is: ?   Next 2 numbers are: ? ?

b) 5, 10, 20, 40, ☐ , ☐   Rule is: ?   Next 2 numbers are: ? ?

c) 17, 21, 25, 29, ☐ , ☐   Rule is: ?   Next 2 numbers are: ? ?

d) 4, 9, 16, 25, ☐ , ☐   Rule is: ?   Next 2 numbers are: ? ?

e) 8, 16, 24, 32, ☐ , ☐   Rule is: ?   Next 2 numbers are: ? ?

f) $\frac{1}{2}$, $\frac{3}{4}$, 1, $1\frac{1}{4}$, ☐ , ☐   Rule is: ?   Next 2 numbers are: ? ?

g) 13.0, 13.5, 14.0, 14.5, ☐ , ☐   Rule is: ?   Next 2 numbers are: ? ?

h) 50, 44, 38, 32, ☐ , ☐   Rule is: ?   Next 2 numbers are: ? ?

Q3. There are 4 machines shown below which always obey a certain rule when a number is put into the top. Whatever number is put into the top of machine A, it will always add on 3. Whatever number is put into the top of machine B, it will always subtract 5, etc.

Example: If 4 is put into the top of machine C, what number will come out? The machine obeys the rule 'Multiply by 10', so the number 40 will come out.

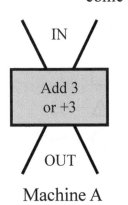

Machine A

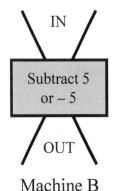

Machine B

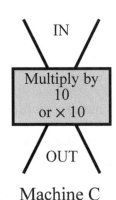

Machine C

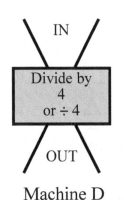

Machine D

Calculate what numbers come out of the machines when the following numbers are put in the top.

i) 8 into machine A
ii) 17 into machine B
iii) 6 into machine C
iv) 20 into machine D
v) 35 into machine A
vi) 24 into machine B
vii) 8 into machine C
viii) 32 into machine D

Q4. A rule has been given connecting the bottom symbol to the top symbol. Write down the missing number in the tables below. This is very similar to Q3.
(**Hint:** The first number in each table has already been done for you.)

a) $\square = \triangle + 5$

$\triangle$	7	8	9	10
$\square$	12			

b) $\square = \triangle - 7$

$\triangle$	30	31	32	33
$\square$	23			

c) $\triangle = \bigcirc \div 4$

$\bigcirc$	40	32	28	20
$\triangle$	10			

d) $\hexagon = \triangle \times 5$

$\triangle$	7	8	10	12
$\hexagon$	35			

e) $\square = \triangle + 3\frac{1}{2}$

$\triangle$	3	4	5	6
$\square$	$6\frac{1}{2}$			

f) $\hexagon = \square - 3.5$

$\triangle$	10	13	16	19
$\hexagon$	6.5			

Q5. Find the value of each symbol ($\square$, $\triangle$, $\bigcirc$, $\hexagon$) in the number sentences shown below.

a) $\square + 5 = 17$

b) $\triangle - 4 = 11$

c) $\bigcirc \times 8 = 24$

d) $\square \div 3 = 6$

e) $\triangle + 1\frac{1}{2} = 2$

f) $6 \times \hexagon = 30$

g) $20 \div \square = 4$

h) $\hexagon - 2.5 = 4$

i) $\square \times \square = 49$

j) $\dfrac{20}{\square} = 4$

k) $\triangle + \triangle + \triangle = 27$

l) $\hexagon \times 7 = 42$

Year 5 Essential Exercises
Warwick Marlin © Five Senses Education

Q1. a) Draw the next set of diamonds in this pattern:

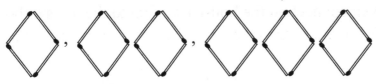

Match sticks were used to construct all the patterns in Q1 and Q2.

b) Complete the table on the right which shows the number of matches needed for each new set of diamonds in the pattern.

Number of diamonds	1	2	3	4	5
Number of matches	4				

c) Write a short rule to describe the pattern.

d) How many matches would be needed for 9 diamond shapes?

Q2. a) Draw the next set of pentagons in this pattern:

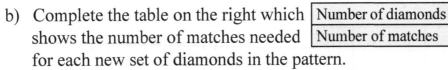

b) Complete the table on the right which shows the number of matches needed for each new set of pentagons in the pattern.

Number of pentagons	1	2	3	4	5
Number of matches	5				

c) Write a short rule to describe the pattern.

d) How many matches would be needed for 12 pentagons?

Q3. a) Draw the next figure represented by blocks in the pattern below.

   ?

Figure 1   Figure 2   Figure 3   Figure 4

This question is more difficult.

b) Complete the table on the right which shows the number of blocks needed for each figure.
(The first 3 have been done for you.)

Figure number	1	2	3	4	5	6
Number of blocks	1	4	9			

c) Write a short rule to describe the pattern.

d) How many blocks would be needed to make Figure 9?

Q4. Briefly explain the rule in each of the following number patterns, and then write down the next two numbers in each pattern:

a) 31, 28, 25, 22, ☐, ☐

b) 21, 28, 35, 42, ☐, ☐

c) 2, 4, 8, 16, ☐, ☐

d) 7, $9\frac{1}{2}$, 12, $14\frac{1}{2}$, ☐, ☐

e) 20.0, 17.5, 15.0, 12.5, ☐, ☐

f) 40, 48, 56, 64, ☐, ☐

Q5. There are 4 different machines below which always obey a certain rule when a number is put into the top. (See level 1, Q3. for a more detailed explanation and an example.)

Machine A   Machine B   Machine C   Machine D

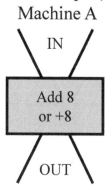 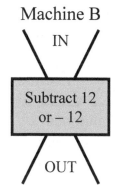 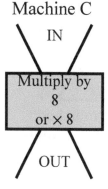 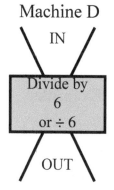

Calculate what numbers come out of the machines when the following numbers are put in the top. The machine will be in brackets after the number.

i) 12 (A)   ii) 30 (B)   iii) 5 (C)   iv) 42 (D)

v) 94 (A)   vi) 84 (B)   vii) 12 (C)   viii) 90 (D)

Q6. Briefly write down the rule connecting the top numbers to the bottom numbers in each of the tables below. Also write down the 2 missing numbers in each table.

a)

Top number	5	6	7	8	9	10
Bottom number	12	13	14	15		

b)

Top number	4	5	6	7	8	9
Bottom number	12	15	18	21		

c)

Top number	25	24	23	22	21	20
Bottom number	19	18	17	16		

d)

Top number	30	27	24	21	18	15
Bottom number	10	9	8	7		

Q7. Find the value of each symbol (☐, △, ◖, ⬡) in the number sentences below:

a) ☐ + 16 = 30

b) △ − 12 = 28

c) ◖ × 9 = 63

d) ☐ ÷ 8 = 15

e) △ + $2\frac{1}{4}$ = 6

f) ⬡ × ⬡ = 64

g) 12 × ◖ = 72

h) ☐ − 3.2 = 1.8

i) $\dfrac{⬡}{4}$ = 15

Year 5 Essential Exercises
Warwick Marlin © Five Senses Education

PROBLEM SOLVING

Q1.   You will see different patterns below which have been made using match sticks.
Write down the number pattern for each question. Then write down the next
two numbers in the pattern, and also write down the 8ᵗʰ number in each pattern.

Example: △ ,   △ △ ,   △ △ △

3 matches   6 matches   9 matches

The number pattern is therefore 3, 6, 9.
The next two numbers in the pattern will be 12 and 15.
3, 6, 9, 12, 15, 18, 21, 24. The 8ᵗʰ number = 24

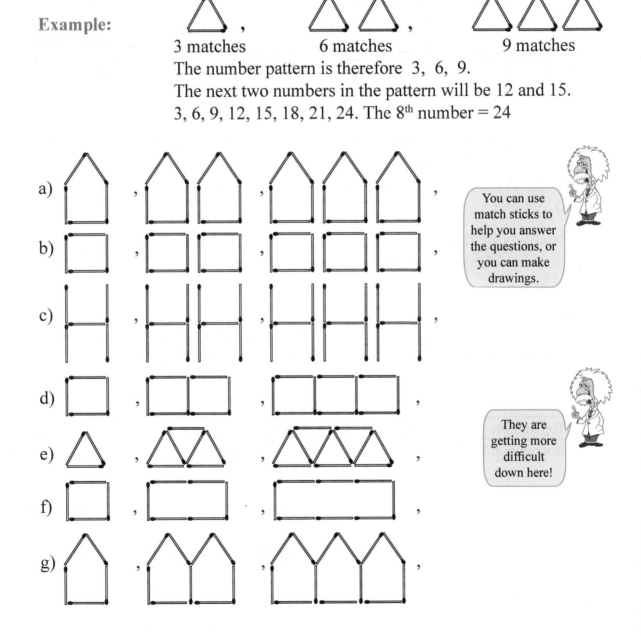

a)

b)

c)

d)

e)

f)

g)

You can use
match sticks to
help you answer
the questions, or
you can make
drawings.

They are
getting more
difficult
down here!

Q2. Find the value of each symbol in the number sentences below:
(Some answers may be fractions).

a) $3 \times \square + 1 = 22$ b) $5 \times \triangle - 3 = 27$ c) $\bigcirc \times 7 = 22$

d) $4 \times \ominus + 5 = 7$ e) $\triangle + \triangle + \triangle = 13$ f) $(\square \div 3) + 5 = 12$

Q3. The number patterns below use one rule to get the first number, then a second rule to get the number after that.

Examples:

8, 12, 11, 15, 14   18, 20, 15, 17, 12
  +4 -1 +4 -1   +2 -5 +2 -5
Add 4 Subtract 1, etc.   Add 2 Subtract 5, etc.

Write the next 2 numbers in the patterns below:

a) 10, 18, 15, 23, 20,   b) 50, 51, 45, 46, 40,
c) 3, 6, 7, 14, 15,   d) 7, 10, 15, 18, 23

Q4. Use the first number as the starting number. Then use the given rule to write down the next 3 numbers in the pattern:

a) 5 "add 7"   b) 38 "subtract 3"   c) 2 "multiply by 3"
d) 64 "divided by 2"   e) 2 "multiply by 4   f) 81 "add 1 and then
                             and subtract 5"   divide by 2"

Q5. A rule has been given connecting the bottom symbol to the top symbol. Write down the missing numbers in the tables below.
(**Hint:** The first number in each table has already been done for you.)

a) $\square = \triangle + 1\frac{1}{2}$

$\triangle$	3	4	$5\frac{1}{2}$	$10\frac{1}{2}$
$\square$	$4\frac{1}{2}$			

b) $\ominus = \triangle + 2.5$

$\triangle$	6	7	8.5	12.5
$\ominus$	8.5			

c) $\bigcirc = \square \div 3$

$\square$	12	15	21	25
$\bigcirc$	4			

d) $\hexagon = \ominus \times 10$

$\ominus$	3.1	4.1	7.2	9.3
$\hexagon$	31			

e) $\square = \triangle \times \triangle$

$\triangle$	5	7	8	12
$\square$	25			

f) $\bigcirc = \ominus - \frac{1}{10}$

$\ominus$	$\frac{3}{10}$	$\frac{5}{10}$	$\frac{7}{10}$	$1\frac{4}{10}$
$\bigcirc$	$\frac{2}{10}$			

Year 5 Essential Exercises
Warwick Marlin © Five Senses Education

Level 4

PATTERNS AND ALGEBRA

Difficult

Q1. Match sticks are joined to make the following patterns of triangle shapes:

a) Draw the next two patterns that follow from the 4 triangles shown.
b) From the diagrams shown above, fill out the rest of the table below:

Number of triangles	1	2	3	4	5	6
Number of matches	3	5				

c) How many matches will be required for 15 triangles?
d) Try to find a rule connecting the number of matches to the number of triangles. The rule should begin like this:

Number of matches = ? ?

Q2. Match sticks are once again joined to make the following patterns of pentagon shapes:

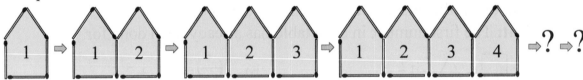

a) Draw the next two patterns that follow from the 4 pentagon shapes shown.
b) From the diagrams shown above, fill out the rest of the table below.

Number of pentagons	1	2	3	4	5	6
Number of matches	5	9				

c) How many matches will be required for 12 pentagons?
d) Try to find a rule connecting the number of matches to the number of the pentagons. The rule should begin like this:

Number of matches = ? ?

Q3. Write a number sentence using symbols (☐, △, etc), and then find the value of the unknown symbol.
a) The sum of a certain number and 12 is 37. What is the number?
b) The difference between a certain number and 15 is 42. What is the number?

c) The product of a certain number and 8 is 20. What is the number?

d) The quotient of a certain number and 2 is $6\frac{1}{2}$. What is the number?

e) A certain number is multiplied by 4 and then 5 subtracted from the product. The answer is 47. What is the number?

f) A certain number is divided by 7, and then 12 is added to the quotient. The answer is 20. What is the number?

Q4. There are 12 people at a party. If every person shakes hand with every other person, how many different handshakes will there be?

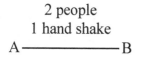
2 people
1 hand shake
A—————B

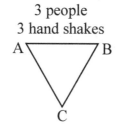
3 people
3 hand shakes

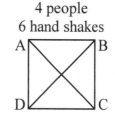
4 people
6 hand shakes

etc.

Try to discover a pattern by completing the table below, in order to work out the answer.

Number of people	2	3	4	5	6	7	8	9	10	11	12
Number of hand shakes	1	3	6								

Q5. A rule has been given connecting the bottom symbol or letter to the top symbol or letter. Write down the missing numbers in each table using the given rule.

a) $\square = (2 \times \triangle) + 5$

△	3	4	7	9
□				

b) ⬡ = (◐ × 4) − 6

◐	2	3	5	10
⬡				

c) $B = (A \div 2) + 4$

A	6	10	12	20
B				

d) $M = (N \times N) - 3$

N	4	5	8	9
M				

e) $Q = (2 \times P) + 3$

P	1.5	2.5	4.5	7.5
Q				

f) $Y = (X \div 2) + \frac{1}{2}$

X	6	9	12	21
Y				

Q6. Find the value of each letter in the number sentences below:
Note: Small alphabetical letters (a, m, x, y) have been used instead of the symbols ($\square$, $\triangle$, $\bullet$, etc.)

a) $3 \times n + 4 = 25$

b) $\frac{a}{3} + 4 = 13$

c) $4 \times m + 5 = 7$

d) $5 \times p = 23$

e) $q \div 4 = 3.5$

f) $(t \div 3) + 4 = 11$

g) $m \times m = 81$

h) $6 \times p - 7 = 35$

i) $\frac{n}{4} - 7 = 3$

Year 5 Essential Exercises
Warwick Marlin © Five Senses Education

USING UNITS OF MEASUREMENT

The "Australian Curriculum Mathematics" (ACM) references for this sub-strand of "Measurement and Geometry" (MG) are below:

☞ Choose appropriate units of measurement for length, area, volume, capacity and mass (ACMMG 108).

☞ Calculate the perimeter and area of rectangles using familiar metric units (ACMMG 109).

☞ Compare 12- and 24-hour time systems and convert between them (ACMMG 110).

❖ LENGTH

In Australia we use the metric system of all units of measurement, except for the units of time. Calculations in the metric system are made very much simpler, because they are based on powers of 10 just like our decimal system. The 3 most important units of length used in everyday living, and their shortened symbols, are listed below.

> 10 millimetres (mm) = 1 centimetre (cm)
> 100 centimetres (cm) = 1 metre (m)
> 1 000 metres (m) = 1 kilometre (km)

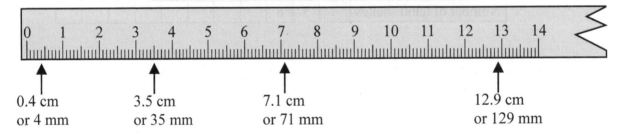

| 0.4 cm | 3.5 cm | 7.1 cm | 12.9 cm |
| or 4 mm | or 35 mm | or 71 mm | or 129 mm |

❖ CHOOSING UNITS OF LENGTH

We use millimetres (mm) for VERY small lengths, like measuring the thickness of an exercise book. We use centimetres (cm) for SMALL lengths, like measuring how long your pen is. The nails on your hand are about 1 cm wide.

We use metres (m) to measure many lengths around the house, like the length and width of your bedroom.

1 large step
Length ≈ 1 metre

Kilometres (km) are used for measuring large distances. We use kilometres for distances between towns and suburbs.

One metre is about the same distance as taking one large step.

❖ PERIMETER

The perimeter of a closed figure is the total distance around the figure. Simply add up the lengths of all the sides.

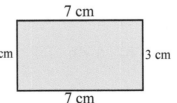

7 cm
3 cm
3 cm
7 cm

The perimeter of the rectangle (not drawn to scale) is
(7 + 3 + 7 + 3) cm
Perimeter = 20 cm

AREA

The area of a figure is the amount of region inside the shape. To find the amount of region, it is necessary to work out how many square units would fill that shape. One could split up a rectangle into square units and then count those units. For example:

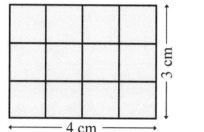

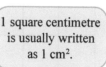 = 1 square centimetre = 1 cm²

By counting the squares:
Area = 12 cm²

1 square centimetre is usually written as 1 cm².

A larger unit of area is the "square metre" written as m². This is useful for measuring many areas around the house. For example, the area of your bedroom maybe about 12 m².

Very large areas are measured in HECTARES. For example, real estate agents and farmers measure area in hectares. The symbol for hectare is ha.

| 1 hectare = 10 000 square metres |
| or 1 ha = 10 000 m² |

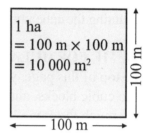

1 ha
= 100 m × 100 m
= 10 000 m²

 FORMULA FOR AREA OF A RECTANGLE (Extension work)

It was stated above that we could find the area of a rectangle by splitting it up into square units, and then simply counting those units. However the above method of counting squares is time consuming and Mathematicians have worked out a formula which gives the area more quickly and easily. We simply multiply the length of the rectangle by the breadth of the rectangle.

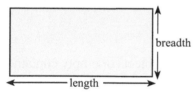

| **Area = length × breadth** |

 IRREGULAR AREAS

The areas of more complicated shapes can only be calculated by splitting them up into 2 or more rectangles. Find the area of each rectangle and then simply add them to find the total area.

Example: A figure is made up of two rectangles joined together as shown in the diagram. Find the total area of both rectangles.

Solution:

Area 1 = length × breadth
= 4 cm × 3 cm
= 12 cm²
Area 2 = length × breadth
= 8 cm × 6 cm
= 48 cm²
Total Area = 12 cm² + 48 cm²
= 60 cm²

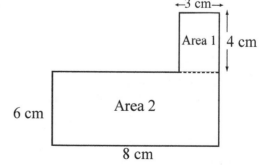

Year 5 Essential Exercises
Warwick Marlin © Five Senses Education

VOLUME

The volume of a rectangular prism (box shape) is the amount of space within the prism. In other words, it is the amount of cubic units which would fit into that space. As with areas, the volume could be calculated by splitting the prism up into cubic units and then counting these units.

Example:

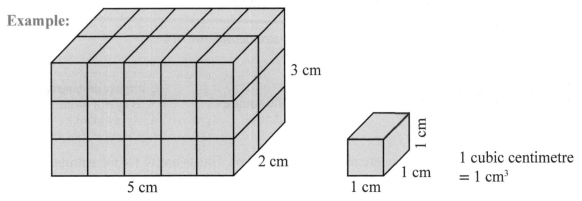

3 cm

2 cm

5 cm

1 cm

1 cm

1 cm

1 cubic centimetre
= 1 cm³

By counting the cube units, it can be seen that the volume of the rectangular prism above is 30 cm3.

VOLUME FORMULA (Extension work)

At the top of this page, you saw that it is quite easy to find the volume of a prism by splitting it up into cubic blocks, and then counting how many blocks fit into the prism.
A very much faster method is to use the simple formula shown below.

Rectangular
Prism
Shape

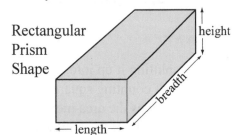

height

breadth

length

$$\text{Volume} = \text{length} \times \text{breadth} \times \text{height}$$

In the example at the top of the page:
Volume = 5 x 3 x 2
= 30 cm³

 CAPACITY

We have seen in the previous section that volumes of solid objects or empty containers are measured in cm³ or m³. However, liquids (water, milk, petrol, soft drinks, etc.) are usually measured in millilitres (mL) or litres (L).

Teaspoon
Capacity ≈ 5 mL of liquid

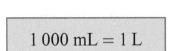

$$1\ 000\ \text{mL} = 1\ \text{L}$$

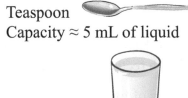

1 L of milk

Glass
Capacity ≈ 300 mL

 MASS

The kilogram is the basic metric unit of mass used in everyday living. The gram is used for small weights, and the tonne is used for larger weights. 'Kilo' means 1 000, and so it is easy to remember that one kilogram is equal to 1 000 grams.

1 000 grams (g) = 1 kilogram (kg)
1 000 kilograms (kg) = 1 tonne (t)

Apple
Mass ≈ 200g

12 year old
Mass ≈ 30 to 40 kg

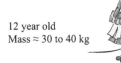

VOLUME, CAPACITY AND MASS (Extension work only)

In previous sections, we saw that the volumes of solid objects are usually measured in cm^3, and the volumes of liquids are measured in millilitres or litres.

There is a very important simple connection between volume and capacity.

$$1 \text{ cm}^3 \text{ (volume)} = 1 \text{ mL (capacity)}$$

$$1\,000 \text{ cm}^3 \text{ (volume)} = 1 \text{ L (capacity)}$$

> A cubic centimetre takes up the same space as 1 millilitre of liquid.

Another useful fact to know is that one litre of pure water weighs one kilogram.

1 litre of water   1 kilogram

 ANALOG TIME

In the past, the main method of stating time of the day has been with the use of the words am and pm.

am - between 12 o'clock midnight and 12 noon

pm - between 12 o'clock noon and 12 midnight

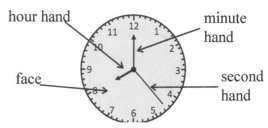

hour hand, minute hand, face, second hand

Therefore 6:15 am means 15 minutes past 6 o'clock in the morning, while 6:15 pm means 15 minutes past 6 o'clock in the evening.

 DIGITAL 24 HOUR TIME

In the last 10 years, there have been an increasing amount of clocks, watches and video recorders which are now using the 24 hour time scale. The main advantage of this scale is that 'am' and 'pm' do not have to be mentioned, and therefore there is less chance of any confusion occurring.

The 24 hour time method is always given as a 4 digit number, with the first two numbers giving the hour past midnight, and the second two numbers giving the minutes.
Sometimes a colon or space is used as a separator between the first two numbers and the second two numbers.

Therefore 6:15 am is written as 0615 or 06:15 or 06 15, and 6:15 pm is written as 1815 or 18:15 or 18 15.

> Students should know how to convert from one system to the other.

 For further reference, see 'Understanding Year 5 Maths' by W. Marlin

Year 5 Essential Exercises
Warwick Marlin © Five Senses Education

Q1. Change the following into the units shown:

a) 6 cm = ☐ mm   b) 3 km = ☐ m   c) 8 m = ☐ cm

d) 90 mm = ☐ cm   e) 7 000 m = ☐ km   f) 400 cm = ☐ m

Q2. Write down the lengths below (where the arrow is pointing) using centimetres (cm) and millimetres (mm). Example: 4 cm and 6 mm.

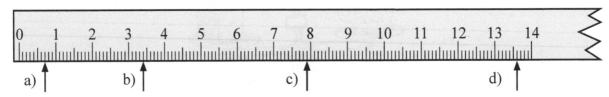

Q3. Write down the answers from Q2. in decimal form using cm only.
(Example: 3 cm and 2 mm = 3.2 cm)

Q4. Measure the lengths of the following lines in cm and mm and write your answers in decimal form:

a)   b)    c)   d)

Q5. Choose the most suitable units of length to measure the following:

a) length of your exercise book   b) length of a swimming pool

c) thickness of 40 sheets of paper   d) distance between Sydney and Canberra

e) your height   f) thickness of this book

Q6. Find the areas of the following figures in cm²:

a) 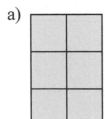   b) 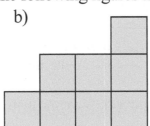   c) 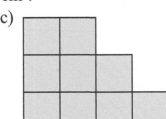   d)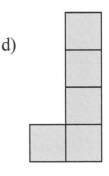

Q7. Find the perimetre of each figure in Question 6.

Q8. Change the following into the units shown:

a) 2 ha = ☐ m²   b) 30 000 m² = ☐ ha   c) 15 ha = ☐ m²

Q9.   Choose the most suitable units of area to measure the following:
   a)   the area of your living room   b)   the area of a sheet of paper
   c)   the area of a bathroom tile   d)   the area of a tennis court
   e)   the area of a cricket oval   f)   the area of a block of a land

Q10.   Each cube below represents a cubic centimetre. Find the volume of the following
       figures in cm³:

   a)   b)   c)

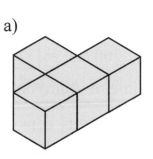   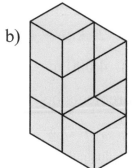   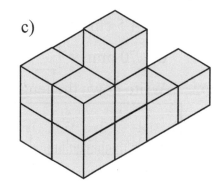

Q11.   Change the following to the units shown:

   a)   3 L = ☐ mL   b)   7 000 mL = ☐ L   c) $\frac{1}{2}$ a litre = ☐ mL

Q12.   Choose the most suitable units of capacity to measure the following:
   a)   capacity of a teaspoon   b)   a large bottle of coke
   c)   filling the car with petrol   d)   a glass of water

Q13.   Change the following to the units shown:

   a)   3 kg = ☐ g   b)   5 000 g = ☐ kg   c) $2\frac{1}{2}$ kg = ☐ g

Q14.   Choose the most suitable units of mass to measure the following:
   a)   mass of a dog   b)   a glass of water
   c)   a steak   d)   a bag of potatoes

Q15.   These digital clocks below show 24-hour time. Rewrite each in 12 hour time using
       am and pm:

   a) [08:00]   b) [14:00]   c) [11:30]   d) [19:00]

Q16.   Write each time below in 24-hour time:

   a) 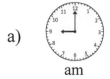   b)    c)   d)
        am   pm   am   pm

Year 5 Essential Exercises
Warwick Marlin © Five Senses Education

Q1. Change the following into the units shown:

a) $4.5 \text{ cm} = \boxed{} \text{ mm}$ b) $2\frac{1}{2} \text{ km} = \boxed{} \text{ m}$ c) $7\frac{1}{2} \text{ m} = \boxed{} \text{ cm}$

d) $70 \text{ mm} = \boxed{} \text{ cm}$ e) $4\ 000 \text{ m} = \boxed{} \text{ km}$ f) $300 \text{ cm} = \boxed{} \text{ m}$

Q2. Write down the length measurements below using millimetres (mm) only:

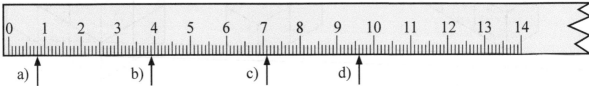

Q3. Write down the answers above in decimal form using cm only.

Q4. With the aid of your ruler, find the perimeter of the following figures and write your answers in decimal form using cm only.

a)  b)  c)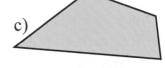

Q5. Choose the most appropriate units to measure the lengths of the following:

a) dining room table   b) length of your toothbrush
c) thickness of a ruler   d) distance from your house
                              to the supermarket.

Another word for 'most suitable units' is to say 'the most APPROPRIATE units'.

Q6. Each of the shapes is drawn on centimetre grid paper. Find the area of each shape in cm².

a) b) c)
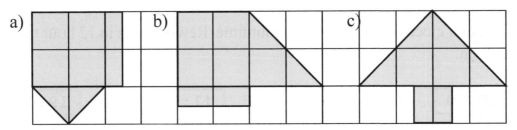

Q7. Choose the most appropriate units of area to measure the following areas:

a) postage stamp   b) farm   c) classroom floor   d) book cover

Q8. Change the following into the units shown:

a) $3\frac{1}{2} \text{ ha} = \boxed{} \text{ m}^2$ b) $40\ 000 \text{ m}^2 = \boxed{} \text{ ha}$ c) $1 \text{ cm}^2 = \boxed{} \text{ mm}^2$

Q9. By splitting each shape up into equal squares (along the marks shown), find the area of each shape in square units:

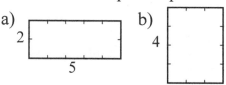

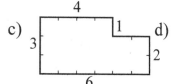

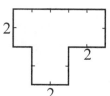

Q10. What is the volume of each solid shape below in cubic units:

a)

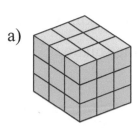

b)

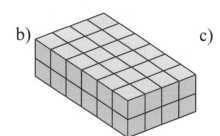

c)

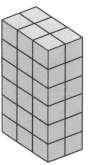

Q11. By splitting each solid shape into cubes (along the marks shown), find the volume of each shape in cubic centimetres (cm³):

a)

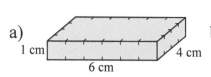

b)

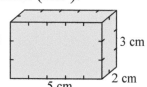

c)

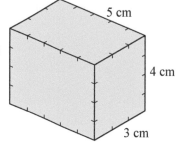

Q12. Change the following to the units shown:

a) $2 L = \boxed{} mL$ b) $5\,000\ mL = \boxed{} L$ c) $\frac{1}{4}$ of a litre $= \boxed{} mL$

d) $5\ kg = \boxed{} g$ e) $3\,000\ g = \boxed{} kg$ f) $\frac{3}{4}$ of a kg $= \boxed{} g$

Q13. Choose the most suitable units of capacity or mass to measure the following:

a) a bucket of water (mL or L)   b) the mass of a pencil (g or kg)

c) a swimming pool (L or kL)   d) the mass of a truck (kg or t)

Q14. These digital clocks below show 24-hour time. Rewrite each in 12-hour time using am or pm.

a) 06:30   b) 16:15   c) 10:25   d) 22:45

Q15. Write each time below in 24-hour time:

a) 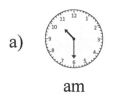   b)   c)   d)

am   pm   am   pm

Year 5 Essential Exercises
Warwick Marlin © Five Senses Education

PROBLEM SOLVING

Q1. If I jog 16 times around a track measuring 250 m, how many km will I run?

Q2. If the perimeter of a square is 32 m, what is the area of the square?

Q3. If I am 1.72 m tall, how many centimetres (cm) is this?

Q4. How many pieces of material 30 cm long can I cut from a length of material measuring 2.4 m long?

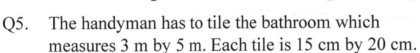

Q5. The handyman has to tile the bathroom which measures 3 m by 5 m. Each tile is 15 cm by 20 cm.
   a) How many tiles will he need?
   b) What will be the cost of the tiles if each one costs $2.50?

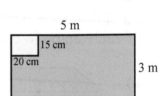

Q6. a) The distance from my house to Taree is 13.5 km. If I travel to Taree and back five times each week for work, what total distance is this?
   b) If my car uses one litre of petrol to travel 15 km, how many litres will I use each week to travel to Taree?

Q7. Firstly calculate the missing lengths and then find the perimeter of the following figures. (All angles are right angles, and the figures have not been drawn accurately.)

   a)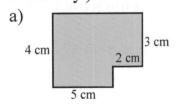
   b)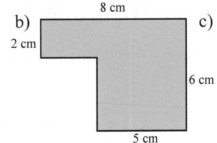
   c)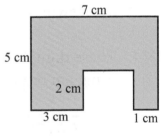

Q8. Write the following times as they would look on a 24-hour digital clock.

   a) quarter past 6 in the morning
   b) quarter past 6 in the afternoon
   c) 20 minutes to 8 in the evening
   d) quarter to 11 in the morning
   e) 11:27 am
   f) 2:35 pm
   g) 10:35 pm
   h) 6:07 am

Q9. Calculate the difference between each pair of times given below.

    a)   2:30 pm, 4:10 pm   b)   7:25 am, 3:15 pm   c)   6:49 am, 8:13 pm

Q10. Jenny wants a new carpet for her bedroom. Her bedroom is rectangular in shape, and it measures 5 m by 4 m. If the carpet costs $37.20 per square metre, how much will it cost for her new carpet?

Q11. Mr. Giovanni wants to put a fence around his rectangular yard. The width is 20 m and the length is one and a half times the width. If the fencing costs $14.35 per metre, how much will it cost to fence his yard.

Q12. I have a jug which can hold 3 litres of water when full.
    a)   How many full glasses (each having a capacity of 400 mL) can I fill with the jug?
    b)   How much water will be left in the jug?

Q13. There are 24 cans of sliced peaches in a carton. If each can has a mass of 500 g what is the mass of the carton in kilograms.

Q14. A labourer is moving some sand using a shovel and wheelbarrow. Each shovel can hold 2.5 kg of sand, and the wheelbarrow can hold 40 kg of sand.
    a)   How many shovels of sand will it take to fill the wheelbarrow?
    b)   If he moves 60 wheelbarrow loads, how many tonnes (t) of sand is this?

Q15. A medicine bottle contains 480 mL of cough mixture. If I take two teaspoons of cough mixture 3 times a day after each meal, how many days will the bottle of cough mixture last? (1 teaspoon = 5 mL of cough mixture)

Q16. By splitting each shape up into equal squares, find the area of each shape in square units. (**Note:** Figures are not drawn to scale.)

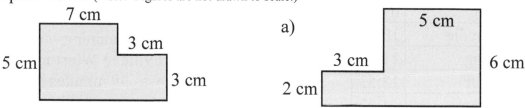

Q17. Find the volume of each solid prism shape in cubic centimetres.

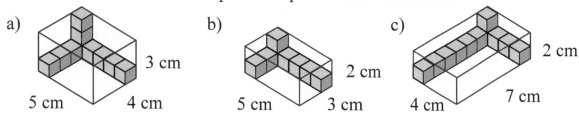

Q1. Change the following into the units shown using decimals.

a) 180 mm = ☐ cm   b) 1 400 m = ☐ km   c) 160 cm = ☐ m

d) 5.3 cm = ☐ mm   e) 2.7 ha = ☐ m²   f) 7 500 m² = ☐ ha

g) 6.25 kg = ☐ g   h) 3 750 g = ☐ kg   i) 4.7 t = ☐ kg

j) 850 g = ☐ kg   k) 7.2 L = ☐ mL   l) 1 750 mL = ☐ L

Q2. By using some logic, find the perimeters of the figures below.
(All angles are right angles and the measurements are in metres.)

a)   4
    2
    3
6   2

b)   3
    2
6   8

c)   8
7   3

Q3. A rectangle measures 3 cm by 5 cm. If the lengths of each side are doubled, how many times larger would the new rectangle be?

Q4. Using your knowledge of fractions, complete the following:

a) $\frac{1}{3}$ h = ☐ min   b) 5 min = ☐ s   c) 3 days = ☐ h

d) 15 s = ☐ min   e) 8 h = ☐ day   f) 4 h = ☐ s

g) 210 s = ☐ min   h) $\frac{1}{10}$ min = ☐ s   i) $\frac{3}{4}$ day = ☐ h

Q5.

TRAIN TIMETABLE	
Stanton	09:18
Dugong	09:57
Trancoville	10:38
Dunning	11:14
Red Hill	12:53
Darley	14:02
Winston	15:37
Stroud	16:29

a) Using 12-hour time (am or pm), what time does the train reach
(i) Dunning   (ii) Winston

b) How long does it take to travel from
(i) Dugong to Dunning
(ii) Trancoville to Winston

c) If the train was 39 minutes late reaching Winston, what time did it arrive?

d) How long does the journey from Stanton to Stroud take according to the time table?

e) Between which two towns was the longest part of the journey? How long did this section take?

Q6. By using the formula, find the area of the shaded figures below. You may have to calculate some unknown lengths.

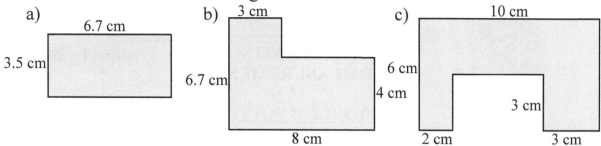

a) 6.7 cm, 3.5 cm

b) 3 cm, 6.7 cm, 8 cm

c) 10 cm, 6 cm, 4 cm, 3 cm, 2 cm, 3 cm

Q7. Find:

a) $\frac{3}{4}$ of 1L

b) $\frac{1}{4}$ of 1 kg

c) $\frac{3}{5}$ of 1 m

d) $\frac{1}{5}$ of 1 ha

e) $\frac{1}{8}$ of 1L

f) $\frac{3}{8}$ of 1 kg

g) $\frac{4}{5}$ of 1 km

h) $\frac{7}{10}$ of 1 t

Q8. By using the volume formula, or by splitting each shape up into cubic units, find the volume of the following prisms in cubic centimeters. (The figures are not drawn to scale.)

a)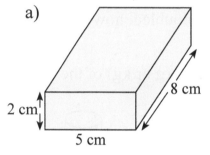
8 cm, 2 cm, 5 cm

b)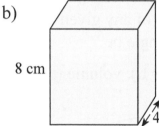
8 cm, 7 cm, 4 cm

c)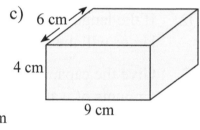
6 cm, 4 cm, 9 cm

Q9. The following questions are testing your knowledge of the relationship between capacity, mass and volume (using water). This is quite difficult extension work. See page 55 to refresh your memory.

Complete the following:

a) 10 mL = ☐ cm³

b) 60 cm³ = ☐ mL

c) 1 L = ☐ mL

d) 1 L = ☐ cm³

e) 10 mL = ☐ g

f) 10 cm³ = ☐ g

g) 3 L = ☐ kg

h) 120 mL = ☐ g

i) 2 000 cm³ = ☐ kg

Q10. A rectangular container is 30 cm high, 80 cm long and 50 cm wide.

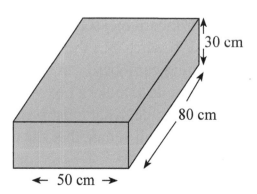
30 cm, 80 cm, 50 cm

a) Find the volume in cubic centimetres (cm³).

b) Find the capacity in milliliters (mL).

c) Find the capacity in litres (L).

d) Find the mass of water in kilogram (kg) which would fill the container.

Year 5 Essential Exercises
Warwick Marlin © Five Senses Education

PROBLEM SOLVING

Q1. A small hobby farm is in the shape of a rectangle, with a length of 500 m and a width of 300 m.

    a) What is the perimeter of the farm in kilometres (km)?

    b) What is the area of the farm in hectares (ha)?

    c) The farmer decides to divide up his land into small square blocks and sell them individually to people who want to build a house. If each square block measures 50 m by 50 m, how many subdivisions can he have on his farm?

    d) What is the area of each subdivision in hectares? If he sells each subdivision for $75 000, how much money will he make altogether?

Q2. If the length and breadth of any given rectangle is doubled, how many times larger will the new rectangle be?

Q3. Give the capacity (mL or L), volume (cm^3) and mass (g or kg) of the following amounts of water:

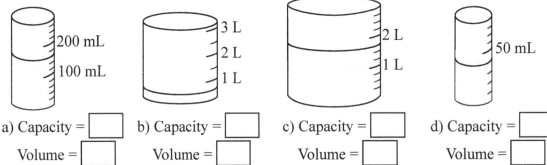

a) Capacity = ☐
    Volume = ☐
    Mass = ☐

b) Capacity = ☐
    Volume = ☐
    Mass = ☐

c) Capacity = ☐
    Volume = ☐
    Mass = ☐

d) Capacity = ☐
    Volume = ☐
    Mass = ☐

Q4.

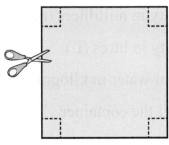

The shaded area of this cube is 64 cm^2.
What is the volume of the cube?

Q5. Amy wants to make a box from a square sheet of cardboard measuring 12 cm by 12 cm. She cuts out four squares (see the dotted lines) so that the remaining cardboard can be folded into a box shape. If she wants to make a box with the LARGEST VOLUME possible, what must be the length of the side of each small square that she cuts out?

Q6. Mr. Chu is preparing a new vegetable patch. He has dug up a large trench measuring 8 m long by $4\frac{1}{2}$ m wide by 50 cm deep. If each cubic metre of soil weighs 1 100 kg, how many tonnes of soil will he need to order?

Q7. An empty rectangular tank is 40 cm long and 30 cm wide. A hose fills the tank with water at the rate of 6 litres/minute.

   a) What will be the height of the water after 5 minutes?
   b) How long (in minutes and seconds) will it take to reach a height of 32 cm.
   c) If the tank itself weighs 15.8 kg, how heavy will it be when he the water reaches a height of 35 cm?

Q8. The rules for finding the area of a right angled triangle, a parallelogram and the third figure have not been explained to you yet. See if you can work out a logical way of finding the shaded areas of the 3 figures.

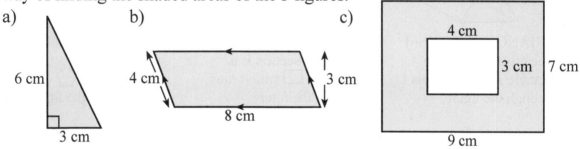

a) 6 cm, 3 cm
b) 4 cm, 8 cm, 3 cm
c) 4 cm, 3 cm, 7 cm, 9 cm

Q9. If the volume of a perfect cube is 343 cm³, find the surface area of the six square faces.

Q10. Builders and architects usually use millimeters in their drawings and plans. Mr. Gatti has some plans drawn for an extension to his house. Find the area in square metres of:
   a) bedroom A
   b) the family room
   c) the complete extension

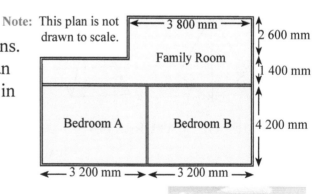

Note: This plan is not drawn to scale.
3 800 mm
2 600 mm
Family Room
1 400 mm
Bedroom A   Bedroom B   4 200 mm
3 200 mm   3 200 mm

Q11. A car is travelling at a constant speed of 60 km/h.
   a) How far will the car travel in $2\frac{1}{5}$ hours?
   b) How many hours and minutes will it take to travel 195 km?

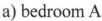

Q12. If it takes 7 men 4 full days (assume a full working day is 10 hours) to paint the outside walls of a house, how many hours will it take 5 men to paint the same house?

Year 5 Essential Exercises
Warwick Marlin © Five Senses Education

SHAPE

The "Australian Curriculum Mathematics" (ACM) reference for this sub-strand of "Measurement and Geometry" (NA) is below:

☞ Connect three-dimensional objects with their nets and other two-dimensional representations (ACMMG III).

❖ PRISMS

Solid shapes can be split into 3 groups:

1. Prisms   2. Pyramids   3. Neither prisms nor pyramids

> A prism is named according to its cross section. The cross-section is the constant shape which runs through the figure.

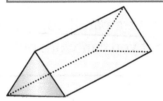   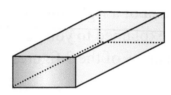   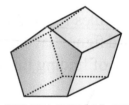

TRIANGULAR PRISM
The cross section is a triangle △ which runs through the figure.

RECTANGULAR PRISM
The cross section is a rectangle ☐ which runs through the figure.

PENTAGONAL PRISM
The cross section is a pentagon ⬠ which runs through the figure.

❖ PYRAMIDS

All pyramids have one face which may not be a triangle. It is this face (square, rectangle, pentagon, etc.) that is used to name the pyramid. If all of its faces are triangular, then it is called a triangular pyramid or a tetrahedron.

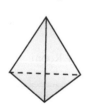      

> The dotted lines show edges which we cannot see.

❖ NAMES OF FEATURES ON A 3-D SHAPE

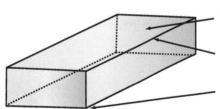

FACE – the flat part of the surface

EDGE – the line where two faces meet

VERTEX – where the three faces meet

> The rectangular prism on the left has:
> 6 faces
> 12 edges
> 8 vertices

CYLINDER   CONE   SPHERE

❖ SOME OTHER 3-D SHAPES

We stated above that some solids are neither prisms nor pyramids. Three very common solids which fall into this group are shown on the right.

❖ INTRODUCTION TO NETS

It is easy to make a solid shape from a piece of paper or cardboard by first drawing a net of the faces of the solid. The net is made up of different plane shapes (rectangles, squares, triangles, etc.) When the net is cut out, and the faces of the net folded along the edges, then the solid is formed.

The easiest net to understand and make is the net for a perfect cube. It has six square faces.

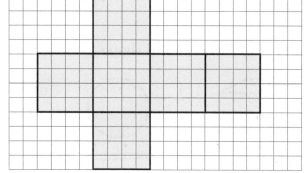

❖ DRAWING SOLID SHAPES

3 dimensional solids can be drawn on paper more easily using square grid paper, triangular grid paper, square dot paper or isometric dot paper. They help to give depth to the solid by showing different projections or viewing points.

"square grid paper"

"triangular grid paper"

"isometric dot grid paper"

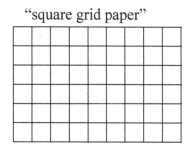
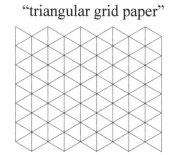
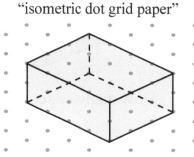

❖ CUBE MODELS AND ISOMETRIC DRAWINGS

Students should be able to explore the different possible combinations of 2, 3, 4, etc. interlocking cubes. They should be able to show all the different combinations on isometric dot paper.

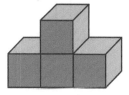
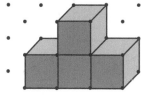
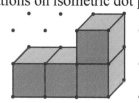

❖ DIFFERENT VIEWS OF SOLIDS

Students should also be able to draw what the cube model would look like from the front, side or top. This kind of activity shows how much a student can visualize and manipulate 3-D images.

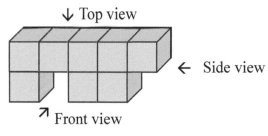

↓ Top view

← Side view

↗ Front view

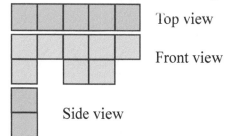

Top view

Front view

Side view

 For further reference, see 'Understanding Year 5 Maths' by W. Marlin

Q1. Name the following solid shapes:

a) 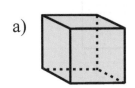   b)   c)   d)

e)   f)   g)   h)

Q2. How many faces do each of the following solids have?

a) 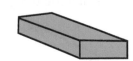   b)   c)

Q3. How many edges do each of the solids have in Q2?

Q4. How many vertices do each of the solids have in Q2?

> Vertices means the same as corners.

Q5. What solid shape can be made from each group of faces below?

a)

b)

c)

d)

e)

Q6. Copy each shaded drawing below on isometric dot paper. Part of the copied drawing has already been done for you.

a)

b)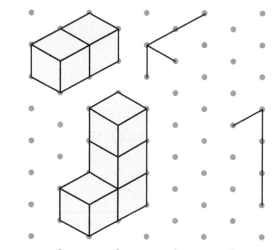

c)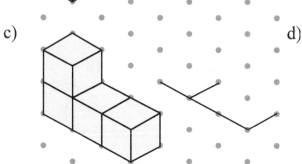

d)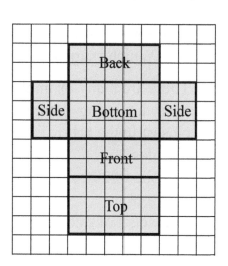

Q7. The net of a certain solid shape has been drawn on squared grid paper on the right hand side of the page.

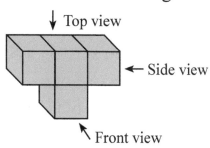

a) If the faces were folded over on the bold lines shown, what solid shape would be formed?

b) Draw a sketch of the solid shape and write in the dimensions of the sides.

c) What is the volume of this solid shape in cubic units (units³)?

d) What is the area of the net in square units (units²)?

Q8. Study the picture of the 4 joined tetracubes shown on the right. Sketch:

a) the front view

b) the side view

c) the top view

↓ Top view
← Side view
↖ Front view

Q9. How many tetracubes are used to build each of these models?

a)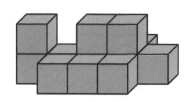

b)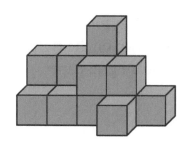

Year 5 Essential Exercises
Warwick Marlin © Five Senses Education

Level 2 — SHAPE — Average

Q1. (i) If you could cut or slice the following solids with a knife (where shown in each picture), what is the shape of the cross-section that you will see?

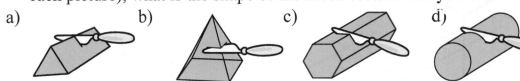

a) b) c) d)

(ii) Which of the solids has the same (or uniform) cross section no matter where you cut it?

(iii) Which of the solids could be called prisms?

(iv) Which shape is neither a prism nor a pyramid?

Q2. There are many examples of solid shapes around the house, and also in our everyday living. Name a solid (cylinder, cone, rectangular, prism, etc.) that is closest to the following:

a) glass

b) party hat

c) tin of baked beans

d) pile of 20 coins

e) volcano

f) soccer ball

g) book

h) ice blocks

i) simple tent

j) packet of rice bubbles

k) orange

l) toblerone chocolate bar

Q3. Name the following solids:

a)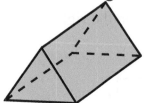

b)

c)

Q4. How many faces do each of the solids in Q3. Have?

Q5. How many edges do each of the solids in Q3. Have?

Q6. How many vertices do each of the solids in Q3. Have?

Q7. Draw the net for the rectangular prism shown on the right on ordinary $\frac{1}{2}$ cm square grid paper.

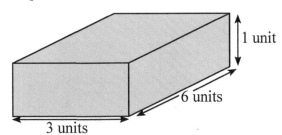

1 unit

6 units

3 units

Q8. Match each solid with its correct net below:

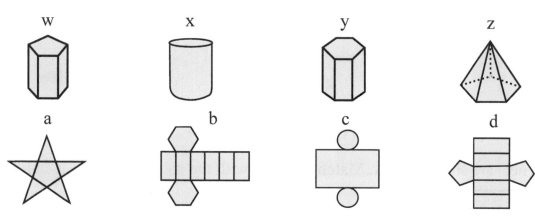

Q9. With the aid of isometric dot paper, redraw the 3 solid shapes shown below:

a)   )   )

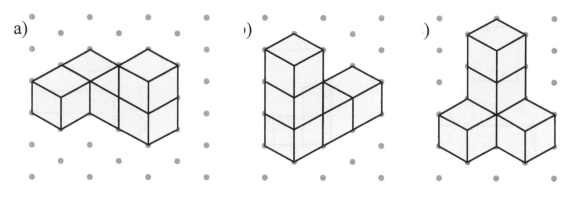

Q10. With the aid of triangular grid paper, redraw the 3 solid shapes below.

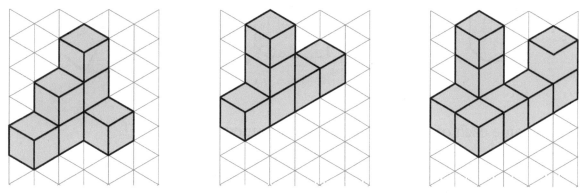

Q11. Thirteen tetracubes have been joined together to make the solid shape on the right. Sketch:

a) the front view

b) the side view

c) the top view

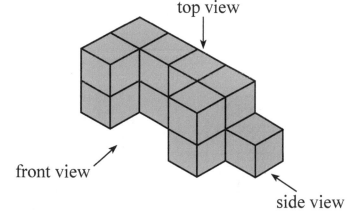

Year 5 Essential Exercises
Warwick Marlin © Five Senses Education

PROBLEM SOLVING

Q1. Six nets are shown below. Match each net with the solid 3-D shape it can form.

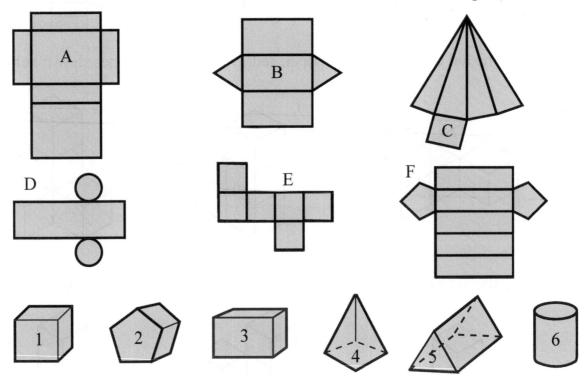

Q2. Name each of the solid 3-D objects formed in Question 1.

1. Name: _____

2. Name _____

3. Name: _____

4. Name _____

5. Name: _____

6. Name _____

Q3.

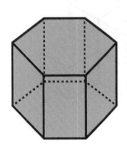

a) Is the solid shape on the left a pyramid or a prism?
b) Explain the reason for your answer in a).
c) How many faces does the solid have?
d) How many edges does the solid have?
e) How many vertices does the solid have?
f) Name the solid.

Q4. Draw the net on ordinary square grid paper shown on the right, for the rectangular prism below.

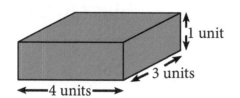

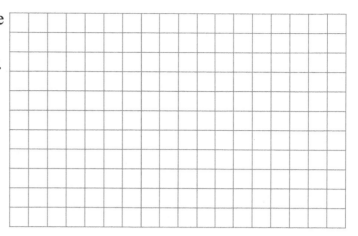

Q5. Redraw the 2 solids below on isometric dot paper.

a)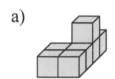

b)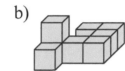

Q6. For each solid below, draw the top view, the front view, and the side view.

Example: Cylinder

a)
Cone

Top view:

b)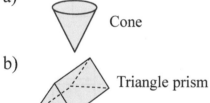
Triangle prism

Front view:

c)
Sphere

Side view:

Q7. a) How many cubes must be subtracted from solid X so that it becomes like solid Y?

b) How many cubes must be added to solid X to make it a perfect 3 × 3 × 3 cube?

c) How many cubes must be added to solid Y to make it a perfect 3 × 3 × 3 cube?

Solid X

Solid Y

Year 5 Essential Exercises
Warwick Marlin © Five Senses Education

Q1. Which two solids have been joined together to make the solid shapes shown on the right?

a)   b)

Q2. In Q1. part (a), how many faces, edges and vertices does the solid have?

Q3. Name the solid shapes below which have the following properties:
a) 7 faces, 15 edges, 10 vertices
b) 7 faces, 12 edges, 7 vertices
c) 2 faces, 1 curved surface, 0 vertex
d) 1 face, 1 curved surface, 1 vertex

The plural of vertex is vertices.

Q4. The figure on the right shows the net of a cube. If the perimeter of the net is 98 cm, find the
a) volume of the cube
b) the total area of the six faces
c) the sum of all the edges of the cube

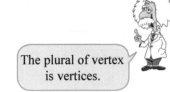

Q5. The diagram on the right shows the net of a rectangular prism with a square base. When the net is folded along the lines, what is the
a) volume of the rectangular prism?
b) total area of the six faces?
c) sum of all the edges of the prism?

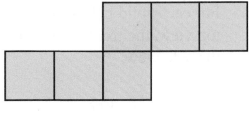

3 cm

10 cm

Q6. The net on the right has been drawn exactly to size using $\frac{1}{2}$ cm square grid paper. When it is folded along the lines shown,
a) what solid is formed
b) draw a sketch of the solid
c) what is the sum of all the lengths of the edges?

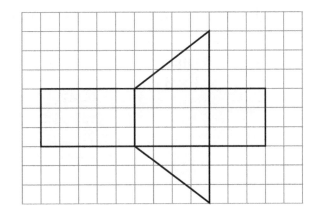

Q7. The net of the die below is folded into a cube. Which solids below will be obtained?

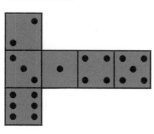

a)   b)

c)   d)

Q8. The net of a cone is made up from 2 shapes. Draw a sketch of the 2 shapes needed.

Q9. 4 different solid shapes are sliced 3 times. The pictures of the front view of each slice (called the cross section) are shown below. Name each of the 4 solid shapes.

a) 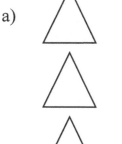 b)   c) 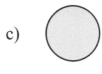 d)

Q10. For the following 3 solids, draw the front view, the top view and the side view.

a) 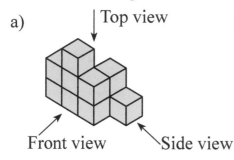 b) c)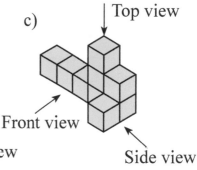

Q11. Redraw each of the solids in Q10 on isometric dotted paper.

Q12. Two different shapes are built using tetracubes, and the different views of each solid are shown below. Sketch each solid using isometric dotted grid paper.

a)  b)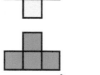

Year 5 Essential Exercises
Warwick Marlin © Five Senses Education

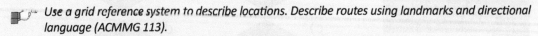

LOCATION AND TRANSFORMATION

The "Australian Curriculum Mathematics" (ACM) references for this sub-strand of "Measurement and Geometry" (MG) are below:

☞ *Use a grid reference system to describe locations. Describe routes using landmarks and directional language (ACMMG 113).*

☞ *Describe translations, reflections and rotations of two dimensional shapes, identify line and rotational symmetries (ACMMG 114).*

❖ **SCALED DRAWING**

A scaled drawing has exactly the same shape of the object they represent, but has a different size (usually very much smaller).
Maps are very good examples of scaled drawings.

SCALE: length on drawing ≡ real length

> The symbol ≡ means equivalent. 1 cm is equivalent to 200 m.

Example:

Typical map scale on the right.

METRES

0   200   400   600   800   1000

SCALE:
1 cm ≡ 200 m

❖ **GRID REFERENCES OR COORDINATES**

To describe an exact position on a page (or any flat surface like a map) we can use a letter and a number. Firstly, we go along the horizontal line to find the letter and then we go up vertically to find the number. The position is written as (letter, number). These are called the **COORDINATES** of the position.

Example: Give the coordinates of the 4 shapes shown in the picture.

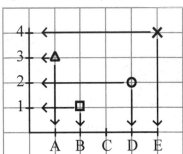

The position of the triangle △ is (A, 3)
The position of the square □ is (B, 1)
The position of the circle ○ is (D, 2)
The position of the cross ✕ is (E, 4)

> Remember to write the letter first (horizontal) and the number second (vertical).

❖ **SYMMETRY**

If one half of the shape can be folded exactly onto the other half, then the shape is said to have a LINE OF SYMMETRY. Shapes which have one or more lines of symmetry are called SYMMETRICAL.

The letter A has
1 line of symmetry.

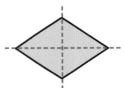

A diamond shape has
2 lines of symmetry.

A square has
4 lines of symmetry.

❖ REFLECTION

In reflection, the mirror line acts in the same way as a line of symmetry. Each point on the image must be directly opposite the object, and also the same distance on the other side of the mirror line.

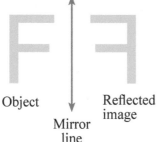

Object   Reflected image

Mirror line

Think of reflection as "flipping the object over".

❖ TRANSLATION

When a shape is moved to another position, without turning or twisting in any way, then it is called a **TRANSLATION.**

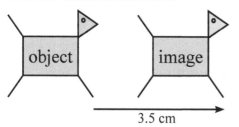

object   image

3.5 cm

Each point on the object has been translated 3.5 cm to the right.

Think of translation as 'a sliding movement'.

❖ ROTATION

Rotation means turning the object through a fixed point in a clockwise direction. The fixed point need not be in the centre of the object, or even on the object.

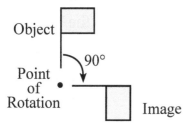

Object

90°

Point of Rotation

Image

The flag has been rotated about the point through 90° or $\frac{1}{4}$ of a turn.

Think of rotation as 'a twisting movement'.

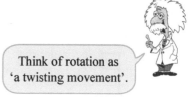

❖ ENLARGEMENT

If you switch a torch on at night, and then place one hand about half a metre away, you will see a bigger shadow of your hand on the wall. This is the same way that enlargement works. We firstly need a point, called the "centre of enlargement". Think of this point as the light bulb sending out rays of light. We also need an object (like your hand), and then we will get some larger image (like the shadow of your hand on the wall).

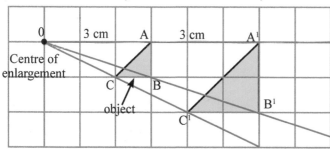

0   3 cm   A   3 cm   A¹

Centre of enlargement

C   B

object

C¹   B¹

In this example, each point on the larger triangle is twice as far from 0 as each point on the smaller triangle.

We say that the original triangle ABC has been enlarged to triangle A¹B¹C¹ by a scale factor of 2. Reflection, translation, rotation and enlargement are called the 4 TRANSFORMATIONS.

 For further reference, see 'Understanding Year 5 Maths' by W. Marlin

LOCATION AND TRANSFORMATION

Easier

Q1. Draw in the lines of symmetry for the following shapes:

a) **T**   b) **E**   c) **H**

Q2. Copy the following shapes and draw the reflections in the mirror lines shown:

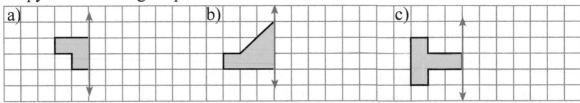

a)   b)   c)

Q3. Translate each of the following shapes by the amounts shown:

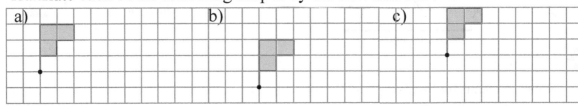

a)   b)   c)

3 units to   2 units up   2 units down
the right   3 units to the left

Q4. Rotate the flags in a clockwise direction around the point (bold) by the amounts shown:

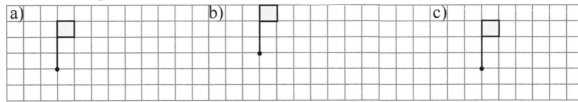

a)   b)   c)

Rotate 90°   rotate 180 °   rotate 270°
($\frac{1}{4}$ turn)   ($\frac{1}{2}$ turn)   ($\frac{3}{4}$ turn)

Q5. Give the grid references (or coordinates) of the following points:

a) △ b) ✗ c) ✚ d) ◓ e) ○

Remember to write the letter first (horizontal) and the number (vertical) second.

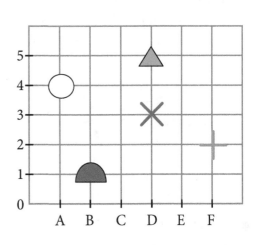

FINDING DIRECTIONS

The four primary directions are North(N), South(S), East(E), West(W).
There is a $\frac{1}{4}$ turn, or 90° angle, between each of the four primary directions.
The 4 major primary directions can
be split up further into 45° angles.
If we turn half way between North
and East, we will face North East (NE).

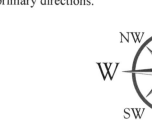

Q6. Look at the picture on the right, and state the position of the objects by writing
north, south, east, or west.

The deer is _____ of the
camping site.
The lake is _____ of the
camping site.
The forest is _____ of the
camping site.
The mountains are _____ of
the camping site.

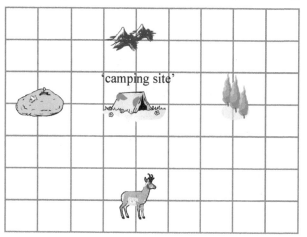

ROTATIONAL SYMMETRY

If a shape can fit onto itself after a certain rotation (not a full one), then it said to have
ROTATIONAL SYMMETRY. The number of times it can fit exactly onto itself in one full revolution
is called the " order of rotational symmetry".

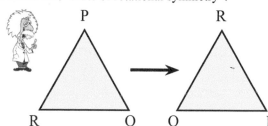

An equilateral triangle (all sides equal) has rotational
symmetry because it can fit exactly onto itself after $\frac{1}{3}$ of a
turn (120°). The triangle has rotational symmetry of
order 3, because it can fit onto itself 3 times.

Q7. Which of the following figures have rotational symmetry?

a) S   b) T   c) ▢   d)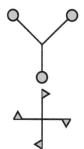

e) ◆   f) ▮   g) Z   h)

Q8. (i) What is the order of rotational symmetry for the square at c) above?
(ii) What is the order of rotational symmetry for the letter Z at g) above?

Year 5 Essential Exercises
Warwick Marlin © Five Senses Education

LOCATION AND TRANSFORMATION

Q1. The scale on a certain map is shown on the right.

1 cm ≡ 50 m

a) How far is 3 cm on land?

b) How far is 8 cm on land?

c) The church lies 350 m away from school. How far will this be on the map?

d) The supermarket is about $\frac{1}{4}$ of a kilometre from our house. How far will this be on the map?

e) If 1 cm on the map is equivalent to 50 m on land (1 cm ≡ 50 m) how much will 1 mm represent on land?

Q2. Using grid paper similar to that shown on the right, mark in the following grid references with a solid bold dot.

i) (C,1) ii) (D,4) iii) (F,2)

iv) (A,5) v) (B,3) vi) (E,0)

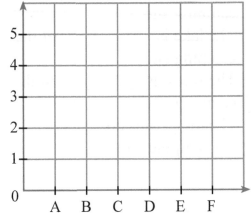

Q3. Draw in the line(s) of symmetry for the following shapes:

a) b) c) d)

Q4. Copy the following shapes and draw the reflections in the mirror lines shown:

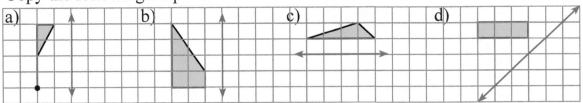

a) b) c) d)

Q5. Translate each of the shapes below by the amounts shown:

a) b)

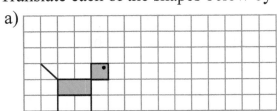 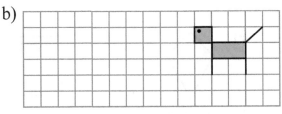

4 units to the right and 1 unit up

5 units to the left and 2 units down

Q6. The letter T shown on the right is rotated clockwise about the point shown (•). Draw its final position after:

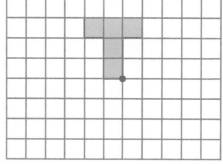

a) A rotation of 90° ($\frac{1}{4}$ turn).

b) A rotation of 180° ($\frac{1}{2}$ turn).

c) A rotation of 270° ($\frac{3}{4}$ turn).

(**HINT:** tracing paper may be very useful.)

Q7. A rectangle ABCD is enlarged to produce an image A¹ B¹ C¹ D¹. The centre of enlargement is at O.

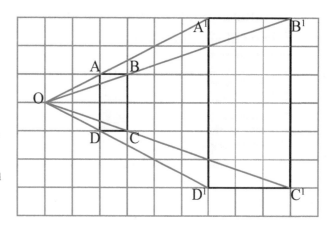

a) What is the length of OA and OA¹?

b) How many times longer is OA¹ compared to OA?

c) How many times longer is A¹B¹ compared to AB?

d) What is the scale factor for this enlargement?

The word NEWS comes from North (N), East (E), West (W), and South (S).

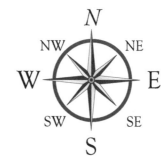

Q8. Name the directions in the figure on the right hand of the page if I walk from:

i) A to B   ii) A to C   iii) A to D
iv) B to A   v) A to E   vi) C to A
vii) D to A   viii) E to A

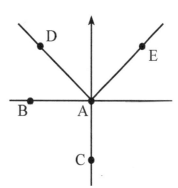

Q9. a) Name 4 important transformations.

b) Which transformation changes the size of the final image?

Year 5 Essential Exercises
Warwick Marlin © Five Senses Education

PROBLEM SOLVING

Q1. The map of the "Pinjarra Cycle Marathon" starts at a town called Pinjarra. There are 8 stages to the race. In the first stage the cyclists head off to the town of Kumari. Study the map and answer the questions below. Please carefully note the scale on the map.

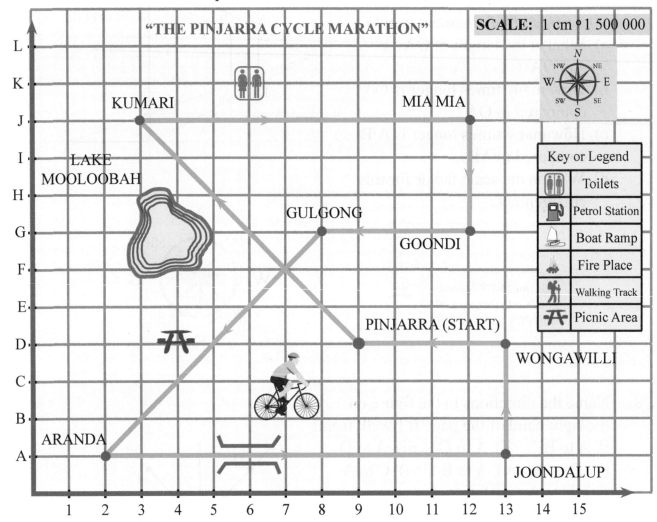

a) The cyclists started at the town of Pinjarra and started cycling towards Kumari. In which direction was this?

b) About two thirds of the way to Kumari, what did they see on the left hand side of the road?

c) What is the grid reference of Kumari?

d) From Kumari to Mia Mia what did they see on the left hand side of the road?

distance they cycled from Kumari to Mia Mia?

rs to cycle from Mia Mia to Goondi, what was their

/hour during this stage?

at a motel in Goondi, and early the next morning they

n what direction was this?

n kilometres from Gulgong to Aranda?

they cycle after Gulgong?

the right hand side at (4, D)?

at Aranda before cycling to Joondalup. What did they

nce of Wongawilli?

cycle the last leg from Wongawilli to Pinjarra.

e speed over this final stage?

n) How many kilometres did they cycle altogether over the 2 full days?

Q2. Which transformation has taken place in each of the following diagrams?

a)
object

image

b)
object image

c)
object image

d)
object

image

Q3. The shaded triangle on the right is
firstly reflected in mirror 1, then
this reflection is reflected for
a second time in mirror 2.
Draw both reflections on the square
grid paper provided.

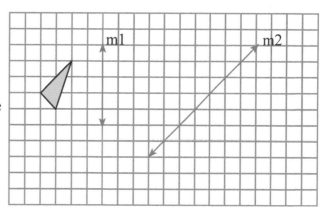

Q4. If 2 figures are said to be CONGRUENT, which of the following is true?

a) The figures have the same shape, but are different in size.
b) The figures have the same size, but are different in shape.
c) The figures are identical (exactly the same) in both size and shape.

Year 5 Essential Exercises
Warwick Marlin © Five Senses Education

The following questions refer to the map of Australia shown below. Some coordinates may not lie exactly on a town or city, so please just give the nearest whole number and letter. **Example:** Kalgoorlie is at approximately (6, H).

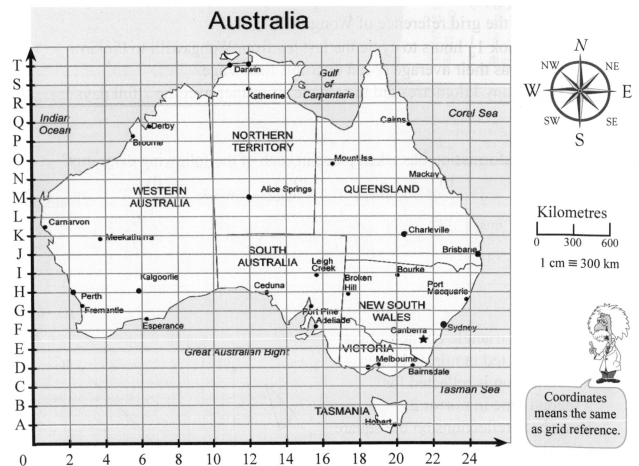

Q1. What are the nearest coordinates for the following cities:

a) Sydney   b) Melbourne   c) Perth   d) Brisbane

Q2. Which towns or cities lie closest to the following grid positions:

a) (12, S)   b) (16, O)   c) (22, N)   d) (15, F)

Q3. a) What town is almost in the middle of Australia?

b) What are the coordinates for this town?

Q4. Which town along the coast line lies about half way between Sydney and Brisbane?

Q5. Which town in NSW lies North West (NW) of Canberra?

Q6. With the aid of the scale and a ruler, what is the straight line distance from Perth to Hobart?

Q7. If an aeroplane can fly at 600 km/h, how many hours and minutes will it take to fly from Perth to Hobart?

Q8. What are the coordinates for Darwin?

Q9. What is the distance from Darwin to Alice Springs using the scale?

Q10. What town in Western Australia lies almost South of Derby?

Q11. Queensland, Northern Territory and South Australia meet at one point. What are the coordinates of this point?

Q12. Reflect each of the following shapes in the lines shown:

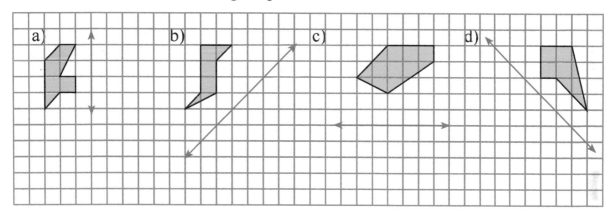

Q13. Translate each of the following shapes by the amounts shown:

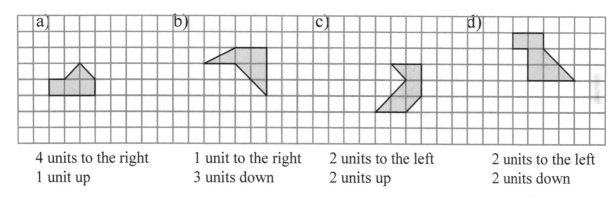

| 4 units to the right | 1 unit to the right | 2 units to the left | 2 units to the left |
| 1 unit up | 3 units down | 2 units up | 2 units down |

Q14. Rotate each flag below through 90° ($\frac{1}{4}$ turn) in a clockwise direction around the the solid dot shown:

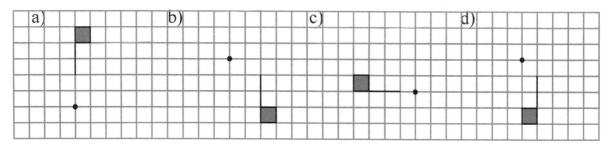

Year 5 Essential Exercises
Warwick Marlin © Five Senses Education

PROBLEM SOLVING

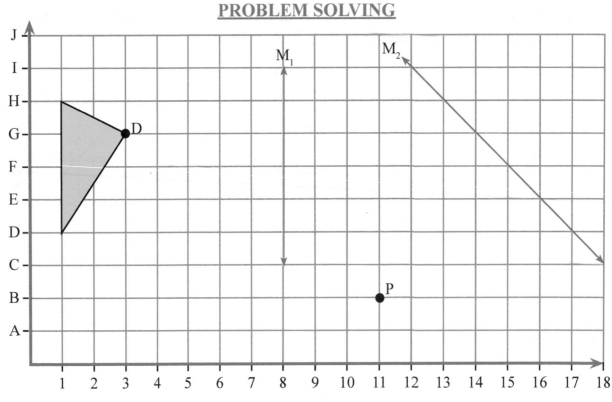

Q1. a) The shaded triangle shown in the grid above has a solid dot in the right hand corner, labelled by the capital letter D. Translate the triangle 4 units to the right and give the new grid position of D.

b) Draw the reflection of this new position in the mirror (M_1). Give the new grid position of D.

c) Rotate this figure 90° ($\frac{1}{4}$ turn) around the point P. Give the new grid position of D.

d) Finally, reflect this image in the second mirror M_2.
Note: there should be 4 drawings of triangles in the grid above.

Q2. The following shapes have rotational symmetry. Give the order of rotational symmetry for each figure.

a)   b)    c) 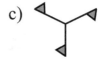   d)

Q3. A triangle ABC is enlarged to produce an image called $A^1B^1C^1$. The centre of enlargement is at O.

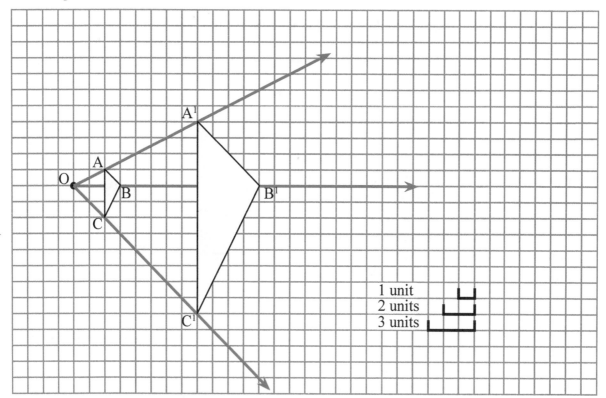

a) What is the length of OB in units?
b) What is the length of OB^1 in units?
c) How many times longer is OB^1 than OB?
d) What is the scale factor for this enlargement?

Q4. On 1 cm squared grid paper, a square ABCD is drawn. The centre of enlargement is at point P. Using a scale factor of 3, draw the new image and label the corners $A^1B^1C^1D'$. These should be in the same relative positions as A, B, C, and D.

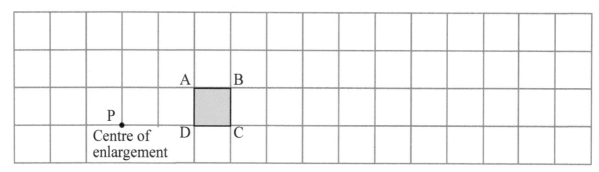

a) How many units long is PD?
b) How many units long is PD^1?
c) What is the area of ABCD in square centimetres?
d) What is the area of $A^1B^1C^1D^1$ in square centimetres?
e) How many times bigger is the area of $A^1B^1C^1D^1$ compared to the original square ABCD?

Year 5 Essential Exercises
Warwick Marlin © Five Senses Education

GEOMETRIC REASONING

The "Australian Curriculum Mathematics" (ACM) reference for this sub-strand of "Measurement and Geometry" (MG) is below:

☞ Estimate, measure and compare angles using degrees. Construct angles using a protractor (ACMMG 112).

❖ POINTS, LINES, INTERVALS & RAYS

A POINT, which is denoted by a capital letter, may be used to show a precise position on the page. The point on the right is read as point C.

•C

A STRAIGHT LINE doesn't have any 'end' points. The symbol is shown by an arrow on either side of the line. The line AB is shown on the right. Sometimes shown as $\overleftrightarrow{AB}$.

An INTERVAL (sometimes called a line interval) has 2 definite end points. The symbols are shown by 2 solid dots or short lines at the end points. The interval PQ is shown using both methods. Sometimes shown as $\overline{PQ}$.

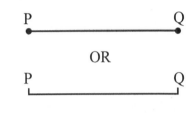

A RAY is a straight line with only one end point. The symbol is shown with a solid dot on one end, and an arrow at the other end. Sometimes shown as $\overrightarrow{MN}$.

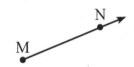

❖ NAMING ANGLES

An angle is made up of 2 rays which meet at a common point called the **VERTEX.**
For example, BA and BC are the rays (or arms) of the angle which meet at the vertex B.
There are 5 main ways of naming the angle shown:

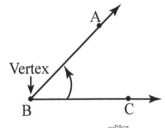

(i)	∠ABC or	∠CBA
(ii)	AB̂C or	CB̂A
(iii)	∠B	

The vertex must always be the middle letter, when using either of the first two methods shown.

NOTE:
(1) Method (i) and (ii) above are used most of the time.
(2) The vertex must always be the middle letter when using methods (i) or (ii).
(3) ∠B can only be used if there is no possibility of confusion—we hardly ever use method (iii).

❖ THE PROTRACTOR

A protractor is an instrument which is used to give an accurate measurement of angle size. Angles are measured in degrees, which is denoted by the symbol °. Most school protractors have 2 different sets of readings on them — a clockwise reading and an anticlockwise reading. You can see that readings on the outside go from 0° to 180° in a clockwise direction, and the readings on the inner part of the protractor go from 0° to 180° in an anticlockwise direction.

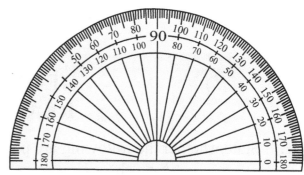

The scale of a protractor is in degrees, usually from 0° to 180°

> The unit of angle measurement is the degree.
> The symbol is °

❖ TYPES OF ANGLES

Angles can be arranged into 6 major types (or groups). You should be able to state what TYPE of angle it is just by looking at it — without the use of a protractor!

DIAGRAM	TYPE	ANGLE SIZE
	Acute angle (called a 'sharp angle' in previous years)	Less than 90°
The symbol for right angle!!	Right angle (called a 'square angle' in previous years)	Exactly 90° (or $\frac{1}{4}$ of a full turn)
	Obtuse angle (called a 'blunt angle' in previous years)	Between 90° and 180°
	Straight angle	Exactly 180° (or $\frac{1}{2}$ of a full turn)
	Reflex angle	Between 180° and 360°
	Revolution	Exactly 360° (or 1 complete turn)

❖ MEASURING, CONSTRUCTING & ESTIMATING ANGLES

The above 3 important geometrical concepts are thoroughly investigated and explained in the book titled "Understanding Year 5 Maths" by the same author. As explained in the introduction, this book primarily focuses on exercises rather than detailed theory and explanations. However, some limited assistance will be provided in the actual exercises, when the above concepts are tested.

 For further reference, see 'Understanding Year 5 Maths' by W. Marlin

Year 5 Essential Exercises
Warwick Marlin © Five Senses Education

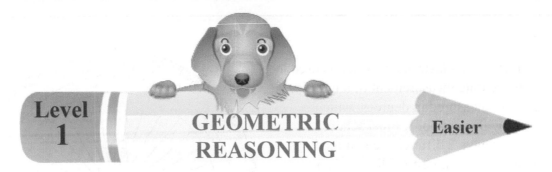

Q1. State whether the following are points, lines, rays or intervals:

a) 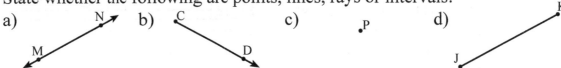 b) c) d)

Q2. Measure the lengths of the following line intervals to the nearest millimetre (mm):

a) P Q b) T U c) W X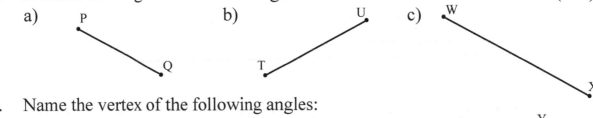

Q3. Name the vertex of the following angles:

a) M N L b) Q R P c) F D E d) Y X Z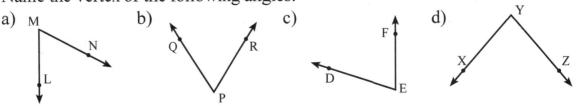

Q4. Use the method of ∠ABC to name the angles in Q3.

Q5. Write down the size of each angle:

(Hint: Each protractor has 2 different sets of readings on them — a clockwise reading on the outside and an anticlockwise reading on the inside. To make sure you select the correct reading, ask yourself "is the angle you are measuring less then, or bigger than 90°?")

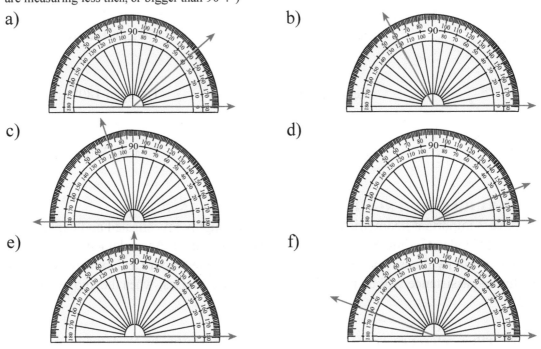

a) b)

c) d)

e) f)

Q6. There are 8 diagrams of different sized angles shown below.

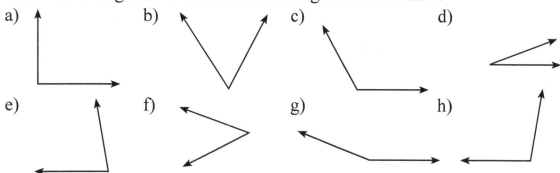

    (i)   Which figure shows the smallest angle?
    (ii)   Which figure shows the largest angle?
    (iii)   Which angle is bigger a) or c)?
    (iv)   Which angle is smaller e) or f)?
    (v)   Which angle is a right angle?
    (vi)   List the 8 angles in order of size (using the letters) from the smallest angle to the largest angle.

Q7. Name each of the following two dimensional shapes, and state how many sides and how many angles each shape has.

a)   b)   c)   d)

Q8. In previous years of schooling, an 'acute angle' was called a 'sharp angle', and an 'obtuse angle' was called a 'blunt angle', and a 'right angle' was called a 'square angle'. State whether the angles shown below are acute, obtuse, or right angles.

a)   b)   c)   d)

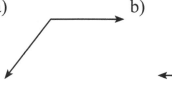

e)   f)   g)   h)

 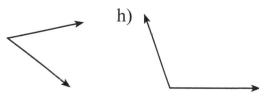

Q9. In the figure on the right (rectangle) I am trying to name the angle shown by)).

    a)   Why can't I simply call it ∠D?
    b)   Give two different methods of naming the angle correctly.

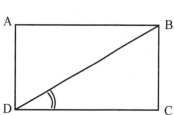

Year 5 Essential Exercises
Warwick Marlin © Five Senses Education

GEOMETRIC REASONING

Q1. Write whether the following are lines, rays or line intervals:

a)   b)   c)   d)

Q2. Use the method $A\widehat{B}C$ to describe the angles shown below.

a) 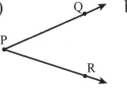   b)   c)   d)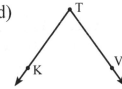

Q3. Write down the size of each angle:

a)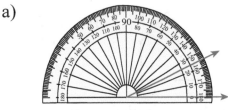

b)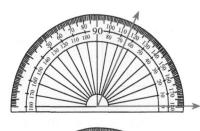

c)

d)

Q4. Measure the following angles by using the STEPS explained below.

> 1. Place the centre of the protractor on the vertex of the angle.
> 2. Make sure the base line on the protractor is lying exactly on top of one of the rays (or arms) of the angle.
> 3. Read off the angle size where the second ray cuts the protractor.

a)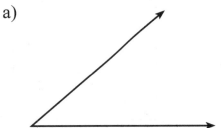

b)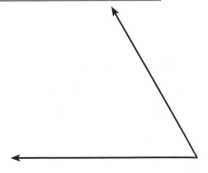

c)   d)

Q5. Construct the following angles by using the STEPS explained below.

> 1. Draw one arm of the angle. (This has been done for you.)
> 2. Place the centre of the protractor at one end of the arm, so that the arm of the angle lies exactly on the base line of the protractor.
> 3. Follow the scale from zero to the angle size you want, and mark this spot.
> 4. Remove the protractor and join this mark to the end of the arm.

a)   50° angle   b)   80° angle

The vertex or corner has been marked with a solid dot.

50°   80°

c)   70° angle   d)   120° angle

70°   120°

Q6. A list of 8 angle sizes has been given below. State whether each angle is acute, obtuse, right angle, straight angle, reflex angle or revolution.

a)   70° _____   b)   180° _____

c)   90° _____   d)   39° _____

e)   142° _____   f)   200° _____

g)   360° _____   h)   100° _____

Year 5 Essential Exercises
Warwick Marlin © Five Senses Education

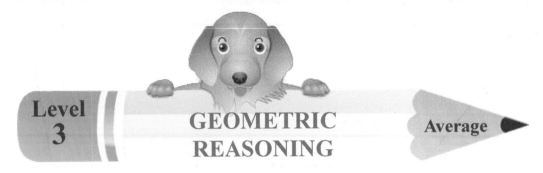

Level 3
GEOMETRIC REASONING
Average

PROBLEM SOLVING

Q1. In the figure shown:
- a) Name 3 line intervals
- b) Name 2 different rays
- c) Name a line
- d) Name a vertical line interval
- e) Name a sloping line interval
- f) Name a horizontal line interval
- g) Name the right angle

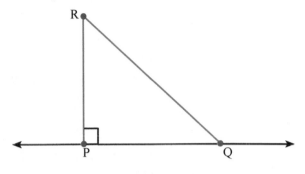

Q2. Without using a protractor, name the types of angles below (acute angle, obtuse angle, right angle, straight angle, reflex angle or revolution).

a)

b)

c)

d)

e)

f)

Q3. Without using a protractor, give an estimate of the angle size of each figure shown below. The approximate answer to each angle will be one of the following: 10° , 80°, 20°, 90°, 135°, 100°, 45°, 300°, 170°.

a)

b)

c)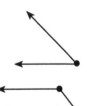

d)   e)   f)

Q4. What is the angle (0⁰ to 180⁰) between the hour hand and the minute hand on the following clocks:
(**Hint:** a complete revolution around the clock face is 360°.)

a)
9 am

b)
8 pm

c)
1 am

d)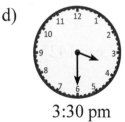
3:30 pm

Q5. Name the angle marked with the "))" in each figure below, using the method of ∠ABC.

a)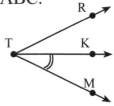

b)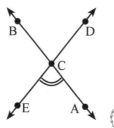

c)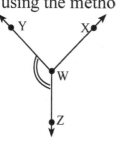

Q6. In geometry, we say that 2 angles are COMPLEMENTARY when they add up to 90°, or form one right angle.

a) Calculate the compliment of 65°.   b) Calculate the compliment of 31°.

Q7. ∠ABC is a right angle in all the figures shown below. The figures are not drawn, accurately to scale. Without using a protractor, calculate the unknown complementary angle.

a)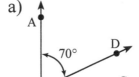

b)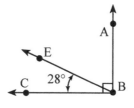

c)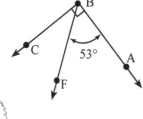

Q8. In geometry, we say that 2 angles are SUPPLEMENTARY when they add up to 180°, or form a straight angle.

a) Calculate the supplement of 110°.   b) Calculate the supplement of 39°.

Q9. PQ̂R is a straight angle in all the figures shown below. The figures are not drawn accurately to scale. Without using a protractor, calculate the unknown supplementary angle.

a) Find SQ̂R

b) Find TQ̂V

c) Find WQ̂P

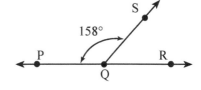

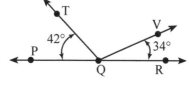

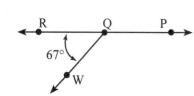

Q10. The following questions relate to the 3 triangles shown below.

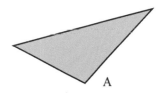

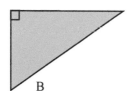

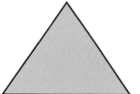

a) Which triangle has 3 acute angles?
b) Which triangle has an obtuse angle?
c) What type of angles does triangle B have?

Year 5 Essential Exercises
Warwick Marlin © Five Senses Education

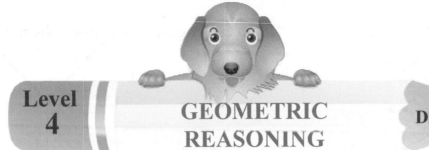

Q1. Use a protractor to measure the size of the following angles.
(**Note:** in some questions you may have to extend the arms of each angle so that you can get a more accurate reading on the protractor face.)

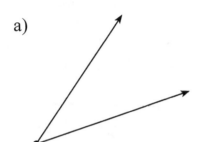

a)

b)

c)

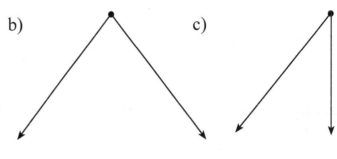

d)

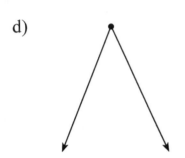

e)

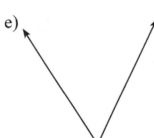

f)

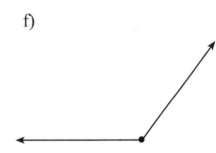

Q2. Construct the following angles:

a) ∠ABC = 55°

b) ∠QPR = 75°

c) ∠MLN = 120°

d) ∠DEF = 160°

e) ∠JHK = 20°

f) ∠XYZ = 95°

Q3. For two angles to be ADJACENT they must lie on opposite order of a common arm (that is an arm which belongs to both angles). The 2 angles must also have the same vertex.

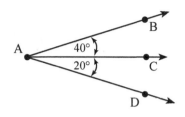

a) Name a pair of adjacent angles.
b) Find the size of ∠BAD.

Q4.

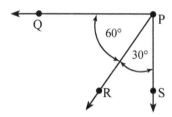

a) Name a pair of adjacent angles.
b) Give a reason why you think that QPS is a right angle.

Q5.

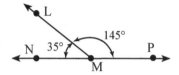

a) Name a pair of adjacent angles.
b) Give a reason why you think that ∠NMP is a straight angle.

Q6. Find the size of ∠PQR in each of the following without using a protractor.

a)

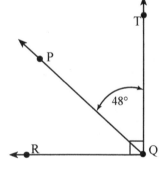

b)

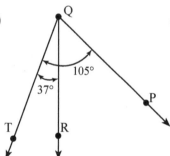

c)

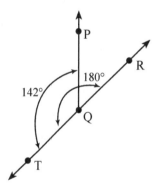

Q7. Without using a protractor, name the types of each angle shown below (acute angle, obtuse angle, right angle, reflex angle, straight angle, or revolution).

a)

b)

c)

d)

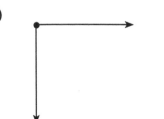

e)

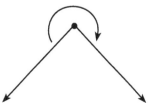

f)

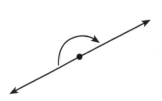

Year 5 Essential Exercises
Warwick Marlin © Five Senses Education

PROBLEM SOLVING

Q1. A bicycle wheel has 24 evenly spaced spokes spreading out from the centre of the wheel to the outer rim. Find the angle between each spoke.

Q2. Study the diagram on the right showing the eight primary directions.
   a) What is the angle made between N and E?
   b) What is the angle made between N and S?
   c) What is the reflex angle made between N and W?
   d) What is the angle between S and SW
   e) If I am facing South, how many degrees must I turn in a clockwise direction to face SE?

Q3. If the minute hand of a clock makes one complete revolution, then it has turned through an angle of 360°.
   a) What angle is made when the minute hand turns through 5 minutes?
   b) What angle is made when the minute hand turns through 1 minute?
   c) What angle is made between the minute hand and the hour hand when the time is 5:12 pm?
   d) What angle is made between the minute hand and the hour hand when the time is 2:36 am?
   e) How many degrees does the hour hand turn through when the minute hand turns through 15 minutes?

Q4. A trundle wheel is a measuring device commonly used by school children to measure approximate distances.
It works by having a wheel which has a circumference of exactly 1 metre, hence one revolution of the wheel equates to 1 metre of distance travelled on the ground, if there is no slip. Every time the wheel makes a rotation, the wheel produces an audible click which is then counted, and therefore the number of clicks that are counted by the user is approximately the number of metres travelled.

Arushi is measuring the distance from the main school gate to her house. If she counts 500 clicks 4 times, and then another 278 clicks, how far in kilometres is her house from the school.

Q5. How many different triangles can you find in this diagram?

(**Hint:** the answer is somewhere between 10 and 18 triangles.)

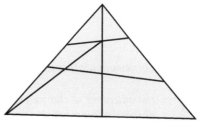

Q6.

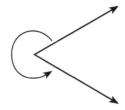

The angle shown on the left is a reflex angle. Find the size of the angle, and briefly explain how you did it by only using an ordinary 180° protractor.

Q7. With the aid of a protractor,
  a) measure XŶZ
  b) measure XẐY
  c) measure YX̂Z
  d) what is the sum of the 3 angles?

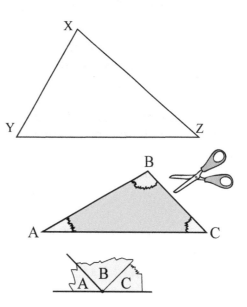

Q8. Here is an interesting and very important practical exercise. Draw any shaped triangle that you like. Then cut off the 3 angles with scissors, and place the 3 corners together as shown on the right. Briefly explain what you notice?

Q9. Draw a line segment AB = 5 cm. Construct a ray of 55° at point A. Construct another ray from point B of 65°. Let the point where the two rays cross each other be called C. You should now have constructed a triangle with the letter A, B and C. Measure AĈB with a protractor.

Explain why your answer should be 60°.

Q10. Without measuring with a protractor, work out the value of the letter in each of the following diagrams:

  a)

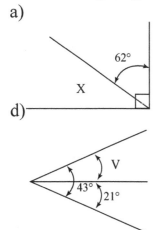

  b)

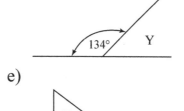

  c)

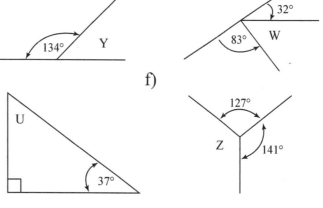

  d)

  e)

  f)

Year 5 Essential Exercises
Warwick Marlin © Five Senses Education

CHANCE

The "Australian Curriculum Mathematics" (ACM) references for this sub-strand of "Statistics and Probability" (SP) are below:

☞ List outcomes of chance experiments involving equally likely outcomes, and represent probabilities of those outcomes using fractions (ACMSP).

☞ Recognise that probabilities range from 0 to 1 (ACMSP 117).

❖ CHANCE OR PROBABILITY

There are many different events taking place in everyday life that involve chance. For example, what is the chance of it raining tomorrow? Is there a high chance or low chance? Maybe it is a 50 -50 or even chance. Another word that we usually use in maths, instead of the word chance, is PROBABILITY.

Therefore, we could ask "What is the probability of it raining tomorrow?" Below you will find some more examples of events that involve chance, which you might hear us use in everyday conversation. Australians love sport of all kinds, and often you will use the word chance, when talking about sports.

Examples: a) What is the chance of our team winning at netball on Saturday?

b) What is the probability that "Royal king" will win the Melbourne Cup?

c) What is the chance of Australia winning the cricket ashes against England?

❖ EQUALLY LIKELY OUTCOMES

When you toss a coin into the air, there are 2 equally likely outcomes of either a head showing, or a tail showing. The chance of getting a head is equal to $\frac{1}{2}$ and the chance of getting a tail is also equal to $\frac{1}{2}$. Both outcomes, or results, are equally likely, and so both fraction are the same.

If I toss a normal 6 sided die, then there are 6 equally possible outcomes (or results).
a) What is the chance of the number 3 being thrown?
b) What is the chance of an even number being thrown?
c) What is the chance of 2 or 5 showing?

Solutions: a) 1 chance out of $6 = \frac{1}{6}$

b) 3 chances out of $6 = \frac{3}{6}$ or $\frac{1}{2}$

c) 2 chances out of $6 = \frac{2}{6}$ or $\frac{1}{3}$

❖ SPINNERS AND CHANCE

There are many different types of spinners that can be made. There are 3 sided ones, 4 sided, 5 sided, 10 sided and even circles. A spinner in made of a background with different colours, or numbers or letters on it. The spinner in the middle is then flicked (or spun) around, and eventually the arrow will land on a particular colour or letter or number.

Circular spinner with numbers in the background

Triangular spinner with 3 colours in the background

THE MAIN RULE
The chance of an outcome occurring $= \dfrac{\text{number of ways the outcome can occur}}{\text{total number of outcomes possible}}$

Example: In a normal pack of 52 playing cards, what is the chance (or probability) of:

    a) drawing the Ace of Spades?   b) drawing any Ace?

    c) drawing a heart?

    a) There is only 1 Ace of Spades.

       Therefore 1 chance in $52 = \dfrac{1}{52}$

    b) There are 4 Aces altogether.

       Therefore 4 chances in $52 = \dfrac{4}{52} = \dfrac{1}{13}$

    c) There are 13 hearts altogether.

       Therefore 13 chances in $52 = \dfrac{13}{52} = \dfrac{1}{4}$

 ALL PROBABILITIES RANGE FROM 0 TO 1

> An impossible event has a probability of 0.
> A certain event has a probability of 1.
> All other probabilities lie between 0 and 1
> $0 \leq$ probabilities/chances ≤ 1

> We are going to use the word probability more and more. Please remember that probability means the same as chance.

Note: If you ever get an answer that is either negative, or larger than 1, then you will know that you have made a mistake in your calculations.

 ORDERING EVENTS ON A NUMBER LINE

A number line is very useful for understanding probability, because it gives us an actual picture or drawing to look at, instead of just a bunch of numbers. If we draw a number line from 0 to 1, then we can divide this line up into either fractions or decimals. In later years, we can also use percentages to describe probabilities or chance.

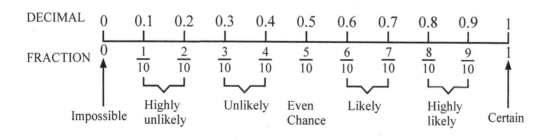

 For further reference, see 'Understanding Year 5 Maths' by W. Marlin

Essential Exercises – Year 5 Maths
Warwick Marlin © Five Senses Education

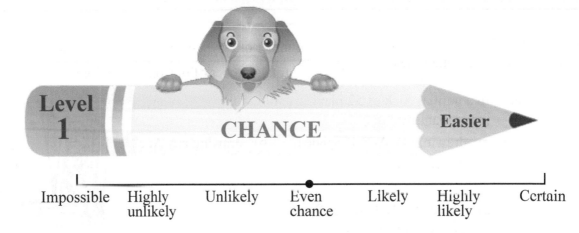

Q1.

Impossible   Highly unlikely   Unlikely   Even chance   Likely   Highly likely   Certain

Use one of the words above to describe the following chances:

a) I will score more than $\frac{8}{10}$ in the next spelling test.

b) My dog will follow me to school.

c) The moon will fall into the sea.

d) The head mistress will cancel school today.

e) We will have our athletics carnival this week.

f) I will have something to eat during the day.

g) Our teacher will be wearing a red dress today.

h) My father waters the garden about every second day, so he might water the garden tonight.

i) We have assembly 4 times a week, so we might have assembly today.

j) We have the same number of boys and girls in our school.

k) Our teacher will laugh at least once during the day.

Q2. A jar contains 50 blue and 50 yellow jelly beans. Jenny puts her hand in the jar and, without looking, takes one jelly bean out.

a) What is the chance that it is blue?

b) What is the chance that it is yellow?

c) What is the chance that it is either blue or yellow?

d) What is the chance that it is green?

Q3. There are 4 different spinners shown below. Each spinner has been split up into EQUAL parts, and each part has been shaded different colours. In each diagram, what is the chance of the spinner pointing to the colour red?

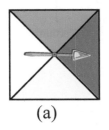 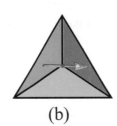 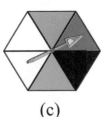 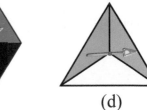

(a)   (b)   (c)   (d)

Q4. Twenty coloured marbles were placed inside a jar. The 4 different colours are yellow, blue, red and green.
How many of the marbles were:

a) yellow   b) blue

c) red   d) green

Lei puts her hand in the jar, and without looking, she takes one marble out.

e) Which colour is most likely to be taken from the jar?

f) Is she more likely to take blue or green?

g) Which colour is least likely to be taken?

h) Order the chance of taking each colour from most likely to least likely.

Q5. In this question, we will ask you about the jar above which has a total of 20 coloured marbles in it.

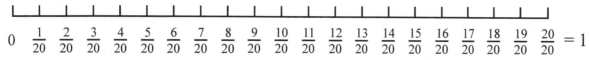

$$0 \quad \frac{1}{20} \quad \frac{2}{20} \quad \frac{3}{20} \quad \frac{4}{20} \quad \frac{5}{20} \quad \frac{6}{20} \quad \frac{7}{20} \quad \frac{8}{20} \quad \frac{9}{20} \quad \frac{10}{20} \quad \frac{11}{20} \quad \frac{12}{20} \quad \frac{13}{20} \quad \frac{14}{20} \quad \frac{15}{20} \quad \frac{16}{20} \quad \frac{17}{20} \quad \frac{18}{20} \quad \frac{19}{20} \quad \frac{20}{20} = 1$$

Using the number line above, work out the chance (using one of the fractions shown) of picking:

a) a yellow marble   b) a blue marble   c) a red marble   d) a green marble

Q6. There are 6 different spinners shown below. Colour each spinner to show the given outcome. If you do not have coloured crayons then simply label the triangle(s) with the first letter of the colour eg. red (R), blue (B) etc.

a)

a $\frac{1}{6}$ chance of spinning blue

b)

a $\frac{1}{2}$ chance of spinning green

c)

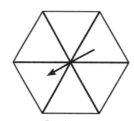

a $\frac{5}{6}$ chance of spinning yellow

d)

a certain chance of spinning red

e)

a $\frac{1}{3}$ chance of spinning black

f)

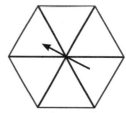

no chance of spinning purple

Essential Exercises – Year 5 Maths
Warwick Marlin © Five Senses Education

Q1. An eight sided spinner is shown on the right.
What fraction of the spinner is:

a) red? b) green? c) blue?

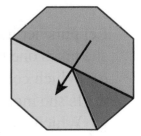

| Impossible | Very unlikely | Unlikely | Even | Likely | Very likely | Certain |

Using one of the words above, describe the chance of the 8 sided spinner pointing to:

d) green e) blue f) red g) blue or green h) yellow

Q2. Jack collected 10 sporting legend swap cards. Six of the cards are cricket cards with a picture of Ricky Ponting. Three of the cards are tennis cards with a picture of Samantha Stosur, and one card is a swimming card with a picture of Ian Thorpe. Jack shuffles the cards and asks his friend Huang to choose one card without looking at the pictures.

a) Which card has the highest chance of being picked?

b) Which card has the least chance of being picked?

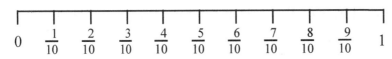

$0 \quad \frac{1}{10} \quad \frac{2}{10} \quad \frac{3}{10} \quad \frac{4}{10} \quad \frac{5}{10} \quad \frac{6}{10} \quad \frac{7}{10} \quad \frac{8}{10} \quad \frac{9}{10} \quad 1$

Work out the chance, using one of the fractions on the number line above, of Huang picking:

c) a swimming card d) a cricket card e) a tennis card f) a hockey card

Q3. Jessica tosses a normal six sided die. What is the probability (or chance) of her tossing:

a) the number 3

b) any odd number

c) a number greater than 2

d) any number which is not 4

e) a number equal to or greater than 3

f) a number greater than 6

Q4. At the local fair ground, one of the side shows involves a large dart board with 16 numbers on it. Each contestant is first blind folded before they throw their dart at the board. Small prizes are given if the dart hits any number greater than 20.

3	8	15	24
21	26	40	9
13	6	10	17
18	32	12	28

a) How many even numbers are there?
b) How many multiples of 3 are there?
c) How many prime numbers are there?
d) How many numbers are greater than 20?

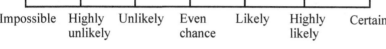

0 — Impossible   Highly unlikely   Unlikely   Even chance   Likely   Highly likely   Certain — 1

Using one of the words on the number line above:

e) What is the chance of the dart hitting a prime number?
f) What is the chance of the dart hitting a multiple of 3?
g) What is the chance of the dart hitting an even number?
h) What is the chance of winning a prize?
i) What is the chance of the dart hitting the number 16?
j) What is the chance of the dart hitting the number 13?
k) What is the chance of the dart hitting a number below 50?

> A prime number has only 2 factors, itself and 1.

Q5. Jenny tosses a coin into the air, and the coin then lands on the ground.

a) What is the probability of a head showing?
b) What is the probability of a tail showing?
c) If Jenny tossed the coin 200 times, approximately how many times will a head show?
d) Is there any chance at all that the coin will not show a head or a tail - this means that the coin lands on its thin edge?

Q6. There are 16 girls and 4 boys in our class. A name is drawn out of a hat to select a runner for our classroom. (Write all final answers as simplified fractions.)

a) Does a boy or a girl have a higher chance of being picked?
b) What is the probability that a girl is picked?
c) What is the probability that a boy is picked?

Essential Exercises – Year 5 Maths
Warwick Marlin © Five Senses Education

PROBLEM SOLVING

Q1.

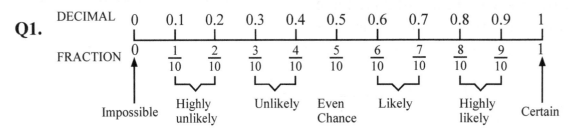

DECIMAL 0 0.1 0.2 0.3 0.4 0.5 0.6 0.7 0.8 0.9 1

FRACTION 0 $\frac{1}{10}$ $\frac{2}{10}$ $\frac{3}{10}$ $\frac{4}{10}$ $\frac{5}{10}$ $\frac{6}{10}$ $\frac{7}{10}$ $\frac{8}{10}$ $\frac{9}{10}$ 1

Impossible   Highly unlikely   Unlikely   Even Chance   Likely   Highly likely   Certain

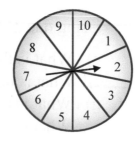

Study the spinner on the right. Answer the following questions using the words (likely, highly likely, certain etc). Also work out the probability using both a fraction and a decimal.

a) What is the probability of the spinner landing on 3?

b) What is the probability of the spinner landing on an even number?

c) What is the probability of the spinner landing on any of the numbers from 1 to 8?

d) What is the probability of the spinner landing on the number 4 or less?

e) What is the probability of the spinner landing on the number 11?

Q2. Use the words shown on the scale in Question 1 (impossible, highly unlikely, unlikely etc) to rate the chance of the following events happening in your life.

a) I will sprint the 100 metres in less than 20 seconds.

b) My first throw of a die will be the number 3.

c) It will snow on Mount Kosciuszko this July.

d) I will see a full moon tonight.

e) My first toss of a coin will show a head.

f) I will do some homework on Xmas Day.

g) I will jump 2 metres high in the next Athletics Carnival.

h) Australia will win the next cricket ashes against England.

i) I drop my slice of bread at breakfast and it falls on the floor with the marmalade side facing up.

Q3. There are 4 different five sided spinners shown below. Shade each spinner to show the given outcome.

a) 60% chance   b) 20% chance   c) 40% chance   d) 80% chance

Q4. There may be some students who have little or no knowledge of a pack of playing cards. Therefore, we must begin by briefly investigating a normal pack of 52 playing cards, and also we are going to assume that all jokers have been removed.

The pack is split up equally into 4 main suits called spades, hearts, diamonds and clubs. Each suit consists of 13 cards, and there are 2 black suits (spades and clubs) and 2 red suits (hearts and diamonds).

♠ Spades	black	Ace, King, Queen, Jack, 10, 9, 8, 7, 6, 5, 4, 3, 2,	(13 cards)
♥ Hearts	red	Ace, King, Queen, Jack, 10, 9, 8, 7, 6, 5, 4, 3, 2,	(13 cards)
♦ Diamonds	red	Ace, King, Queen, Jack, 10, 9, 8, 7, 6, 5, 4, 3, 2,	(13 cards)
♣ Clubs	black	Ace, King, Queen, Jack, 10, 9, 8, 7, 6, 5, 4, 3, 2,	(13 cards)

TOTAL = 52 cards

The highest card in each suit is the Ace, then comes the king, queen, etc. all the way down to the lowest card in each suit, which is the two. So each pack contains 4 different Aces, 4 different kings, 4 different queens, etc.

Questions: Consider a normal pack of playing cards. If I shuffle the cards and then pick one out of the pack, work out the following chances.

a) What is the probability of picking the ace of spades?
b) What is the probability of picking any ace?
c) What is the probability of picking any diamond card?
d) What is the probability of picking any red card?
e) What is the probability of picking any honour card?
   (An honour card is 10, J, Q, K or Ace)

Note: Simplify fractional answers when possible.

Essential Exercises – Year 5 Maths
Warwick Marlin © Five Senses Education

Q1. Twenty coloured balls are placed inside a jar.
The 4 different colours are yellow, blue, red
and green. Firstly, count how many balls of
each colour there are. Then work out the chance
(using PERCENTAGE) of picking out the
following colours.

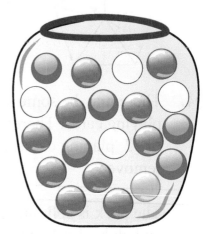

a) a yellow ball
b) a blue ball
c) a red ball

Final answers to be
written as a percentage!

d) a green ball
e) which colour has an EVEN chance of being picked?
f) which colour is most unlikely to be picked?

Q2. There are 8 different spinners shown below. Using a pencil, shade each spinner
grey to show the given outcome.

a) $\frac{3}{8}$ chance   b) 25% chance   c) $\frac{3}{4}$ chance   d) 50 % chance

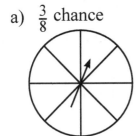   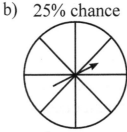   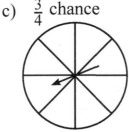   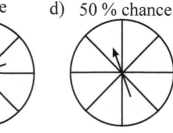

e) 0.75 chance   f) $12\frac{1}{2}$ % chance   g) 0.375 chance   h) 100% chance

Q3. Stefan has a normal pack of 52 playing cards, and the pack contains no jokers.
He shuffles the cards, and picks one card out without looking.
What is the probability that the card is:

Simplify all
fractions where
possible.

a) any club   b) the 7 of diamonds?
c) the 7 of any suit?   d) any black card (spade or club)
e) 2 or 3 or 4 from any suit?   f) ace, king, queen, or jack from any suit?

Q4. When we toss 2 coins into the air, there are actually 4 different possibilities, or outcomes that could take place. This is shown in the table on the right. A head on coin 1 and a tail on coin 2 is a different outcome to a tail on coin 1 and a head on coin 2. We can use a shortened form of Head (H) and Tail (T) and list the 4 outcomes as { HH, HT, TH, TT}. Knowing the above results, if we toss 2 coins into the air, work out the probability of tossing:

Coin 1	Coin 2
Head	Head
Head	Tail
Tail	Head
Tail	Tail

a) { Head, Head }   b) { Head or Tail in any order}   c) { Tail, Tail}

Note: The above explanation should help you to have a better understanding of question 5 in Level 3.

Q5. a) If we take a sample of families who only have one child, what is the chance of this child being a boy?
   b) What is the chance of this child being a girl?
   c) Would you agree that working this theory out is similar to tossing one coin in the air?
   d) If we take a sample of families who have only 2 children, what is the chance of both children being boys?
   e) What is the chance of having a daughter and son in any order?
   f) What is the chance of both children being girls?
   g) Would you agree that working this theory out is the same as tossing one coin twice (or tossing 2 coins together)?
   h) If we interview 1 000 families who have only 2 children, how many of these families would you expect to have 2 daughters?

Q6. When we toss 2 dice, it is similar to tossing 2 coins. If you understand that idea, then it will also be easy for you to understand that a 3 on die 1 and a 5 on die 2 is a different outcome from a 5 on die 1 and a 3 on die 2. In the diagram on the top right, we have die 1 in white and die 2 in grey shading.

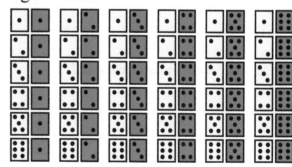

When you toss a pair of normal 6 sided dice, there is a total of 36 different outcomes.

   a) Looking at the table on the right, how many times does the total of 4 come up?
   b) How many times does the total of 12 come up?
   c) If you rolled 2 dice 36 times, how many times would you expect to get a total of 7?
   d) How many times would you expect to get a total of 5?
   e) If you rolled 2 dice 36 times, which total has the highest chance of happening?
   f) Which total(s) have the least chance of happening?

Essential Exercises – Year 5 Maths
Warwick Marlin © Five Senses Education

DATA REPRESENTATION AND INTERPRETATION

The "Australian Curriculum Mathematics" (ACM) references for this sub-strand of "Statistics and Probability" (SP) are below:

☞ Pose questions and collect categorical data by observation and survey (ACMSP 118).

☞ Construct displays, including column graphs, dot plots and tables, appropriate for data type, with and without the use of digital technologies (ACMSP 119).

☞ Describe and interpret different data sets and context (ACMSP 120).

❖ INTRODUCTION

Graphs are used a great deal in many areas of Science, Geography, Economics and everyday living. It is often much easier to understand a set of results by looking at a graph, than it is by searching through a maze of figures. As you will see, there are several types of graphs, which depend on the information being presented.

A graph is an easier, quicker way of showing people information in the form of a diagram or picture.

❖ NUMERAL AND CATEGORICAL DATA

There are many different types of data, but we will explain 2 main types, which are best understood by studying the example below.

Example: Ten children in grade 6 are asked the following two questions:

QUESTION	DATA COLLECTED
Q1. What did you score in the last spelling test?	7, 8, 10, 6, 8, 7, 9, 9, 8, 6
Q2. What is your favourite subject?	english, art, music, maths, italian maths, english, geography, music

The first question involves numbers, and therefore the information we obtain is called **'numerical data'**. We could put the results in order from lowest to highest, and we could also find the class average.

The second question involves different categories (english, art, maths, etc.). We cannot calculate any average for these categories, and we cannot put them in any definite order. Therefore this data is called **'categorical data'**.

❖ THE PICTOGRAM OR PICTURE GRAPH

Each symbol in a pictogram stands for a certain (approximate) amount of items. The symbol (picture) should have some basic similarity to the product.

Example: The following pictogram shows the number of new houses which were built in N.S.W. over a period of 4 years.

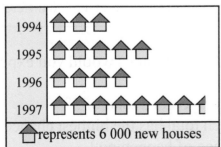

As you can see the symbol ⌂ does look basically like a house. Pictograms are also easy to understand at a quick glance.

❖ THE COLUMN GRAPH

Usually the column graph uses vertical columns with spaces in between each column as shown in the example below. However, some column graphs are drawn with no spaces between the columns, and some are also drawn HORIZONTALLY.

Example: Stanley Primary School conducted a survey on the Year 5 students to find out how each of them travelled to school each day. The results are shown in the column graph below.

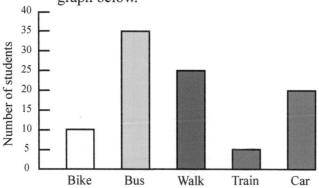

Sometimes there are no spaces between each column, and sometimes you will see them drawn horizontally.

❖ DOT PLOTS

As the name suggests, this graph uses dots to represent data. This is one of the simplest and more basic types of graphs, and there is usually only one horizontal number line or axis. Each dot represents one piece of data, and this is plotted directly above one of the numbers.

Example: The school computer club has 35 members, and their ages are shown below.

13, 15, 12, 13, 14, 14, 14, 16, 13, 12, 16, 15,
14, 13, 14, 15, 14, 13, 14, 16, 14, 15, 17, 16,
14, 12, 14, 13, 15, 16, 12, 13, 15, 14, 17

Use a dot plot to show the ages of the students in the computer club and discuss the results.

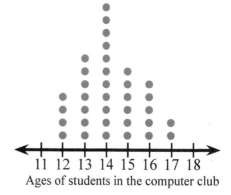

Ages of students in the computer club

❖ LINE GRAPHS

Line graphs have a horizontal and vertical axis with different scales and units.
By reading the unit along one axis, it is easy to find the value of the unit on the other axis.

Example: The temperature was recorded every 4 hours at Broken Hill over a 24 hour period. The information was recorded on the line graph on the right.

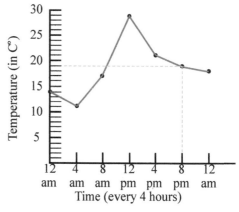

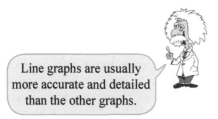

Line graphs are usually more accurate and detailed than the other graphs.

 For further reference, see 'Understanding Year 5 Maths' by W. Marlin

Year 5 Essential Exercises
Warwick Marlin © Five Senses Education

DATA REPRESENTATION AND INTERPRETATION

Easier

Q1. At Cabramatta Primary School, all the students were asked which mode of transport they used to come to school. The results are shown in the picture graph on the right.

Bicycle	
Car	
Bus	
Train	
Walk	

represents 30 students

a) Is the data numerical or categorical?

b) How many students travelled to school by bicycle?

c) How many more students walk to school rather than coming by cars?

d) How many students catch the public bus?

e) How many students were involved in the data?

Q2. A class of Year 8 students were asked about what time they usually went to bed at night. The results are shown on the bar graph on the right.

a) How many students went to bed at 11 p.m.?

b) How many students went to bed at 9:30 p.m.?

c) What was the most popular bed time?

d) How many students went to bed after 10 p.m.?

e) How many students were involved in the survey?

f) Was the information above obtained by SURVEY or OBSERVATION.

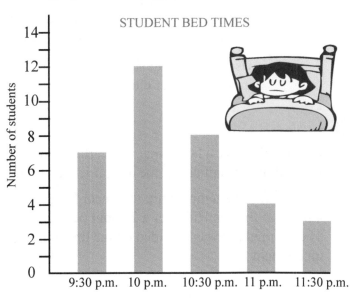

STUDENT BED TIMES

Number of students

9:30 p.m.   10 p.m.   10:30 p.m.   11 p.m.   11:30 p.m.

There are 2 main ways of collecting data. We can conduct SURVEYS on particular topics by interviewing a group of people and asking them questions. Or we can obtain data by experiment and OBSERVATION. For example, if we toss 2 coins one hundred times and record the results, then this data has been collected by experiment and observation.

Q3. The dot plot shown on the right was obtained from a class of Grade 5 students who sat for a spelling test out of 10. Each dot represents 1 student.

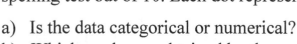

a) Is the data categorical or numerical?

b) Which mark was obtained by the most students?

c) How many students sat for the test?

d) If $\frac{7}{10}$ was considered the pass mark, how many students passed the spelling test?

e) Complete the tally table on the right of the page.

f) Find the class average correct to one decimal place by adding up all the marks and dividing this total by the total number of students in the class.

Score mark	Tally	Total
4		
5		
6		
7		
8		
9		
10		

Q4. A Grade 5 class of 30 students were asked to name their favourite pet animal. A tally of their answers from the survey is shown on the right.

Favourite Pet	Tally	Total
Dog	ЖН ЖН	
Cat	ЖН |||	
Fish	||	
Bird	ЖН		
Hamster	||||	

a) Complete the total (or frequency) column in the table.

b) Draw a column graph of the results. (Use a space between each column.)

c) Is the data numerical or categorical?

d) Which was the third most popular pet?

e) How many more students preferred dogs to hamsters?

Q5. The line graph on the right shows the daily sales of books at a bookstore.

a) How many books were sold on Friday?

b) On what day was the second highest number of books sold?

c) How many more books were sold on Saturday compared to Thursday?

d) Why do you think the most books were sold on Saturday?

e) Find the average number of books sold each day. (Hint: This is calculated by finding the total number of books sold, and dividing by the number of days.)

f) Is the data 'categorical' or 'numerical'?

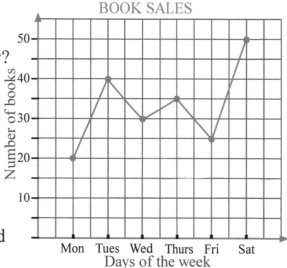

Year 5 Essential Exercises
Warwick Marlin © Five Senses Education

Q1. The picture below shows the number of food items sold on a particular day in a bakery.

a) If 60 muffins were sold during the day, how many items of food does each picture represent?

b) How many cakes were sold during the day?

c) How many loaves of bread were sold during the day?

d) How many more pies were sold than cakes?

Pie	
Pizza	
Cake	
Muffin	
Bread	
	represents **?** items of food

e) Do you think the owner should continue making pizzas? Give a brief reason for your answer.

Q2. We surveyed all the students in our school, and asked them which sports electives they have chosen for term 2. The results of the survey are shown in the horizontal column graph below.

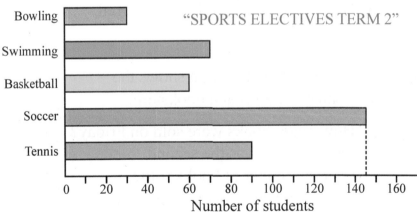

a) Which was the least popular sport?

b) How many more students chose tennis compared to basketball?

c) How many students chose soccer?

d) What is the total number of students?

e) Is the information presented 'numerical' or 'categorical'?

f) Was the information obtained by 'survey' or 'observation'?

g) If I wanted to show that 62 students have elected to play basketball, is this type of graph accurate enough to show smaller detail?

Q3. Students in class 5E were surveyed and asked how many siblings (brothers and sisters) they have in their family. The results of the survey are shown on the dot graph on the right.

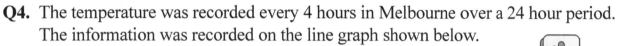

Number of siblings in the family

a) How many families have 3 siblings?
b) Which is the most frequent (popular) number of siblings in each family?
c) How many families have 2 or less siblings?
d) What is the total number of students in the survey?
e) How many families have 8 siblings?
f) How many families have 4 or more siblings?
g) Is the data 'categorical' or 'numerical'?

Q4. The temperature was recorded every 4 hours in Melbourne over a 24 hour period. The information was recorded on the line graph shown below.

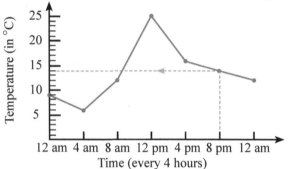

a) What was the temperature at 8 p.m.?
b) What time did the temperature first reach 18°C?
c) What was the lowest temperature and what time did it occur?
d) By how much did the temperature fall between 12 p.m. and 4 p.m.?
e) What was the temperature range over the 24 hours?
f) What was the temperature difference between 12 p.m. and 8 a.m.?

Q5. Amy stands at the side of the road and observes and records the colour of each car as it goes past her. She records all her data using a tally and frequency table.

a) Complete the frequency column.
b) How many cars went past her in total?
c) How many more blue cars than green cars went past her?
d) Why do you think white is the most popular colour in Australia?
e) Draw a vertical column graph of the results with no spaces between each column.

COLOUR	TALLY	FREQUENCY
Blue	ЖЖ ЖЖ I	
Red	ЖЖ III	
Black	ЖЖ II	
White	ЖЖ ЖЖ ЖЖ	
Gold	ЖЖ IIII	
Green	III	

Year 5 Essential Exercises
Warwick Marlin © Five Senses Education

DATA REPRESENTATION AND INTERPRETATION

Average

PROBLEM SOLVING

Q1. The table on the right shows the number of new houses built in Queensland over a period of 5 years.

a) Construct a picture graph of the data, and let  represent 4 000 new houses.

b) How did you show 2 000 new houses if  represents 4 000 new houses?

c) If you wanted to show 5 000 new houses, would this be easy to do?

d) From your picture graph, what conclusion immediately becomes obvious about the number of new houses being built each year?

e) Why do you think the construction of new houses is steadily decreasing from 2007 to 2011. Give a brief reason.

f) A world wide financial recession started in 2008. Do you think that this may have also contributed to the decline of new houses? Discuss briefly.

Year	New houses
2007	28 000
2008	20 000
2009	18 000
2010	14 000
2011	10 000

🏠 represents 4 000 new houses

Q2. Jenny tossed 2 coins and recorded the results using a tally table.

Result	Tally	Total
Head, Head (HH)		
Tail, Tail (TT)		
Head or Tail (HT)		

She got the following results:

HH, HT, HT, TT, HT, HT, TT, HT, HT, HT, HH, HT, HT, TT, HH, HT, HT, HT, HT, TT, HT, HH, HH, TT, HT, HT, HH, HH, HT, TT, HT, TT, HT, HH, HT, TT, HH, TT, TT, HT

a) Record the results using the tally table above.

b) Draw a vertical column graph of the result with a space between each column.

c) How many times did Jenny toss the coins?

d) How many times did a head and tail combination occur?

e) Why do you think a head and tail combination had approximately double the frequency of the other 2 outcomes? Give a brief reason for your answer.

Q3. A class of students were asked by the school tuck shop committee to name their favourite fruit. The results were as follows:

banana, orange, mango, peach, banana, mango, orange,
mango, peach, orange, apple, mango, banana, mango,
peach, orange, mango, peach, mango, mango, apple, orange,
banana, peach, mango, orange, peach, mango, peach, banana

a) Complete a tally table for the results.
b) Construct a dot plot for the table.
c) Is the data numerical or categorical?
d) The tuck shop committee is considering which fruit to stock for students. It is not mango or peach season, so which fruit do you think they should sell? Give a brief reason.
e) How many students were involved in the survey?
f) Was the data collected by 'observation' or 'survey'?

Q4. A survey was conducted on 100 men and 100 women just before an election. In the opinion poll they were asked to rate two politicians, as shown in the table below. Study the table and answer the following questions:

a) How many women thought that Mr. Goodman was average?
b) How many men thought that Mr. Trusting was poor?
c) How many more women thought that Mr. Trusting was excellent, compared to Mr. Goodman?

Rating	Mr. Goodman		Mr. Trusting	
	Men	Women	Men	Women
Excellent	23	18	13	28
Good	27	16	16	19
Average	22	31	33	39
Poor	10	9	28	8
Unsure	18	26	10	6

d) Because there were exactly 100 men and 100 women involved in the survey, it is easy to convert the numbers to percentages. For example, 18% of men are unsure of Mr. Goodman. What is the total percentage of men and women who are still unsure of Mr. Goodman?

e) What is the total percentage of men and women who are still unsure of Mr. Trusting.

f) On the whole, who is more popular with the women voters?

g) Which group (men or women) is Mr. Goodman more popular with?

h) Who do you think will win the election vote based on the table of results. Give a brief reason for your answer.

Year 5 Essential Exercises
Warwick Marlin © Five Senses Education

Q1. The picture graph on the right shows the number of books borrowed from the school library during the week.

LIBRARY BOOKS

Mon	📗 📗
Tue	📗 📗 📗 📗
Wed	📗 📗 📗 📗
Thur	📗 📗 📗
Fri	📗 📗 📗 📗 📗 📗

Number of books borrowed

   a) If 14 books were borrowed on Wednesday, what does each 📗 represent?

   b) What day was the least number of books borrowed?

   c) What was the total number borrowed during the week?

   d) Give a brief reason why more books would be borrowed on Friday?

Q2. For this question, please refer back to Question 1 above. Using the results of the pictogram above, complete the frequency table on the right. Then draw a horizontal bar column graph, with no spaces between each bar, to show the number of books borrowed during the week.

('Books borrowed' on the horizontal axis, and 'days of the week' on the vertical axis.)

Day	Tally of books borrowed	Total
Mon		
Tue		
Wed		
Thur		
Fri		

Q3. The line graph below is taken from the hospital chart of a sick girl. Read the scale carefully and then answer the following questions:

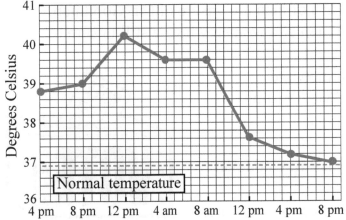

   a) What was the girl's temperature when she first went into hospital?

   b) If our normal body temperature is 37°C, how much higher than normal was her temperature when she first went in?

c) What was her highest temperature?
d) During what time did the temperature remain the same?
e) At what time did she start to dramatically improve?
f) At what time was her temperature 38.4°C?
g) How much did the temperature drop between 8 am and 12 pm?

Q4. The Serengeti National Park in Tanzania (Africa) is one of the great wild life national parks in the world. Every 5 years, since 1950, the park rangers take a census of the amount of elephants sighted during that year. These sightings are recorded by the rangers and the results are shown in the table below.

Year	Number of elephants
1950	3 200
1955	3 000
1960	3 000
1965	2 600
1970	2 800
1975	2 700
1980	2 800
1985	2 400
1990	2 400
1995	1 800
2000	1 900
2005	2 000
2010	2 000

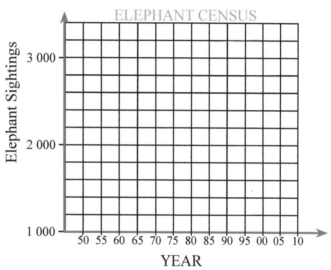

a) Using the data in the table, draw a line graph of the results using the scaled grid paper on the right.
b) Using the graph, estimate how many elephants were in the park in 1993.
c) Looking at the graph, what was happening to the elephant population between 1950 and 1995?
d) There was a big advertising campaign to save the elephants. Which year do you think this campaign started?
e) Each elephant eats between 300 kg and 400 kg of tree leaves, bark, corn and grass each day. The Africans are burning down their forests for firewood and more arable land to grow food crops. Using this information, explain why elephant populations are rapidly declining around the world?
f) Give another reason why elephants and rhinoceroses are cruelly and senselessly killed?

"Save our beautiful, majestic elephants".

119

APPENDIX

Note: Some reminders of important basic concepts have been given on the pages to follow. For further reference to the complete chapters, please see "Understanding Year 5 Maths" by W. Marlin.

Year 5 Essential Exercises
Warwick Marlin © Five Senses Education

INTRODUCTION TO PROBLEM SOLVING

Solving problems is becoming an important part of mathematics both in Primary School as well as in High School, because it involves a certain amount of original or lateral thinking. It is also a difficult topic to teach, because there are no clear rules for finding the answer to a particular problem. Some students might use one method, while others might arrive at the same correct answer by using a different method. Some gifted students might be able to answer some of the problems quickly and mentally, but most students will have to do some working (multiplication, division, diagrams, tables, charts, etc.) and 'wrestle with the problem' for some time before they arrive at the answer.

10 USEFUL HINTS FOR SOLVING PROBLEMS

1. Read the question carefully — maybe even two or three times.
2. Decide what you are asked to find.
3. Write down information that may be helpful.
4. Try to find a pattern or a clever shortcut method.
5. You may have to try several other methods if the first one doesn't work.
6. Use any method that will help you. (pictures, tables, drawings, working backwards, etc.)
7. Think of it as a challenging puzzle — don't give up on it!
8. Show any working that you do (adding, subtracting, multiplying, dividing, pictures, etc.)
9. Write your final answer out clearly.
10. Check to see if your answer makes sense.

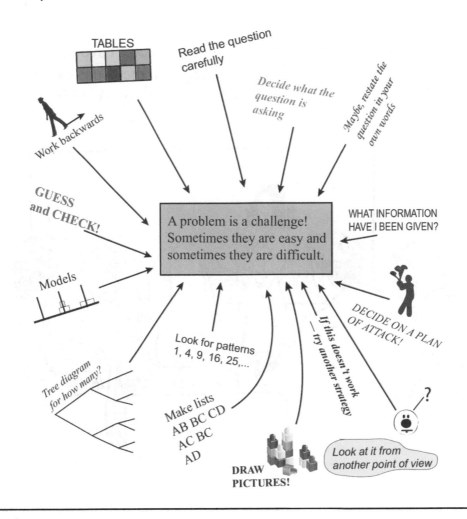

SOME IMPORTANT WORDS IN MATHS

SUM means ADD or TOTAL.

The sum of 17 and 21 is $17 + 21 = 38$

DIFFERENCE means SUBTRACT.

The difference between 10 and 4 is $10 - 4 = 6$

PRODUCT means MULTIPLY.

The product of 9 and 6 is $9 \times 6 = 54$

QUOTIENT means DIVIDE.

The quotient of 24 and 3 is $24 \div 3 = 8$

INCREASE means to ADD ON.

Increase 10 by 7 means $10 + 7 = 17$

DECREASE means to SUBTRACT FROM.

Decrease 23 by 8 means $23 - 8 = 15$

= means EQUALS.

$3 + 5 = 8$

≠ means NOT EQUAL TO.

$3 + 5 \neq 10$

> means LARGER THAN.

$8 > 5$

< means LESS THAN.

$3 < 4$

∴ means THEREFORE

$\square + 5 = 7 \therefore \square = 2$

If you do not understand the meaning of these words, then you will not be able to answer many questions in mathematics.

SQUARED means POWER OF 2.

Four squared means $4^2 = 4 \times 4 = 16$

CUBED means POWER OF 3.

Ten cubed means $10^3 = 10 \times 10 \times 10 = 1000$

AVERAGE means MIDDLE.

The average of 6 and 10 is 8

ASCENDING ORDER means the given numbers are arranged from smallest to highest.

3, 5, 7, 10, 11

DESCENDING ORDER means the given set of numbers are arranged from highest to smallest.

11, 10, 7, 5, 3

Example 1: Find the sum of the first five odd numbers, and then decrease this total by 4.
The Sum of first five number means $1 + 3 + 5 + 7 + 9 = 25$
Decrease this by 4 means $25 - 4 = 21$

Example 2: Find the product of the first three even numbers, and increase this total by 7.
Product of the first 3 even numbers means $2 \times 4 \times 6 = 48$
Increase this by 7 means $48 + 7 = 55$

Example 3: The difference of 14 and 9 is subtracted from the quotient of 28 and 4.
The difference of 14 and 9 means $14 - 9 = 5$
The quotient of 28 and 4 means $28 \div 4 = 7$
5 subtracted from 7 leaves an answer $= 2$

Year 5 Essential Exercises
Warwick Marlin © Five Senses Education

AVERAGE

The average of a set of different numbers is "approximately the MIDDLE" number. If Ann scored 8 out of 10 in one spelling test, and 6 out of 10 in a second spelling test, then her average mark is 8 out of 10.

> Average of a set of scores (or numbers) = $\dfrac{\text{add up all the scores}}{\text{total number of scores}}$

Example 1: Find the average of 3, 5, 9 and 11.

$$\text{Average} = \frac{3 + 5 + 9 + 11}{4}$$

$$= \frac{28}{4}$$

$$= 7$$

Add up all the scores (28) and divide by the number of scores (4).

Example 2: In 3 cricket matches, Peter scored 40 runs, 35 runs and 54 runs. What is his batting average for the 3 games.

$$\text{Average} = \frac{40 + 35 + 54}{3}$$

$$= 43$$

Peter has a batting average of 43 runs per game.

Example 3: Sally has a part time job at McDonalds. In one week she worked 5 days and earned the following amounts: $17, $24, $45, and $32. What was her average daily wage?

$$\text{Average} = \frac{\text{add up all the scores}}{\text{total number of scores}}$$

$$= \frac{17 + 24 + 38 + 45 + 32}{5}$$

$$= \frac{156}{5}$$

$$= 31.2$$

Average can be written using decimals or fractions.

Her average daily usage is $ 31.20

THE ORDER OF OPERATIONS

Mathematicians around the world have agreed on a definite order of doing brackets and the 4 operations (+ − × ÷), otherwise confusion would occur.

For example, which is the correct answer to the problem below?

$$6 + 2 \times 4 = 32$$ **or** $$6 + 2 \times 4 = 14$$

Do we add the 6 + 2 and then multiply this by 4 to equal 32?

Do we multiply the 2 times 4, and then add the six to equal 14?

THE AGREED ORDER OF OPERATIONS

First, work out the answer to the brackets.

Secondly, work out any division and multiplication as they occur from left to right in the number sentence.

Thirdly, work out any additional subtraction as they occur from left to right in the given number sentence.

This is often remembered by students as:

Equal priority-
depends which comes first.

Equal priority-
depends which comes first.

B   **O**   **D**   **M**   **A**   **S**

Brackets   of   Division   Multiplication   Addition   Substraction

Note: Do not worry about the letter O = of at this stage!!

Example 1: $6 + 2 \times 4$ Multiplication first.
$= 6 + 8$ Addition next.
$= 14$

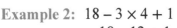

Try to memorise the word BODMAS.

Example 2: $18 - 3 \times 4 + 1$ Multiplication first.
$= 18 - 12 + 1$ Then addition & subtraction as they occur
$= 6 + 1$ from left to right in the given number sentence.
$= 7$ In this example, the subtraction must be done before the addition.

Example 3: $(3 + 18) - 40 \div 5$ Brackets first.
$= 21 - 40 \div 5$ Division next.
$= 21 - 8$ Subtraction last.
$= 13$

Year 5 Essential Exercises
Warwick Marlin © Five Senses Education

PERCENTAGES, DECIMALS AND FRACTIONS

We can write hundredths in 3 different ways which all have exactly the same meaning. To make this idea very clear, we have shaded in different amounts of the larger squares in the diagrams below. On the right hand side, the EQUIVALENT (means equal) percentage, decimal and fraction of the shaded area has been given. Many fractions can be simplified.

	PERCENTAGE	=	DECIMAL	=	FRACTION	=	SIMPLIFIED FRACTION (where possible)

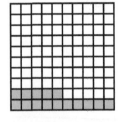 15% = 0.15 = $\dfrac{15}{100}$ = $\dfrac{3}{20}$

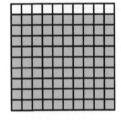 90% = 0.90 = $\dfrac{90}{100}$ = $\dfrac{9}{10}$

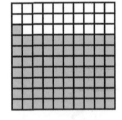 71% = 0.71 = $\dfrac{71}{100}$ = Not possible to simplify

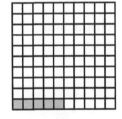 5% = 0.05 = $\dfrac{5}{100}$ = $\dfrac{1}{20}$

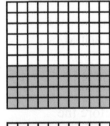 40% = 0.40 = $\dfrac{40}{100}$ = $\dfrac{2}{5}$

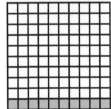 10% = 0.10 = $\dfrac{10}{100}$ = $\dfrac{1}{10}$

IMPORTANT PERCENTAGE CONVERSIONS

As we have seen on the previous page, percentages can be written in their equivalent decimal or fraction form. Some of these occur so regularly in everyday living (as well as in tests), that they should be memorised. The most important conversions are listed below.

PERCENTAGE	DECIMAL	FRACTION	SIMPLIFIED FRACTION
25%	0.25	$\dfrac{25}{100}$	$\dfrac{1}{4}$
50%	0.50	$\dfrac{50}{100}$	$\dfrac{1}{2}$
75%	0.75	$\dfrac{75}{100}$	$\dfrac{3}{4}$
100%	1.00	$\dfrac{100}{100}$	1
10%	0.1	$\dfrac{10}{100}$	$\dfrac{1}{10}$
20%	0.2	$\dfrac{20}{100}$	$\dfrac{1}{5}$
30%	0.3	$\dfrac{30}{100}$	$\dfrac{3}{10}$
40%	0.4	$\dfrac{40}{100}$	$\dfrac{2}{5}$
60%	0.6	$\dfrac{60}{100}$	$\dfrac{3}{5}$
70%	0.7	$\dfrac{70}{100}$	$\dfrac{7}{10}$
80%	0.8	$\dfrac{80}{100}$	$\dfrac{4}{5}$
90%	0.9	$\dfrac{90}{100}$	$\dfrac{9}{10}$

Try to memorise these important conversions.

Example: Find 25% of $300

Method (i): $\dfrac{25}{100} \times \dfrac{300}{1} = \$75$ Change to a fraction, multiply and cancel down.

Method (ii): $25\% = \dfrac{1}{4}$ as a simplified fraction (see table above)

$\dfrac{1}{4} \times \dfrac{300}{1} = \dfrac{300}{4} = \$75$

The word "OF" in Maths means "MULTIPLY".

Year 5 Essential Exercises
Warwick Marlin © Five Senses Education

SOME EVERYDAY MEASUREMENTS

Note: All these measurements are approximate because they are based on average sizes only. The symbol in Maths for approximate is ≈.

Average sized man
Height ≈ 178 cm
or 1.78 m
Mass ≈ 75 kg

Apple
Mass ≈ 200g

Steak
Mass ≈ 250 g

12-year-old
Height ≈ 145 cm
or 1.45 m
Mass ≈ 30 to 40 kg

Normal body temperature 37°C

Tall basketball
player
Height ≈ 2 m
or 200 cm
Mass ≈ 85 kg

1 large step
Length ≈ 1 metre

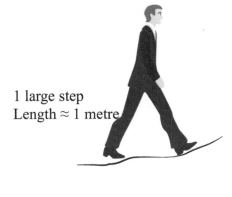

Average walking
speed ≈ 5 km/h

Teaspoon
Capacity ≈ 5 mL of liquid

Pencil
Length ≈ 15 cm
Mass 15 ≈ g

Spoon
Capacity ≈ 10 mL to 12 mL

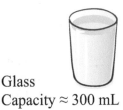

Glass
Capacity ≈ 300 mL

1 L of milk

1 L of Soda

Bucket of water
Capacity ≈ 5 L

Block of land
Area ≈ 0.1 ha
or 1 000 m³

Freezing temperature of
ice cubes = 0°C

Boiling point of
water = 100°C

Tub of margarine
Mass ≈ 500 g

Tennis Court
Area ≈ 270 m²

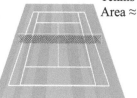

Car
Mass ≈ 1 000 kg to 1 500 kg

Swimming pool
Capacity ≈ 100 000 L or 100 kL

Middle-sized truck
Mass ≈ 1 500 kg to 2 500 kg

Bath capacity ≈ 120 L

Large truck
Mass ≈ 10 000 kg to 12 000 kg or 10 t to 12 t

Middle-sized dog
Mass ≈ 25 kg

A4 Page
Area ≈ 630 cm²

Arctic temperatures
From −6°C to −40°C

Year 5 Essential Exercises
Warwick Marlin © Five Senses Education

USEFUL UNITS AND METRIC CONVERSION

Some of the metric conversions shown below (and their abbreviations) are each explained more thoroughly in "Understanding Year 5 Maths" by the same author.

	1 Litre	=	1 000 millilitres
or	1 L	=	1 000 mL
	1 kilometre	=	1 000 metres
or	1 km	=	1 000 m
	1 metre	=	100 centimetres
or	1 m	=	100 cm
	1 centimetre	=	10 millimetres
or	1 cm	=	10 mm
	1 kilogram	=	1 000 grams
or	1 kg	=	1 000 g
	1 hectare	=	10 000 square metres
or	1 ha	=	10 000 m²

Some important prefixes:

kilo means 1 000 ⟹ **kilo**gram = 1 000 grams

⟹ **kilo**metre = 1 000 metres

centi means $\frac{1}{100}$ ⟹ **centi**metre = $\frac{1}{100}$ of a metre

milli means $\frac{1}{1\ 000}$ ⟹ **milli**gram = $\frac{1}{1\ 000}$ of a gram

⟹ **milli**metre = $\frac{1}{1\ 000}$ of a metre

SOLUTIONS

Note: Most of the solutions, particularly the problem solving questions, show the working and the steps required to get each answer.

Essential Exercises – Year 5 Maths
Warwick Marlin © Five Senses Education

These are the answers!

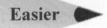

Q1. a) 4 132 b) 9 274 c) 6 309

Q2. Write the following numbers on the place value chart shown:

a) 7 531 b) 6 284

c) 5 076 d) 4 309

Thousands	Hundreds	Tens	Units
7	5	3	1
6	2	8	4
5	0	7	6
4	3	0	9

Q3. a) 30 b) 3 c) 3 000 d) 300

Q4. a) 7 321, 7 312, 7 231, 7 132, 7 123 b) 4 906, 4 690, 4 609, 4 096, 4 069

Q5. a) One thousand and ninety seven b) Three thousand, five hundred and ninety two

c) Six thousand, eight hundred and three d) Two thousand, five hundred and sixty

Q6. a) 4 648 b) 2 705

Q7. a) 4 863 b) 7 498

Q8. a) $2\,498 = (2 \times 1\,000) + (4 \times 100) + (9 \times 10) + (8 \times 1)$

b) $5\,365 = (5 \times 1\,000) + (3 \times 100) + (6 \times 10) + (5 \times 1)$

c) $6\,803 = (6 \times 1\,000) + (8 \times 100) + (0 \times 10) + (3 \times 1)$

d) $9\,760 = (9 \times 1\,000) + (7 \times 100) + (6 \times 10) + (0 \times 1)$

> The brackets involving zero can be left out if you wish.

Q9. a) 8 = { 1, 2, 4, 8 } b) 10 = { 1, 2, 5, 10 }

c) 20 = { 1, 2, 4, 5, 10, 20 } d) 17 = { 1, 17 }

Q10. a) HCF = 2 b) HCF = 4

c) HCF = 10 d) HCF = 5

Q11. a) { 10, 20, 30, 40 }

b) { 4, 8, 12, 16, 20, 24 }

c) { 6, 12, 18, 24, 30 }

Q12. a) LCM = 20 b) LCM = 12 c) LCM = 30

Q13. a) 70 b) 140 d) 100

> With 5 always round up.

Q14. a) $497 + 308 = 500 + 300$ (rounded to nearest 100) = 800 (estimate)

b) $602 - 389 = 600 - 400$ (rounded to nearest 100) = 200 (estimate)

c) $89 \times 11 = 90 \times 10$ (rounded to nearest 10) = 900 (estimate)

d) $53 \div 9 = 50 \div 10$ (rounded to nearest 10) = 5 (estimate)

Q15. Find;

a)
```
  ₁
  387
+ 295
─────
  682
```

b)
```
  ₁₁
  694
+ 127
─────
  821
```

c)
```
   ₁
 2 483
+3 347
──────
 5 830
```

d)
```
 ₁ ₁₁
 5 479
+2 586
──────
 8 065
```

Q16. Find:

a)
$$879 \\ -\ 365 \\ \overline{514}$$

b)
$$996 \\ -\ 546 \\ \overline{450}$$

c)
$$3\ 5\overset{6}{\cancel{7}}{}^{1}4 \\ -\ 1\ 239 \\ \overline{2\ 335}$$

d)
$$7\ 6\overset{8}{\cancel{9}}{}^{1}2 \\ -\ 4\ 468 \\ \overline{3\ 224}$$

Q17. Find:

a)
$$\overset{2}{9}7 \\ \times\ 3 \\ \overline{291}$$

b)
$$\overset{2}{8}9 \\ \times\ 6 \\ \overline{534}$$

c)
$$\overset{5\,2}{3}63 \\ \times\ 8 \\ \overline{2\ 904}$$

d)
$$\overset{4\,6}{5}69 \\ \times\ 7 \\ \overline{3\ 983}$$

Q18. Find:

a) $7\overline{)84}$ = 12

b) $3\overline{)54}$ = 18

c) $5\overline{)85}$ = 17

d) $7\overline{)30}$ = 4 r 2

These are the **answers!**

Level 2

NUMBER AND PLACE VALUE

Average

Q1. a) 70   b) 3 000   c) 20 000   d) 400

Q2. a) 4 123, 4 213, 4 231, 4 312, 4 321   b) 6 789, 6 798, 6 879, 6 897, 6 978

Q3. a) Seven hundred & fifty two   b) One thousand & six

  c) Twenty three thousand, seven hundred & eighty nine

  d) Eighteen thousand and seventy four

Q4. a) 7 205   b) 39 823

Q5. a) 8 305   b) 40 967

Q6. a) 7 305 = (7 × 1 000) + (3 × 100) + (5 × 1)

  b) 6 082 = (6 × 1 000) + (8 × 10) + (2 × 1)

  c) 13 049 = (1 × 10 000) + (3 × 1 000) + (4 × 10) + (9 × 1)

  d) 10 073 = (1 × 10 000) + (7 × 10) + (3 × 1)

Q7. a) 34 271 = (3 × 10 000) + (4 × 1 000) + (2 × 100) + (7 × 10) + (1 × 1)

  b) 29 053 = (2 × 10 000) + (9 × 1 000) + (5 × 10) + (3 × 1)

  c) 82 530 = (8 × 10 000) + (2 × 1 000) + (5 × 100) + (3 × 10)

Q8. a) 12 = { 1, 2, 3, 4, 6, 12 }   b) 20 = { 1, 2, 4, 5, 10, 20 }

  c) 29 = { 1, 29 }   d) 24 = { 1, 2, 3, 4, 6, 8, 12, 24 }

Q8. a) 12 = { 1, 2, 3, 4, 6, 12 }   b) 20 = { 1, 2, 4, 5, 10, 20 }

  c) 29 = { 1, 29 }   d) 24 = { 1, 2, 3, 4, 6, 8, 12, 24 }

Q9. a) { 9 , 18, 27, 36 }   b) {8, 16, 24, 32, 40}   c) { 21, 24, 27, 30 }

Q10. a) 18 = { 1, 2, 3, 6, 9, 18 }   b) 27 = { 1, 3, 9, 27 }   c) HCF = 9

Q11. a) HCF = 4   b) HCF = 4   c) HCF = 12

Q12. a) LCM = 40   b) LCM = 45   c) LCM = 56

Q13. Round off each number below to the nearest ten, and then ESTIMATE the final answer.

a)   157 + 42   b)   94 − 38   c)   174 − 52

Round off 160 + 40   Round off 90 − 40   Round off 170 − 50

Estimate = 200   Estimate = 50   Estimate = 120

Essential Exercises – Year 5 Maths
Warwick Marlin © Five Senses Education

Q14. Round off each number below to the nearest hundred, and then ESTIMATE the final answer.

a)   426 + 189   b)   853 − 248   c)   761 + 928
     Round off 400 + 200   Round off 900 − 200   Round off 800 + 900
     Estimate = 600   Estimate = 700   Estimate = 1 700

Q15. Find:

a) $^{1}{}^{1}135$ b) $^{1}784$ c) $^{1}498$ d) $^{1}758$
    + 269   + 359   + 746   + 999
     404   1 143   1 244   1 757

Q16. Find:

a)   938   b)   327   c)   674   d)   427
  − 425   − 145   − 379   − 358
   513   182   295   69

Q17. Find:

a)   374   b)   678   c)   453   d)   692
  ×   8   ×   9   ×   12   ×   23
 2 992   6 102   906   2 076
                                         + 4 530   + 13 840
                                         5 436   15 916

Q18. Find:

a) $7\overline{)91}$ quotient 13   b) $6\overline{)1158}$ quotient 193   c) $8\overline{)5913}$ quotient 739 r 1   d) $5\overline{)2453}$ quotient 490 r 3

Q19.
a) Add one zero onto 27   b) Add one zero onto 318
     Answer = 270   Answer = 3 180
c) Add two zeros onto 48   c) Add three zeros onto 73
     Answer = 4 800   Answer = 73 000

Q20.
a) $9 \neq 12$ b) $6 < 3 + 4$
c) $\therefore 5^2 = 25$ d) $18 > 3 \times 5$
e) $12 \div 3 \leq 4$ f) $\therefore x = 10$
     or $\dfrac{12}{3} \geq 4$

These are the **answers!**

Level 3

NUMBER AND PLACE VALUE

Average

Q1. Divide 135 into 2 nearly equal parts.
We start with 68 ladies and 67 men. We then keep on adding 1 to the number of ladies, and subtracting 1 from the number of men, until there are 11 more ladies than men.

     69 ladies and 66 men – not correct!
     70 ladies and 65 men etc.
     Finally, 73 ladies and 62 men.
∴ 62 men were standing.

Trial and error, or guess and check method.

Q2.

$$3\ 075$$
$$-\ 2\ 798$$
$$\overline{277}$$

Subtract 2 798 from 3 075.

Therefore 277 paving stones are left over.

Q3.

$$389$$
$$249$$
$$+\ 436$$
$$\overline{1\ 074}$$

a) Add up all the kilometres = 1 074 km

b) Average = $\dfrac{1\ 074}{3}$ = 358 km / day (Divide by 3 days)

Q4.

$$43\ 073$$
$$+\ 1\ 074$$
$$\overline{44\ 147}$$

Odometer would show 44 147 at the end of the trip.

Q5.

$$\begin{array}{r} 1\ 728 \\ 8\overline{)13\ 824} \end{array}$$

Divide $ 13 824 by 8.

Therefore each person will get $1 728.

Q6.

a)

$$\begin{array}{r} 140 \\ \times\ \ \ 7 \\ \hline 980 \end{array}$$

He can lay
980 bricks
in one day.

b)

$$\begin{array}{r} 980 \\ \times\ \ \ 5 \\ \hline 4\ 900 \end{array}$$

He can lay
4 900 bricks
in 5 days.

Q7.   7 145 rounded off to the nearest thousand = 7 000 calls

8 cents rounded off to the nearest ten = 10 cents

∴ Estimate = 7 000 × 10 cents = 70 000 cents = $700 . 00

Q8.   Add the 3 marks, and divide by 3
to find the average.

∴ Average = 76%

$$\begin{array}{r} 87 \\ 73 \\ +\ 68 \\ \hline 228 \end{array}$$

$$\begin{array}{r} 76 \\ 3\overline{)228} \end{array}$$

Q9.   Multiply 138 by 6.

Factory makes 828

openers in 6 days.

$$\begin{array}{r} 138 \\ \times\ \ \ 6 \\ \hline 828 \end{array}$$

Q10. Multiply 7 by 365 days

∴ Zac sends out 2 555

text messages in one year.

$$\begin{array}{r} 365 \\ \times\ \ \ 7 \\ \hline 2\ 555 \end{array}$$

The symbol ∴
means therefore.

Q11. Add the heights of the first & second
days. subtract this total from 8 850
to find the height they still have to climb

∴ The team still has to climb 4 273m.

$$\begin{array}{r} 2\ 731 \\ +\ 1\ 846 \\ \hline 4\ 577 \end{array}$$

$$\begin{array}{r} 8\ 850 \\ -\ 4\ 577 \\ \hline 4\ 273 \end{array}$$

Q12. Add the distance together, and then subtract
the total from 1 000 km.

∴ He still needs to cycle 692 km

$$\begin{array}{r} 83 \\ 129 \\ +\ 96 \\ \hline 308 \end{array}$$

$$\begin{array}{r} 1\ 000 \\ -\ 308 \\ \hline 692 \end{array}$$

Q13. Sue has saved one quarter of Judy.
Therefore divide $180 by 4.

Now add the 2 amount together.

∴ Both of them have saved $225.

$$\begin{array}{r} 45 \\ 4\overline{)180} \end{array}$$

$$\begin{array}{r} 45 \\ +\ 180 \\ \hline 225 \end{array}$$

Essential Exercises – Year 5 Maths
Warwick Marlin © Five Senses Education

Q14.
$$\underbrace{7 + 8 + 9}_{24} \quad + \quad \underbrace{7 + 8 + 9}_{24} \quad + \quad \underbrace{7 + 8 + 9}_{24} \quad \text{etc.}$$

$$\begin{array}{r} 24 \\ \times \ 6 \\ \hline 144 \end{array}$$

The pattern $7 + 8 + 9$ repeats 6 times.

∴ Multiply 24 by 6. = 144

Q15. 9 780 rounded off to the nearest thousand = 10 000

$9.45 rounded off to the nearest dollar = $9.00

∴ Estimate = 10 000 × $9 = $90 000

Q16. The best way to do this problem is by GUESS and CHECK.

1st guess: Kate = 15 and Jess = 10 ⟹ 2 × 15 + 3 × 10 = 60 Wrong – too low!

2nd guess: Kate = 20 and Jess = 15 ⟹ 2 × 20 + 3 × 15 = 95 Wrong – too high!

3rd guess: Kate = 18 and Jess = 13 ⟹ 2 × 18 + 3 × 13 = 75 Correct!!

                  Therefore Kate is 18 years old and Jess is 13 years old.

Q17. Once again, GUESS and CHECK is the best method.

Try 6 and 4. $6 \times 4 = 24$ and $6 + 4 = 10$ Wrong.

Try 12 and 2 $12 \times 2 = 24$ and $12 + 2 = 14$ Wrong.

Try 8 and 3 $8 \times 3 = 24$ and $8 + 3 = 11$ Correct!!

                  The two numbers are 8 and 3.

Q18.
a) $10 \times 23 = 230$

c) $85 \div 7 = 12 \text{ rem } 1$

e) $9 = 9 \times 9 = 81$

g) $\dfrac{12 + 20}{2} = \dfrac{32}{2} = 16$

b) $1\ 482 + 3\ 976 = 5\ 458$

d) $3\ 821 - 1\ 963 = 1\ 858$

f) $4 \text{ cubed} = 4 \times 4 \times 4 = 64$

h) $3\ 712 - 1\ 584 = 2\ 128$

Q19.
a) 789, 798, 879, 897, 978, 987

b) 987, 978, 897, 879, 798, 789

c) 897 is the third largest number

Q20.
a)
$$\begin{array}{r} 147 \\ \times \ \ 5 \\ \hline 735 \end{array}$$
Susan earns $735 in 5 days.

b)
$$\begin{array}{r} 124 \\ + \ 28 \\ \hline 152 \end{array} \qquad \begin{array}{r} 735 \\ - \ 152 \\ \hline 583 \end{array}$$
Susan has $583 left over.

Q21. In 4 years, I will be 40 years old. This will be twice the age of my son.

Therefore my son will be 20 in 4 years time.

He must be 16 years old now.

Q22.
$$\begin{array}{r} 369 \\ \times \ \ 7 \\ \hline 2\ 583 \end{array}$$
The farmer sold his pigs for $2 583, but he still has to pay $258 and $183.

$$\begin{array}{r} 258 \\ + \ 183 \\ \hline 441 \end{array} \qquad \begin{array}{r} 2\ 583 \\ - \ \ 441 \\ \hline 2\ 142 \end{array}$$
The farmer has $2 142 left over.

These are the **answers!**

NUMBER AND PLACE VALUE

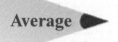

Average

Q1. a) 3 000　　　b) 20 000　　　c) 400 000　　　d) 500

Q2. a) 57 269　　　b) 490 786　　　c) 7 606 403　　　d) 9 067 048

Q3. a) 7 325　 = (7 × 1 000) + (3 × 100) + (2 × 10) + (5 × 1)

b) 17 291　 = (1 × 10 000) + (7 × 1 000) + (2 × 100) + (9 × 10) + (1 × 1)

c) 2 071 803　 = (2 × 1 000 000) + (7 × 10 000) + (1 × 1 000) + (8 × 100) + (3 × 1)

d) 18 306 027 = (1 × 10 000 000) + (8 × 1000 000) + (3 × 100 000) + (6 × 1 000) +
(2 × 10) + (7 × 1)

Q4. a) Nine thousand, four hundred and eighty three

b) Seventeen thousand, two hundred and ninety one

c) Two million, seventy one thousand, eight hundred and three

d) Eighteen million, three hundred and six thousand and twenty seven

Q5. a) 3 805　　　b) 68 027　　　c) 2 374 902

Q6. 25 576 938,　25 657 398,　25 756 983,　25 765 389,　25 765 398

Q7. 34 532 198,　34 523 189,　34 352 891,　34 325 981,　34 235 891

Q8. a) 40 = { 1, 2, 4, 5, 8, 10, 20, 40 }　　　b) 36 = { 1, 2, 3, 4, 6, 9, 12, 18, 36 }

c) 45 = { 1, 3, 5, 9, 15, 45 }　　　d) 60 = { 1, 2, 3, 4, 5, 6, 10, 12, 15, 20, 30, 60 }

Q9. a) HCF = 20　　　b) HCF = 4　　　c) HCF = 15　　　d) HCF = 9

Q10. a) { 12, 24, 36, 48, 60, 72 }　　　b) { 15, 30, 45, 60, 75, 90, 105 }

c) { 20, 40, 60, 80, 100 }　　　d) { 27, 36, 45, 54 }

Q11. a) LCM = 36　　　b) LCM = 60　　　c) 42　　　d) 140

Q12. a) 300　　　b) 700　　　c) 3 500　　　d) 7 300

Q13. a) 7 000　　　b) 10 000　　　c) 5 000　　　d) 19 000

Q14. a)　 648 + 259
= 600 + 300 (Rounding)
= 900　　　(Estimate)

b) 739 − 452
= 700 − 500 (Rounding)
= 200　　　(Estimate)

c) 7 348 − 852
= 7 300 − 900 (Rounding)
= 6 400　　　(Estimate)

d) 641 × 78
= 600 × 100 (Rounding)
= 60 000　　(Estimate)

> 5 is always rounded up.

Q15. a) 792 − 203
= 790 − 200 (Rounding)
= 590　　　(Estimate)

b) 739 ÷ 8
= 740 ÷ 10 (Rounding)
= 74　　　(Estimate)

c) 824 × 12
= 820 × 10 (Rounding)
= 8 200　　(Estimate)

d) 1 618 + 783
= 1 620 + 780 (Rounding)
= 2 400　　(Estimate)

Q16.

a)	b)	c)	d)
931	17 821	36	271
8 926	987	7 832	34 712
14 039	3 574	19 087	16
+ 27	+ 2 589	+ 5 369	2 094
23 923	24 971	32 324	+ 8
			37 101

Essential Exercises – Year 5 Maths
Warwick Marlin © Five Senses Education

Q17.
a)
$$\begin{array}{r} 7\ 028 \\ -\ 3\ 259 \\ \hline 3\ 769 \end{array}$$

b)
$$\begin{array}{r} 6\ 734 \\ -\ 4\ 789 \\ \hline 1\ 945 \end{array}$$

c)
$$\begin{array}{r} 11\ 703 \\ -\ 2\ 536 \\ \hline 9\ 167 \end{array}$$

d)
$$\begin{array}{r} 14\ 381 \\ -\ 7\ 426 \\ \hline 6\ 955 \end{array}$$

Q18.
a)
$$\begin{array}{r} 47 \\ \times\ 29 \\ \hline 423 \\ +\ 940 \\ \hline 1\ 363 \end{array}$$

b)
$$\begin{array}{r} 127 \\ \times\ 15 \\ \hline 635 \\ +\ 1\ 270 \\ \hline 1\ 905 \end{array}$$

c)
$$\begin{array}{r} 320 \\ \times\ 47 \\ \hline 2\ 240 \\ +\ 12\ 800 \\ \hline 15\ 040 \end{array}$$

d)
$$\begin{array}{r} 639 \\ \times\ 78 \\ \hline 5\ 112 \\ +\ 44\ 730 \\ \hline 49\ 842 \end{array}$$

Q19.
a) $8\overline{)5\ 872}$ 734

b) $7\overline{)38\ 346}$ 5 478

c) $5\overline{)6\ 298}$ 1 259 rem 3

d) $9\overline{)12\ 348}$ 1 372

Q20.
a) 71×10
= 710
Add 1 zero

b) 38×100
= 3 800
Add 2 zeros

d) $25 \times 1\ 000$
= 25 000
Add 3 zeros

d) $230 \div 10$
= 23
Subtract 1 zero

Q21.
a) $8 + 2 \times 5$
= 8 + 10
= 18

b) $16 + 10 \div 2$
= 16 + 5
= 21

c) $(8 + 2) \times 5$
= 10 × 5
= 50

d) $10 + 2 \times 3 - 4$
= 10 + 6 − 4
= 12

e) $8 \times 3 - 2 \times 4$
= 24 − 8
= 16

f) $20 \div (2 + 3)$
= 20 ÷ 5
= 4

g) $10 - 4 \times 2$
= 10 − 8
= 2

h) $8 \div 2 + 3 \times 4$
= 4 + 12
= 16

Q22.
a) $4 \times 5 + 13$
= 20 + 13
= 33

b) $7^2 - 13$
= 49 − 13
= 36

c) $63 \div 7 - 9$
= 9 − 9
= 0

d) $(8 + 12) + 40 \div 5$
= 20 + 8
= 28

These are the **answers!**

Level 5

NUMBER AND PLACE VALUE

Difficult

Q1.
a) Room A = 7 000 books
Room B = 5 000 books
Room C = 6 000 books

Estimate of total = 7 000 + 5 000 + 6 000
= 18 000 books

b) Exact total = 18 360 books
c) Average = 18 360 ÷ 3 = 6 120
d) School still needs 25 000 − 18 360 = 6 640 books

Q2.
a) Mango = $3   Rye bread = $6   Margarine = $3   Peach jam = $7
Estimate = 4 × $3 + $6 + $3 + $7 = $28
b) Exact price = 4 × $2.85 + $5.64 + $3.45 + $6.87 = $27.36
c) Change = $50 − $27.36 = $22.64 = $22.65 (Rounded to nearest 5c)

Q3.
Guess 1 : 2 × $12 + 4 × $4 = $40 Too low.
Guess 2 : 2 × $15 + 4 × $5 = $50 Too low.
Guess 3 : 2 × $18 + 4 × $6 = $60 Correct!!
Each adult ticket cost $18 and each child ticket cost $6.

Q4. 3 hamburgers + 4 cokes = 1 850 cents

8 hamburgers + 4 cokes = 4 100 cents   (double the price of 4 hamburgers + 2 cokes)

Therefore the 5 extra hamburgers cost 4 100 – 1 850 = 2 250 cents

∴ 1 hamburger cost 2 250 ÷ 5 = 450 cents = $4.50

It is easy now to work out the price of 1 coke = $1.25

Q5. □ + □ + △ = 73   (line 1)

□ + △ + △ = 65   (line 2)

□ + □ + △ + △ + △ + △ = 130 line 3 (double line 2)

If we look at line 1 and line 3, we can see that the extra triangles in line 3 must add upto 57.

Therefore △ + △ + △ = 57 ⇒ △ = 19

Therefore □ + □ + 19 = 73 ⇒ □ = 27

Q6. Guess 1 : 20 × 15 + 10 × 25 = 550 Too high.

Guess 2 : 21 × 15 + 9 × 25 = 540 Still too high.

Guess 3 : 22 × 15 + 8 × 25 = 530 Correct!!

Therefore there were 8 return tickets, and 22 one way tickets sold.

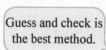
Guess and check is the best method.

Q7. This another problem where you will have to 'guess' and 'check'.

On the first guess, let us assume Josh gets 30 correct answers and 20 wrong answers.

Therefore Jess, who has 4 extra mistakes, will get 26 correct answers and 24 wrong answers.

Josh : 30 correct and 20 incorrect = 30 × 7 – 20 × 4 = 210 – 80 = 130 } Total = 216

Jess : 26 correct and 24 incorrect = 26 × 7 – 24 × 4 = 182 – 96 = 86 } Far to low.

Josh : 40 correct and 10 incorrect = 40 × 7 – 10 × 4 = 280 – 40 = 240 } Total = 436

Jess : 36 correct and 14 incorrect = 36 × 7 – 14 × 4 = 252 – 56 = 196 } Too high.

Josh : 37 correct and 13 incorrect = 37 × 7 – 13 × 4 = 259 – 52 = 207 } Total = 370

Jess : 33 correct and 17 incorrect = 33 × 7 – 17 × 4 = 231 – 68 = 163 } Correct!!

Therefore Jess got 33 correct answers.

Q8. After 6 matches, Ricky has scored   6 × 21 = 126 runs

After 7 matches, Ricky needs to score   7 × 25 = 175 runs

Therefore, in the 7th match, Ricky needs to score 175 – 126 = 49 runs

Q9. This another problem where you can 'guess and check' or 'trial and error'.

For the first guess, let us assume there are 7 sunny days and 7 rainy days.

Guess 1 : 7 × 20 + 7 × 16 = 140 + 112 = 252 run   too low.

Guess 2 : 8 × 20 + 6 × 16 = 160 + 96 = 256 run   still slightly too low.

Guess 3 : 9 × 20 + 5 × 16 = 180 + 80 = 260 run   correct!!

Therefore there were 9 sunny days during the 2 weeks.

Essential Exercises – Year 5 Maths
Warwick Marlin © Five Senses Education

Q10.   Guess 1 : Let James be 20 and Susan 14.

$3 \times 20 + 4 \times 14 = 60 + 56 = 116$ too low.

Guess 2 : Let James be 21 and Susan 15.

$3 \times 21 + 4 \times 15 = 63 + 60 =$ correct!!

Therefore James is 21 years old and Susan is 15 years old.

Q11.   Let us start our first guess with 20 cows = 80 legs. Therefore there must be 31 chickens to make a total of 142 legs.

Guess 1 : $20 \times 4 \ + \ 31 \times 2 \ = \ 80 + 62 \ = \ 142$ legs

$31 \times 4 \ + \ 20 \times 2 \ = \ 124 + 40 \ = \ 164$ legs $\Rightarrow$ too low.

Guess 2 : $19 \times 4 \ + \ 33 \times 2 \ = \ 76 + 66 \ = \ 142$ legs

$33 \times 4 \ + \ 19 \times 2 \ = \ 132 + 38 \ = \ 170$ legs $\Rightarrow$ still too low.

Guess 3 : $18 \times 4 \ + \ 35 \times 2 \ = \ 72 + 70 \ = \ 142$ legs

$35 \times 4 \ + \ 18 \times 2 \ = \ 140 + 36 \ = \ 176$ legs $\Rightarrow$ correct!!

Therefore the farmer had 18 cows and 35 chickens.

Q12.

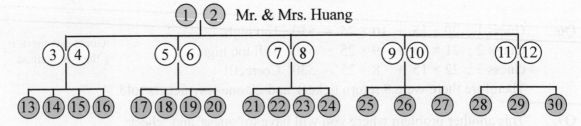

This question is best answered by drawing a picture like the one above.
Then it is easy to see that there are 30 people in the Huang family.

Q13.   We could do this problem easily by 'guess' and 'check'.

However, we can also work backwards from the final answer by doing the opposite or reverse operations.

55 add 8 = 63 and 63 divided by 9 = 7 (Add is opposite to subtract, and divide is the
opposite operation to divide,)

Therefore the number I thought of is 7.

Q14. $1 + 3 + 5 + 7 + 9 \cdots\cdots\cdots\cdots\cdots\cdots\cdots + 95 + 97 + 99$

We can pair up $1 + 99 = 100$, and $3 + 97 = 100$, and $5 + 95 = 100$ etc.
There are 25 pairs adding upto 100. Therefore the answer is $25 \times 100 = 2\,500$.

Q15.   The quotient $\times$ divisor + remainder = dividend
Therefore $628 \times 6 + 2 = 3\,770$
The dividend = $3\,770$

Q16. $7 + 2 + 9 + 0 = 18$, therefore zero is one of the possible digits.
$7 + 2 + 9 + 1 = 19$, therefore 1 is not one of the possible digits.
$7 + 2 + 9 + 3 = 21$, therefore 3 is one of the possible digits.
$7 + 2 + 9 + 6 = 24$, therefore 6 is one of the possible digits.
$7 + 2 + 9 + 9 = 27$, therefore 9 is one of the possible digits.
The 4 possible 1-digit numbers are 0, 3, 6, and 9.

Q17. a) All the corner cubes have 3 sides painted. Therefore 8 cubes have 3 sides painted.
b) All the edges (except for the corner cube) have 2 sides painted. Therefore 16 cubes have 2 sides painted.
c) On each face, 4 cubes have only 1 side painted. There are 6 faces, and therefore 24 cubes have 1 side painted.
d) There are 8 cubes, right in the very middle, which have no sides painted.

Q18. 6 789, 6 798, 6 879, 6 897, 6 978, 6 987, 7 689 etc
There are 24 different combinations in total. The sixth smallest number is 6 987 shown above.

Q19. The numbers larger than 20, with a remainder of 2, after dividing by 7 are : 23, 30, 37, 44, 51, etc. The numbers larger than 20, with a remainder of 1, after dividing by 4 are : 21, 25, 29, 33, 37, 41, etc. Therefore the smallest number which follows both conditions is 37.

Essential Exercises – Year 5 Maths
Warwick Marlin © Five Senses Education

These are the **answers!**

FRACTIONS AND DECIMALS

Easier

Q1. a) $\frac{3}{5}$ b) $\frac{1}{4}$ c) $\frac{7}{10}$ d) $\frac{1}{4}$

e) $\frac{5}{16}$ f) $\frac{2}{3}$ g) $\frac{5}{6}$ h) $\frac{3}{8}$

Q2. a) $\frac{1}{4} = \frac{2}{8}$ b) $\frac{1}{2} = \frac{3}{6}$ c) $\frac{2}{3} = \frac{4}{6}$ d) $\frac{3}{4} = \frac{6}{8}$

Q3. a) $\frac{10}{12} = \frac{5}{6}$ b) $\frac{4}{6} = \frac{2}{3}$ c) $\frac{6}{10} = \frac{3}{5}$ d) $\frac{18}{20} = \frac{9}{10}$

Q4. a) $\frac{1}{2} = \frac{6}{12}$ b) $\frac{1}{4} = \frac{3}{12}$ c) $\frac{3}{4} = \frac{9}{12}$

Q5. a) $\frac{7}{12} > \frac{6}{12}$ b) $\frac{5}{12} < \frac{1}{2}$ c) $\frac{10}{12} > \frac{3}{4}$ d) $\frac{1}{4} = \frac{3}{12}$

Q6. a) $2\frac{3}{4}$ b) $1\frac{1}{3}$ c) $2\frac{4}{5}$

Q7. a) $\frac{11}{4}$ b) $\frac{4}{3}$ c) $\frac{14}{5}$

Q8. a) $\frac{5}{8}$ b) $\frac{7}{12}$ c) $\frac{4}{5}$ d) $\frac{4}{7}$

Q9. a) $1\frac{1}{4} = \frac{5}{4}$ b) $2\frac{1}{3} = \frac{7}{3}$ c) $3\frac{1}{2} = \frac{7}{2}$ d) $2\frac{3}{5} = \frac{13}{5}$

Q10. a) $\frac{7}{3} = 2\frac{1}{3}$ b) $\frac{11}{4} = 2\frac{3}{4}$ c) $\frac{9}{2} = 4\frac{1}{2}$ d) $\frac{8}{5} = 1\frac{3}{5}$

Q11. a) $\frac{4}{10} = 0.4$ b) $\frac{78}{100} = 0.78$ c) $\frac{7}{100} = 0.07$

Q12. a) 52.43 b) 73.95 c) 15.07

Q13. a) $\frac{8}{100}$ b) $\frac{8}{10}$ c) $\frac{8}{1000}$ d) 80

Q14. a) 0.9 b) 0.41 c) 0.008 d) 3.17

Q15. a) $4.18 b) $26.08 c) $9.40 d) $0.27

Q16. a) 783.492 b) 860.759 c) 6 409.083

Q17. a) $\frac{7}{10}$ b) $\frac{23}{100}$ c) $\frac{593}{1000}$ d) $1\frac{9}{10}$

These are the **answers!**

Level 2 — **FRACTIONS AND DECIMALS** — **Average**

Q1. a) Shade in $\frac{2}{5}$

b) Shade in $\frac{5}{8}$

c) Shade in $\frac{3}{5} = \frac{6}{10}$

d) Shade in $\frac{3}{4} = \frac{12}{10}$

Q2. a) $\frac{1}{4} = \frac{5}{20}$ b) $\frac{2}{5} = \frac{6}{15}$ c) $\frac{2}{3} = \frac{20}{30}$ d) $\frac{3}{4} = \frac{9}{12}$

Q3. a) $\frac{8}{20} = \frac{2}{5}$ b) $\frac{12}{15} = \frac{4}{5}$ c) $\frac{15}{20} = \frac{3}{4}$ d) $\frac{21}{28} = \frac{3}{4}$

Divide by 4   Divide by 3   Divide by 5   Divide by 7

Q4. a) $\frac{1}{5} = \frac{3}{15}$ b) $\frac{2}{5} = \frac{6}{15}$ c) $\frac{3}{15} = \frac{9}{15}$ d) $\frac{12}{15} = \frac{4}{5}$

Q5. a) $\frac{2}{5} > \frac{5}{15}$ b) $\frac{4}{5} = \frac{12}{15}$ c) $\frac{8}{15} < \frac{3}{5}$ d) $\frac{4}{5} > \frac{11}{15}$

Q6. a) $\frac{5}{2}$ b) $\frac{5}{4}$ c) $\frac{12}{5}$

Q7. a) $2\frac{1}{2}$ b) $1\frac{1}{4}$ c) $2\frac{2}{5}$

Q8. a) $\frac{7}{8}$ b) $\frac{7}{15}$ c) $\frac{7}{5} = 1\frac{2}{5}$ d) $\frac{11}{7} = 1\frac{4}{7}$

Q9. a) $\frac{4}{9}$ b) $\frac{8}{10} = \frac{4}{5}$ c) $\frac{2}{4} = \frac{1}{2}$ d) $\frac{3}{12} = \frac{1}{4}$

Q10. a) $\frac{7}{4}$ b) $\frac{17}{5}$ c) $\frac{5}{2}$ d) $\frac{34}{10}$

Q11. a) $2\frac{2}{3}$ b) 2 c) $2\frac{4}{5}$ d) $4\frac{3}{4}$

Q12. a) 24.153   b) 52.403   c) 63.041

Q13. a) $\frac{8}{100}$ b) $\frac{2}{1000}$ c) 900   d) $\frac{3}{10}$

Q14. a) $\frac{7}{10} = 0.7$ b) $\frac{341}{1000} = 0.341$ c) $3\frac{28}{100} = 3.28$ d) $15\frac{6}{100} = 15.06$

Q15. a) 5 308.74   b) 9 006.248   c) 4 070.609

Q16. a) $5.96 = (5 \times 1) + (9 \times \frac{1}{10}) + (6 \times \frac{1}{100})$

b) $7.832 = (7 \times 1) + (8 \times \frac{1}{10}) + (3 \times \frac{1}{100}) + (2 \times \frac{1}{1000})$

c) $39.604 = (3 \times 10) + (9 \times 1) + (6 \times \frac{1}{10}) + (4 \times \frac{1}{1000})$

d) $872.039 = (8 \times 100) + (7 \times 10) + (2 \times 1) + (3 \times \frac{1}{100}) + (9 \times \frac{1}{1000})$

Essential Exercises – Year 5 Maths
Warwick Marlin © Five Senses Education

Q17.   a) $7.28   b) $13.06   c) $0.59   d) $83.00

Q18.   a)   7.138, 7.318, 7.803, 7.813, 7.831

        b)   9.147, 9.4, 9.407, 9.417, 9.471

Q19.   a) $0.9 = \dfrac{9}{10}$ b) $0.38 = \dfrac{38}{100}$ or $\dfrac{19}{50}$

        c) $1.92 = 1\dfrac{92}{100}$ or $1\dfrac{23}{25}$ d) $0.365 = \dfrac{365}{1000}$ or $\dfrac{73}{200}$

These are the **answers!**

PROBLEM SOLVING

Q1. $\dfrac{1}{4}$ of $80 = \dfrac{1}{4} \times \dfrac{80}{1} = 20$. He gave 20 marbles to his best friend.

Q2. $\dfrac{1}{3}$ of $12 = \dfrac{1}{3} \times \dfrac{12}{1} = 4$. She gave 4 eggs to her neighbor, so she still has 8 eggs left.

Q3. $\dfrac{7}{8}$ of $24 = \dfrac{7}{8} \times \dfrac{24}{1} = 21$. She got 21 correct, therefore she got 3 wrong.

Q4.   Complete the number line below using improper fractions on the top part of the line, and mixed fractions on the bottom part of the line. Also where possible, simplify any mixed fractions on the bottom line.

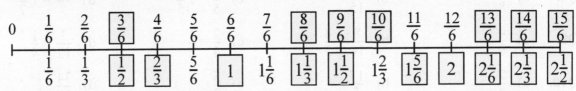

Q5.   a) $\dfrac{1}{3} < \dfrac{3}{6}$ b) $\dfrac{13}{6} = 2\dfrac{1}{6}$ c) $1\dfrac{2}{3} > \dfrac{9}{6}$ d) $\dfrac{14}{6} = 2\dfrac{1}{3}$

Q6.   a) $\dfrac{1}{3}$ is to the right of $\dfrac{1}{4}$ on the number line $\Rightarrow \dfrac{1}{3}$ is bigger than $\dfrac{1}{4}$.

          or $\dfrac{1}{3} = \dfrac{4}{12}$ and $\dfrac{1}{4} = \dfrac{3}{12} \Rightarrow \dfrac{4}{12}$ is bigger than $\dfrac{3}{12}$.

        b) $\dfrac{5}{12}$ is to the left of $\dfrac{1}{2}$ on the number line $\Rightarrow \dfrac{5}{12}$ is smaller than $\dfrac{1}{2}$.

          or $\dfrac{1}{2}$ can be written as $\dfrac{6}{12} \Rightarrow \dfrac{5}{12}$ is smaller than $\dfrac{6}{12}$.

        c) $\dfrac{3}{4}$ is to the right of $\dfrac{2}{3}$ on the number line $\Rightarrow \dfrac{3}{4}$ is bigger than $\dfrac{2}{3}$.

          or $\dfrac{3}{4} = \dfrac{9}{12}$ and $\dfrac{2}{3} = \dfrac{8}{12} \Rightarrow \dfrac{9}{12}$ is bigger than $\dfrac{8}{12}$.

        d) $\dfrac{5}{6}$ is equal to $\dfrac{10}{12}$ on the number line.

Q7. It will take Stuart 7 lots of $\frac{1}{4}$ of an hour $= 7 \times \frac{1}{4} = \frac{7}{1} \times \frac{1}{4}$

$= \frac{7}{4}$ or $1\frac{3}{4}$ hours.

or 4 rooms will take exactly one hour, and the other 3 rooms will take $\frac{3}{4}$ of an hour

⟹ giving a total of $1\frac{3}{4}$ hours or 1 hour and 45 minutes.

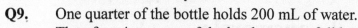

The symbol ∴ means therefore. It is used a great deal when doing solutions.

Q8. Two thirds of the job = 30 tiles

∴ One third of the job = 15 tiles

∴ Three thirds of the whole job = 3 × 15 = 45 tiles

∴ He will have to lay down 15 more tiles to complete the task.

Q9. One quarter of the bottle holds 200 mL of water.

Therefore 4 quarters of the bottle, or one full bottle, holds 4 × 200 mL = 800 mL

Q10. 21 quarters were given away. 20 quarters = 5 whole apples and there is still one quarter left over. Therefore $5\frac{1}{4}$ apples were given away.

or $21 \times \frac{1}{4} = \frac{21}{1} \times \frac{1}{4} = \frac{21}{4} = 5\frac{1}{4}$ apples were given away.

Q11. If we sleep for $\frac{1}{3}$ of the day $= \frac{1}{3}$ of 24 hours = 8 hours each day.

In 7 days we will sleep 7 × 8 = 56 hours in total.

Q12. a) $\frac{1}{4}$ of \$40 = \$10 and $\frac{2}{5}$ of \$40 $= \frac{2}{5} \times \frac{40}{1} = 16.

She has spent \$26, and therefore she has \$14 left.

b) \$14 out of \$40 $= \frac{14}{40} = \frac{7}{20}$. She has $\frac{7}{20}$ left.

Q13. a) What is $30 \div 5 = \boxed{6}$ b) What is $1000 \div 8 = \boxed{125}$ c) $\frac{125}{1000}$

$\frac{2}{5} \times \frac{\boxed{6}}{\boxed{6}} = \frac{12}{30}$ $\frac{1}{8} \times \frac{\boxed{125}}{\boxed{125}} = \frac{125}{1000}$ $= 0.125$

Q14. a) $5 \times \frac{1}{2} = 2\frac{1}{2}$ b) $9 \times \frac{1}{4} = 2\frac{1}{4}$ c) $7 \times \frac{1}{3} = 2\frac{1}{3}$

Q15. a) There are 12 quarters in 3.

b) If I divide 3 by $\frac{1}{4}$, then my answer is 12.

c) $3 \div \frac{1}{4} = 12$

Q16. a) There are 10 fifths in 2.

b) If I divide 2 by $\frac{1}{5}$, then my answer is 10.

c) $2 \div \frac{1}{5} = 10$.

Q17. We can write $\frac{2}{3}$ as an equivalent fraction of $\frac{8}{12}$.

Therefore what fraction is half way between $\frac{7}{12}$ and $\frac{8}{12}$?

Therefore what fraction is half way between $\frac{14}{24}$ and $\frac{16}{24}$?

The answer is $\frac{15}{24}$.

Essential Exercises – Year 5 Maths
Warwick Marlin © Five Senses Education

Q18. a) 100 metres in 15 seconds ➡ 400 metres in one minute or 60 seconds.

b) 400 metres in 1 minute ➡ one hour he can run 60 × 400 = 24 000 metres.

c) 24 000 metres in 1 hour ➡ $\dfrac{24\,000}{1\,000}$ km in 1 hour ➡ 24 kilometres/hour.

Q19. Jim is $\dfrac{4}{5}$ of the way $= \dfrac{4}{5} \times 100 = 80$ metres

Sam is $\dfrac{3}{4}$ of the way $= \dfrac{3}{4} \times 100 = 75$ metres

Therefore Jim is 5 metres ahead of Sam at this stage of the race.

These are the **answers!**

Level 4 — FRACTIONS AND DECIMALS — Difficult

Q1. a) $\dfrac{4}{5} = \dfrac{80}{100}$ b) $\dfrac{1}{4} = \dfrac{25}{100}$ c) $\dfrac{13}{20} = \dfrac{65}{100}$ d) $\dfrac{3}{8} = \dfrac{375}{1000}$

Q2. a) $\left(\dfrac{3}{5}\,or\right)\ \dfrac{6}{10} < \dfrac{7}{10}$ b) $\left(\dfrac{3}{4}\,or\right)\ \dfrac{9}{12} > \dfrac{8}{12}$ c) $\left(\dfrac{4}{5}\,or\right)\ \dfrac{16}{20} < \dfrac{17}{20}$ d) $\dfrac{13}{20} < \dfrac{14}{20}\left(or\ \dfrac{7}{10}\right)$

e) $\dfrac{8}{12} = \dfrac{2}{3}\left(or\ \dfrac{8}{12}\right)$ f) $\left(\dfrac{3}{4}\,or\right)\ \dfrac{15}{20} > \dfrac{12}{20}\left(or\ \dfrac{3}{5}\right)$ g) $\left(\dfrac{5}{6}\,or\right)\ \dfrac{25}{30} > \dfrac{24}{30}\left(or\ \dfrac{4}{5}\right)$

h) $\left(\dfrac{2}{3}\,or\right)\ \dfrac{20}{30} < \dfrac{21}{30}\left(or\ \dfrac{7}{10}\right)$

Q3. a) $\dfrac{3}{4} = \dfrac{9}{12},\ \dfrac{11}{12},\ \dfrac{5}{6} = \dfrac{10}{12},\ \dfrac{2}{3} = \dfrac{8}{12} \Rightarrow \dfrac{2}{3},\ \dfrac{3}{4},\ \dfrac{5}{6},\ \dfrac{11}{12}$ in ascending order

b) $\dfrac{1}{2} = \dfrac{9}{18},\ \dfrac{5}{6} = \dfrac{15}{18},\ \dfrac{2}{3} = \dfrac{12}{18},\ \dfrac{11}{18} \Rightarrow \dfrac{1}{2},\ \dfrac{11}{18},\ \dfrac{2}{3},\ \dfrac{5}{6}$ in ascending order

c) $\dfrac{1}{4} = \dfrac{5}{20},\ \dfrac{2}{5},\ = \dfrac{8}{20},\ \dfrac{3}{10} = \dfrac{6}{20},\ \dfrac{7}{20} \Rightarrow \dfrac{1}{4},\ \dfrac{3}{10},\ \dfrac{7}{20},\ \dfrac{2}{5}$ in ascending order

Q4.
a) $\dfrac{1}{3} + \dfrac{5}{12}$
$= \dfrac{4}{12} + \dfrac{5}{12}$
$= \dfrac{9}{12} = \dfrac{3}{4}$

b) $\dfrac{3}{4} + \dfrac{7}{20}$
$= \dfrac{15}{20} + \dfrac{7}{20}$
$= \dfrac{22}{20} = 1\dfrac{1}{10}$

c) $\dfrac{2}{3} + \dfrac{1}{4}$
$= \dfrac{8}{12} + \dfrac{3}{12}$
$= \dfrac{11}{12}$

d) $1\dfrac{1}{3} + \dfrac{5}{6}$
$= 1\dfrac{2}{6} + \dfrac{5}{6}$
$= 1\dfrac{7}{6} = 2\dfrac{1}{6}$

e) $2\dfrac{1}{5} + 1\dfrac{3}{10}$
$= 2\dfrac{2}{10} + 1\dfrac{3}{10}$
$= 3\dfrac{5}{10} = 3\dfrac{1}{2}$

f) $1\dfrac{1}{2} + 3\dfrac{7}{10}$
$= 1\dfrac{5}{10} + 3\dfrac{7}{10}$
$= 4\dfrac{12}{10} = 5\dfrac{1}{5}$

g) $\dfrac{2}{3} + \dfrac{2}{5}$
$= \dfrac{10}{15} + \dfrac{6}{15}$
$= \dfrac{16}{15} = 1\dfrac{1}{15}$

h) $1\dfrac{1}{3} + 3\dfrac{4}{5}$
$= 1\dfrac{10}{15} + 3\dfrac{12}{15}$
$= 4\dfrac{22}{15} = 5\dfrac{7}{15}$

Q5.
a) $\dfrac{3}{4} - \dfrac{5}{12}$
$= \dfrac{9}{12} - \dfrac{5}{12}$
$= \dfrac{4}{12} = \dfrac{1}{3}$

b) $\dfrac{11}{15} - \dfrac{2}{3}$
$= \dfrac{11}{15} - \dfrac{10}{15}$
$= \dfrac{1}{15}$

c) $\dfrac{17}{20} - \dfrac{3}{4}$
$= \dfrac{17}{20} - \dfrac{15}{20}$
$= \dfrac{2}{20} = \dfrac{1}{10}$

d) $1\dfrac{1}{2} - \dfrac{1}{6}$
$= 1\dfrac{3}{6} - \dfrac{1}{6}$
$= 1\dfrac{2}{6} = 1\dfrac{1}{3}$

e) $2\frac{3}{4} - 1\frac{5}{8}$

$= 2\frac{6}{8} - 1\frac{5}{8}$

$= 1\frac{1}{8}$

f) $\frac{3}{4} - \frac{2}{3}$

$= \frac{9}{12} - \frac{8}{12}$

$= \frac{1}{12}$

g) $\frac{5}{2} - \frac{5}{6}$

$= \frac{15}{6} - \frac{5}{6}$

$= \frac{10}{6} = 1\frac{2}{3}$

h) $\frac{13}{4} - \frac{9}{5}$

$= \frac{65}{20} - \frac{36}{20}$

$= \frac{29}{20} = 1\frac{9}{20}$

Q6. a) $\frac{17}{3} = 5\frac{2}{3}$ b) $\frac{29}{8} = 3\frac{5}{8}$ c) $\frac{19}{5} = 3\frac{4}{5}$ d) $\frac{25}{7} = 3\frac{4}{7}$

Q7. a) $0.8 = \frac{8}{10} = \frac{4}{5}$ b) $0.45 = \frac{45}{100} = \frac{9}{20}$ c) $0.75 = \frac{75}{100} = \frac{3}{4}$ d) $0.56 = \frac{56}{100} = \frac{14}{25}$

Q8. a) $\frac{3}{5} = \frac{6}{10} = 0.6$ b) $\frac{17}{1000} = 0.017$ c) $\frac{7}{20} = \frac{35}{100} = 0.35$ d) $\frac{39}{50} = \frac{78}{100} = 0.78$

Q9. a) 249.6 b) 270.86 c) 914.19 d) 6169.48

Q10. a) 247.08 b) 77.05 c) 81.03 d) 358.63

Q11. Move decimal point to the right 1 place (×10), 2 places (×100) or 3 places (×1000).
Move decimal point to the left 1 place (÷10), 2 places (÷100) or 3 places (÷1000).
  a) $3.72 \times 10 = 37.2$ b) $0.678 \times 1000 = 678$ c) $3.12 \times 100 = 312$
  d) $67.831 \times 100 = 6783.1$ e) $57.3 \div 10 = 5.73$ f) $137.0 \div 1000 = 13.7$
  g) $6321.0 \div 1000 = 6.321$ h) $3.2 \div 100 = 0.032$

Q12. a) \$38.51 b) \$627.32 c) \$84.2 d) \$3.67

Q13. a) $\frac{1}{4}$ of 20 b) $\frac{2}{3}$ of 30 c) $\frac{3}{5}$ of 20 d) $\frac{3}{4}$ of 60

$= \frac{1}{4} \times \frac{20}{1}$ $= \frac{2}{3} \times \frac{30}{1}$ $= \frac{3}{5} \times \frac{20}{1}$ $= \frac{3}{4} \times \frac{60}{1}$

$= 5$ $= 20$ $= 12$ $= 45$

> Remember that 'OF' in Maths means 'Multiply'.

Q14. a) 4 months of the year $= \frac{4}{12} = \frac{1}{3}$

  b) 25 cents out of \$2.00 $= \frac{25}{200} = \frac{1}{8}$

  c) 45 cm out of 1 metre $= \frac{45}{100} = \frac{9}{20}$

> When comparing fractions, we must convert all quantities to the same units.

  d) 200g out of 1 kg $= \frac{200}{1000} = \frac{1}{5}$

Q15. a) (×10) 3.21 cm = 32.1 mm b) (×1000) 6.32 kg = 6320 g
  c) (÷1000) 3450 m = 3.45 km d) (÷1000) 534 mL = 0.534 L
  e) (×100) 6.354 m = 635.4 cm f) (÷1000) 3460 g = 3.46 kg

Q16. a) Firstly change $\frac{1}{4}$ to 0.25 and $\frac{1}{5}$ to 0.2

  0.352, 0.325, 0.253, 0.25($\frac{1}{4}$), 0.235, 0.2 ($\frac{1}{5}$) in descending order.

  b) First change $6\frac{4}{5}$ to 6.8 and $\frac{69}{10} = 6\frac{9}{10}$ to 6.9

  6.9 (or $\frac{69}{10}$), 6.893, 6.839, 6.83, 6.8 (or $6\frac{4}{5}$), 6.389 in descending order.

  c) Firstly change $73\frac{1}{2}$ to 73.5 and $73\frac{2}{5}$ to 73.4

  73.594, 73.549, 73.5 (or $73\frac{1}{2}$), 73.495, 73.45, 73.4 (or $73\frac{2}{5}$) in descending order.

Essential Exercises – Year 5 Maths
Warwick Marlin © Five Senses Education

PROBLEM SOLVING

Q1. Original number = 7.832   New number = 7.382
The difference between the number is 7.932 – 7.382 = 0.45

Q2. The difference between $\frac{3}{5}$ and $\frac{1}{3}$ is $\frac{3}{5} - \frac{1}{3} = \frac{9}{15} - \frac{5}{15} = \frac{4}{15}$

$\therefore \frac{4}{15}$ of the glass is equivalent to 80 mL.

$\therefore \frac{1}{15}$ of the glass is equivalent to 20 mL.

$\therefore \frac{15}{15}$ or one full glass is equivalent to 300 mL.

Q3. 4 pizzas shared by 6 people $\Rightarrow$ each person will get $4 \div 6 = \frac{4}{6} = \frac{2}{3}$ of a pizza.

Q4. One lawn to mow takes $\frac{3}{4}$ of an hour

7 lawns to mow takes $7 \times \frac{3}{4} = \frac{7}{1} \times \frac{3}{4} = \frac{21}{4} = 5\frac{1}{4}$ hours

Q5. $275 in 10 hours $\Rightarrow$ $275 \div 10 in 1 hour = $27.50 per hour.

Q6. In 7 weeks she will lose 7×1.5 kg = 10.5 kg
Therefore 67.8 kg subtract 10.5 kg = 57.3 kg.
In 7 weeks her weight will be 57.3 kg

Q7. a) Average time for each lap = $\frac{96.74}{4}$ = 24.185 seconds

b) Rounded off to the nearest tenth or 0.1, the time is 24.2 seconds.
(Is 24.185 closer to 24.1 or closer to 24.2?)

Q8. The total length of the 2 cut pieces = 6.8 + 13.9 = 20.7 m.
The amount left on the roll = 27.3 – 20.7 = 6.6 m.

Q9. One lady donates $\frac{1}{5}$ of a day wage to the shelter.

Therefore 37 ladies donate $37 \times \frac{1}{5} = \frac{37}{5} = 7\frac{2}{5}$ days pay to the shelter.

Q10. We can really ask how many thirds in $7\frac{2}{3}$ pages?

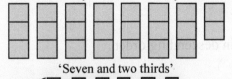

'Seven and two thirds'

It can be seen from the pictures on the left that there are 23 thirds in $7\frac{2}{3}$.

Therefore Todd drew 23 graphs.

Q11. $\frac{3}{8}$ {

'Eight coke bottles'

Let each picture on the left represent one coke bottle divided into eighths. How many lots of $\frac{3}{8}$ are there in the 6 bottles? By counting, the answer is 16. Therefore 16 glasses can be filled from the 6 bottles.

Q12. Steve walks 16.47 metres in 9 seconds.

∴ he walks $16.47 \div 3 = 5.49$ metres in 3 seconds.

∴ he walks $5.49 \times 20 = 109.8$ metres in 60 seconds.

Q13. In one hour Tess earns $7.40

∴ in 50 hours Tess earns $50 \times \$7.40 = \$370.00$

Q14. For one dollar Greta has to pay 34 cents tax.

∴ For 350 dollars Greta has to pay $350 \times 34 = 11\ 900$ cents

∴ She has to pay $119.00 tax.

Q15. a) 15 minutes = one quarter of an hour = $\frac{1}{4}$ of an hour = 0.25 of an hour.

∴ 3 hours and 15 minutes = 3.25 hours

   b) 12 minutes = one fifth of an hour = $\frac{1}{5}$ of an hour = 0.2 of an hour

∴ 6 hours and 12 minutes = 6.2 hours

Q16. To find the average, add up the 6 times, and divide by the six races

∴ Average time = $\dfrac{10.7 + 10.5 + 10.8 + 10.9 + 11.0 + 10.3}{6} = \dfrac{64.2}{6} = 10.7$

Q17. a) $5\frac{3}{10}$ cm = 5.3 cm

   b) $4\frac{75}{1000}$ kg = 4.075 kg

   c) $3\frac{8}{1000}$ L = 3.008 L

   d) $27\frac{18}{100}$ m = 27.18 m

   e) $6\frac{37}{1000}$ km = 6.037 km

   f) $3\frac{451}{1000}$ kg = 3.451 kg

Q18. a) In 5 days, Anne plays for 11.8 hours.

∴ In 1 day, Anne plays for $11.8 \div 5 = 2.36$ hours

   b) 2.36 hours = $2\frac{36}{100}$ hours = $2\frac{9}{25}$ hours.

$\frac{36}{100}$ simplifies to $\frac{9}{25}$

Q19. $\frac{3}{5}$ of 15 matches were won by more than 1 goal.

∴ $\frac{3}{5} \times \frac{15}{1} = 9$ matches were won by more than 1 goal.

∴ $\frac{9}{21} = \frac{3}{7}$ of all matches were won by more than 1 goal.

Q20. a) $\frac{1}{4} + \frac{2}{3} + \frac{3}{5} = \frac{15}{60} + \frac{40}{60} + \frac{36}{60} = \frac{91}{60} = 1\frac{31}{60}$

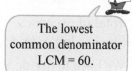

The lowest common denominator LCM = 60.

   b) $5\frac{1}{3} - 2\frac{5}{12} = 5\frac{4}{12} - 2\frac{5}{12} = 4\frac{16}{12} - 2\frac{5}{12} = 2\frac{11}{12}$

   c) $37.28 + 14.91 = 52.19 \Rightarrow 60 - 52.19 = 7.81$

   d) $11 \times \frac{2}{5} = \frac{11}{1} \times \frac{2}{5} = \frac{22}{5} = 4\frac{2}{5}$

   e) $5\frac{1}{2} \div \frac{1}{4}$ means how many quarters are there in $5\frac{1}{2}$?

There are 22 quarters in $5\frac{1}{2}$. Therefore $5\frac{1}{2} \div \frac{1}{4} = 22$.

Essential Exercises – Year 5 Maths
Warwick Marlin © Five Senses Education

Level 1

MONEY AND FINANCIAL MATHEMATICS

Easier

Q1.
a) $58.01
b) $32.17
c) $78.08
d) $1.52
e) $96.88
f) $17.33
g) $487.10
h) $5.968 = $5.97

Q2.
a) $4.73 is closer to $4.75 than $4.70   Therefore answer = $4.75
b) $29.68 is closer to $29.70 than 29.65   Therefore answer = $29.70
c) $13.47 is closer to $13.45 than $13.50   Therefore answer = $13.45
d) $159.72 is closer to $159.70 than $159.75   Therefore answer = $159.70

Q3.
a) 5   apples for 40c ⟹ 1 apple = 8c
    6   apples for 54c ⟹ 1 apple = 9c
    10 apples for 70c ⟹ 1 apple = 7c
    Therefore 10 apples for 70 cents is the best buy.

b) 8   oranges for 80c ⟹ 1 orange = 10c
    12 oranges for $1.32 ⟹ 1 orange = 11c
    5   oranges for 60 cents ⟹ 1 orange = 12c
    Therefore 8 oranges for 80 cents is the best buy.

c) 10 pears for $1.20 ⟹ 1 pears = 12c
    8   pears for 88c ⟹ 1 pears = 11c
    18 pears for $2.34 ⟹ 1 pears = 13c
    Therefore 8 pears for 88c is the best buy.

Q4.
They collected in cash a total of 420 × $2.00 = $840.00
But they have to subtract all their expenses which add up to $375.00
Therefore their profit = $840.00 – $375.00 = $465.00

Q5.
a) New balance
   = $130 + $40
   = $170
b) New balance
   = $130 + $125
   = $255
c) New balance
   = $130 – $80
   = $50

Q6.
His net wage = gross wage – taxes
   = $520 – $85
   = $435

Q7.
a) GST = 10% of $60
      = $6.00
b) GST = 10% of $35
      = $3.50
c) GST = 10% of $45
      = $4.50
d) GST = 10% of $12
      = $1.20

Q8.
Total of expenses = $90 + $140 + $35 + $38 + $45 = $348
She has left over $520 – $348 = $172.

Q9.
We have to divide $2 000 by $172.
$2000 ÷ $172 = 11.6 weeks
It will take her just over $11\frac{1}{2}$ weeks to save up, or 12 full weeks.

Q10.
a) 90 blocks = 90% out of 100
b) 25 blocks = 25% out of 100
c) 73 blocks = 73% out of 100
d) 75 blocks = 75% out of 100

Q11.

a) $90\% = \frac{90}{100} = \frac{9}{10}$
b) $25\% = \frac{25}{100} = \frac{1}{4}$
c) $73\% = \frac{73}{100}$
d) $75\% = \frac{75}{100} = \frac{3}{4}$

Q12.

a) 25% of $40
$= \frac{1}{4} \times \frac{40}{1}$
$= \$10.00$

b) 10% of $80
$= \frac{1}{10} \times \frac{80}{1}$
$= \$8$

c) 50% of $120
$= \frac{1}{2} \times \frac{120}{1}$
$= \$60$

d) 75% of $20
$= \frac{3}{4} \times \frac{20}{1}$
$= \$15$

e) 20% of $30
$= \frac{1}{5} \times \frac{30}{1}$
$= \$6$

f) 80% of $40
$= \frac{4}{5} \times \frac{40}{1}$
$= \$32$

Q13.

a) discount $= \frac{1}{5}$ of $40
$= \$10$

b) discount $= \frac{1}{4}$ of $120
$= \$30$

c) discount $= \frac{1}{4}$ of $60
$= \$15$

d) discount $= \frac{1}{4}$ of $80
$= \$20$

25% discount
$= \frac{25}{100} = \frac{1}{4}$.
So we must find $\frac{1}{4}$ of each item.

Q14.

a) Gross profit $= 230 \times \$15 = \$3\,450$ (total money taken from sales)

b) Expenses $= 230 \times \$6 = \$1\,380$ (total cost of t-shirts)

c) Net profit $=$ Gross profit less expenses
$= \$3\,450 - \$1\,380$
$= \$2\,070$

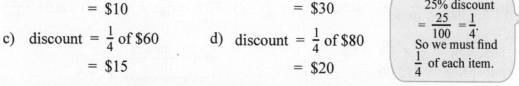

These are the **answers!**

Level 2 **MONEY AND FINANCIAL MATHEMATICS** Average

Q1.

a) Total cost of the 4 items
$= \$18.40 + \$16.85 + \$28.49 + \$14.53$
$= \$78.27$

b) Exact change $= \$100.00 - \$78.27 = \$21.73$

c) Change to the nearest 5 cents $= \$21.75$

Q2.

a) 5 exercise books cost $12.40
$\therefore$ 1 exercise book costs $\frac{\$12.40}{5} = \$2.48$
$\therefore$ 7 exercise books cost $7 \times \$2.48 = \$17.36$

b) 3 hamburgers cost $13.05
$\therefore$ 1 hamburger costs $\frac{\$13.05}{3} = \$4.35$
$\therefore$ 5 hamburgers cost $5 \times \$4.35 = \$21.75$

c) In 7 hours he earns $107.52
In 1 hour he earns $\frac{\$107.52}{7} = \$15.36$
In 9 hours he earns $9 \times \$15.36 = \$138.24$

d) She reads 6 pages in 42 minutes
She reads 1 page in 7 minutes
She reads 28 pages in $28 \times 7 = 196$ minutes
196 minutes = 3 hours and 16 minutes.

Q3.

a) $3.78 is closer to $3.80 than $3.75   Therefore answer = $3.80
b) $15.34 is closer to $15.35 than $15.30   Therefore answer = $15.35
c) $19.62 is closer to $19.60 than $19.65   Therefore answer = $19.60
d) $8.37 is closer to $8.35 than $8.40   Therefore answer = $8.35

Q4.

a) Total cost $= 2 \times \$0.74 + 5 \times \$0.42 + 2 \times \$0.37$
$= \$4.32$

b) Exact change from $10.00 $= \$10.00 - \$4.32 = \$5.68$

c) Change after rounding off $= \$5.70$

Essential Exercises – Year 5 Maths
Warwick Marlin © Five Senses Education

Q5.
a) 500 g of steak cost $7.80. Therefore 2 kg cost 4 × $7.80 = $31.20
We can see that 2 kg at $29.40 is the best buy.

b) 1 kg of potatoes cost $3.90. Therefore 10 kg cost 10 × $3.90 = $39.00
We can see that 10 kg at $37.50 is the best buy.

c) 250 g of chocolate cost $4.70 Therefore 1.5 kg cost 6 × $4.70 = $28.20
We can see that 250 g at $4.70 is the best buy.

Q6.
a) 10 blocks = 10% out of 100
b) 40 blocks = 40% out of 100
c) 60 blocks = 60% out of 100
d) 80 blocks = 80% out of 100

Q7.
a) $10\% = \frac{10}{100} = \frac{1}{10}$
b) $40\% = \frac{40}{100} = \frac{2}{5}$
c) $60\% = \frac{60}{100} = \frac{3}{5}$
d) $80\% = \frac{80}{100} = \frac{4}{5}$

Q8.
a) Discount $= \frac{2}{5} \times \frac{20}{1} = \$8$
Sale price $= \$12.00$

b) Discount $= \frac{2}{5} \times \frac{30}{1} = \$12$
Sale price $= \$18$

$40\% = \frac{40}{100} = \frac{2}{5}$
So we must subtract $\frac{2}{5}$ of the cost from each item.

c) Discount $= \frac{2}{5} \times \frac{18}{1} = \$7.20$
Sale price $= \$10.80$

d) Discount $= \frac{2}{5} \times \frac{12}{1} = \$4.80$
Sale price $= \$7.20$

e) 4 t-shirts normally cost 4 × $12 = $48
4 t-shirts at discounted price cost 4 × $7.20 = $28.80
The saving is $48 − $28.80 = $19.20

Q9.
a) GST $= \frac{1}{10}$ of $30 = $3
Price $= \$33.00$

b) GST $= \frac{1}{10}$ of $25 = $2.50
Price $= \$27.50$

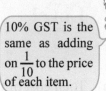

10% GST is the same as adding on $\frac{1}{10}$ to the price of each item.

c) GST $= \frac{1}{10}$ of $43.00 = $4.30
Price $= \$47.30$

d) GST $= \frac{1}{10}$ of $27 = $2.70
Price $= \$29.70$

Q10.
a) Net wage after paying tax = $480.00 − $135.00 = $345.00
b) Total expenses = $37 + $42 + $26.50 + $128 + $68 = $301.50
c) The amount she will have left = $345.00 − $301.50 = $43.50

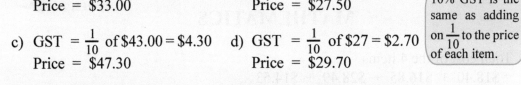

These are the **answers!**

Level 3   MONEY AND FINANCIAL MATHEMATICS   Average

Q1.
a) $82.50
b) $7.50
c) $82.50 − $7.50 = $75.00
d) 78 935
e) GST = 10% of $38 $= \frac{1}{10}$ of $38 = $3.80

Q2.
a) $38.23 is closer to $38.25 than $38.20   Therefore answer = $38.25
b) $16.28 is closer to $16.30 than $16.25   Therefore answer = $16.30
c) $124.17 is closer to $124.15 than $124.20   Therefore answer = $124.15
d) $69.42 is closer to $69.40 than $69.45   Therefore answer = $69.40

Q3.
a) $380.00
b) 8. 4. 12 or 8th April
c) $230.00
b) Total withdrawal = $75.00 + $180.00 = $255.00
e) Total deposits = $200.00 + $230.00 + $245.00 = $675.00

f) Balance = $555.00

g) She gets paid on Mondays.

h) She gets paid fortnightly or every two weeks on a Monday.

i) Net wages = $560.00 – $145.00 – $38.00 = $377.00

j) Her total expenses = $130 + $85 + $35 + $48 + $64 = $362
   The amount she will have left over = $377 – $362 = $15

k) Her new balance will be $800 + $15 = $815.00

Q4. a) Her total budget = $198.00

b) Her actual spending = $210.00

c) She over spent on her clothes by $20.00

d) She spent $10 more on Cafe items.

e) She spent $5 less on make up.

f) The 2 biggest extra expenses over her budget were clothes and Cafe.
   She has to be more careful about over spending on clothes and snacks.

These are the **answers!**

Level 4   MONEY AND FINANCIAL MATHEMATICS   Difficult

Q1. a) Gross profit = total money received = 380 × $3.00 = $1 140.00

b) Bread = 400 × 15c   BBQ sauce = 6 × $5   Mustard = 4 × $2.50
        = $60.00   = $30   = $10.00

   Cooking oil = 5 × $7   Minced meat = 13 × $9   Onions = 8 × $1.50
             = $35   = $117   = $12

   Serviettes = 8 × 50c   Gas = $35.00
            = $4

   Total expenses = $60 + $30 + $10 + $35 + $117 + $12 + $4 + $35
                  = $303.00

c) Net profit = Gross profit less expenses
             = $1 140.00 – $303.00
             = $837.00

d) They were only $30 short of their goal of making $867.00.

e) The highest expense was the minced meat.

f) They need another $30 to reach their goal.
   Therefore they needed to sell 10 more hamburgers.

Q2. a) Discount = $\frac{1}{10}$ of $45 = $4.50.   Therefore sale price = $45 – $4.50 = $40.50

b) Discount = $\frac{1}{5}$ of $35 = $7.00.   Therefore sale price = $35 – $7. = $28.00

c) Discount = $\frac{3}{10}$ of $70 = $21.00.   Therefore sale price = $70 – $21 = $49.00

Q3. 3 t-shirts = 3 × $8.30 = $25.02
5 key rings = 5 × $3.72 = $18.60   } Total = $76.98
4 basketball caps = 4 × $8.34 = $33.36
Change = $100 – $76.98 = $23.02
Change (rounded to the nearest 5 cents) = $23.00

Essential Exercises – Year 5 Maths
Warwick Marlin © Five Senses Education

Q4. a) GST = $\frac{1}{10}$ of $4.30 = 43 cents. ⟹ Price after GST = $4.73

b) GST = $\frac{1}{10}$ of $15.60 = $1.56 ⟹ Price after GST = $17.16

c) GST = $\frac{1}{10}$ of $3.40 = 34 cents ⟹ Price after GST = $3.74

d) GST = $\frac{1}{10}$ of 30c = 3 cents ⟹ Price after GST = 33 cents

Q5. This is a tricky question. To find the actual GST we have to divide by 11 and NOT 10.

a) GST = $88 ÷ 11 = $8 ⟹ price before GST = $80.00

b) GST = $110 ÷ 11 = $10 ⟹ price before GST = $100.00

c) GST = $16.50 ÷ 11 = $1.50 ⟹ price before GST = $15.00

d) GST = $49.50 ÷ 11 = $4.50 ⟹ price before GST = $45.00

Q6. a) 2 kg for $15.00 ⟹ 1 kg for $7.50

3 kg for $22.80 ⟹ 1 kg for $7.60

5 kg for $36.00 ⟹ 1 kg for $7.20

} It is now easy to see that 5 kg for $36.00 represents the best buy.

b) 500 kg for $1.35 ⟹ 1 kg for $2.70

2 kg for $4.90 ⟹ 1 kg for $2.45

5 kg for $11.00 ⟹ 1 kg for $2.20

} It is now easy to see that 5 kg for $11.00 represents the best buy.

c) In this question it is easier to find the price of 3 kg of each.

500 kg for $2.10 ⟹ 3 kg for $12.60

1.5 kg for $5.85 ⟹ 3 kg for $11.45

3 kg for $12.42 ⟹ 3 kg for $12.42

} It is now easy to see that 1.5 kg for $5.85 represents the best buy.

Q7. Opening balance = $756.47

Balance after deposit and 2 withdrawals = $756.47 + $325.48 (deposit) − $238.46 (withdrawal) − $190.88 (withdrawal) = $652.61

Q8. Cost of equipment plus repairs = $85 + $67 + $47.30
= $199.30

His profit = $260 subtract expenses = $260 − $199.30 = $60.70

Q9. Total cost of meal = $34.80 (Peking Duck) + $22.40 (Sweet &Sour Pork)
+ $3.45 (tea) + $3.45 (tea) + $6.80 (desert) + $6.80 (desert)
+ $5 (tip to waitress)
= $82.70

The change from $100.00 = $100.00 − $82.70
= $17.30

These are the **answers!**

Q1.
a) Total estimated expenses = $200.00
b) Savings = wages – expenses = $300 – $200 = $100.00
c) Total of actual expenses = $289.00
d) Savings = wages – expenses = $340.00 – $289.00 = $51.00
e) Clothes was the expense that was $12 higher than her budget.
f) If she hadn't earned the extra $40 , then she would have only saved $11.00
g) Presents were double what she budgeted for.
h) Gloria hasn't kept to her budget very well. The extra $40 in wages helped her, otherwise she would have only saved $11.00 instead of saving $100.00 which was in her budget.

Q2.
a) $185 + $\frac{1}{10}$ of $185
   = $185 + $18.50
   = $203.50

b) $38.50 + $\frac{1}{10}$ of $38.50
   = $38.50 + $3.85
   = $42.35

c) $19.80 + $\frac{1}{10}$ of $19.80
   = $19.80 + $1.98
   = $21.78

Q3.
a) Anna = $5 + $20 + $5 = $30 (Rounding each item to nearest $5)
   Giovanni = $10 + $20 + $10 + $5 = $45 (Rounding each item to nearest $5)
   Carmella = $15 + $5 + $5 = $25 (Rounding each item to nearest $5)
   Total = $100.00
b) Anna = $5.00 + $18.50 + $3.50 = 27.00
   Giovanni = $17.80 + $11.00 + $4.80 = $33.60
   Carmella = $16.40 + $4.80 = $27.20
   Total amount (without GST) = $87.80
c) GST = 10% of $87.80 = $8.78
   Total of bill = $87.80 + $8.78 = $96.58
d) The exact change = $100.00 – $96.58 = $3.42
   Rounded to the nearest 5 cents, he will receive $3.40

Q4.
Balance + deposit = $380.40 + $320.75 = $701.15
Withdrawal = $701.15 – $512.45 = $188.70
She withdrew $188.70

Q5.
a) $35 less $\frac{1}{10}$ of $35
   = $35 – $3.50
   = $31.50

b) $75 less $\frac{1}{4}$ of $75
   = $75 – $18.75
   = $56.25

c) $58 less $\frac{3}{10}$ of $58
   = $58 – $17.40
   = $40.60

Q6.
a) GST = $792 ÷ 11
        = $72
b) GST = $132 ÷ 11
        = $12
c) GST = $165 ÷ 11
        = $15

To find the GST amount we divide by 11 not 10!!

Level 1

PATTERNS AND ALGEBRA

 Easier

Q1. a) { 31, 33, 35, 37, 39 } b) { 52, 54, 56, 58 }
c) { 1, 3, 6, 10, 15 } d) { 25, 36, 49 }
e) { 12, 16, 20, 24, 28 }

Q2. a) Subtract 2 from the previous number ⇒ next 2 numbers are 10 and 8.
b) Double the previous number ⇒ next 2 numbers are 80 and 160.
c) Add 4 to the previous number ⇒ next 2 numbers are 33 and 37.
d) These are all squares numbers ⇒ next 2 square numbers are 36 and 49.
e) Add 8 to the previous number, or multiples of 8 ⇒ next 2 numbers are 40 and 48.
f) Add $\frac{1}{4}$ to the previous number ⇒ next 2 numbers are $1\frac{1}{2}$ and $1\frac{3}{4}$.
g) Add 0.5 to the previous number ⇒ next 2 numbers are 15.0 and 15.5.
h) Subtract 6 from the previous number ⇒ next 2 numbers are 26 and 20.

Q3. i) $8 + 3 = 11$ ii) $17 - 5 = 12$ iii) $6 \times 10 = 60$ iv) $20 \div 4 = 5$
v) $35 + 3 = 38$ vi) $24 - 5 = 19$ vii) $8 \times 10 = 80$ viii) $32 \div 4 = 8$

Q4. a) □ = △ + 5

| △ | 7 | 8 | 9 | 10 |
| □ | 12 | 13 | 14 | 15 |

b) □ = △ − 7

| △ | 30 | 31 | 32 | 33 |
| □ | 23 | 24 | 25 | 26 |

c) △ = ◐ ÷ 4

| ◐ | 40 | 32 | 28 | 20 |
| △ | 10 | 8 | 7 | 5 |

d) ⬡ = △ × 5

| △ | 7 | 8 | 10 | 12 |
| ⬡ | 35 | 40 | 50 | 60 |

e) □ = △ + $3\frac{1}{2}$

| △ | 3 | 4 | 5 | 6 |
| □ | $6\frac{1}{2}$ | $7\frac{1}{2}$ | $8\frac{1}{2}$ | $9\frac{1}{2}$ |

f) ⬡ = △ − 3.5

| △ | 10 | 13 | 16 | 19 |
| ⬡ | 6.5 | 9.5 | 12.5 | 15.5 |

Q5. Find the value of each symbol (□ , △ , ◐ , ⬡) in the number sentences shown below.

a) □ + 5 = 17
∴ □ = 12

b) △ − 4 = 11
∴ △ = 15

c) ◐ × 8 = 24
∴ ◐ = 3

d) $\square \div 3 = 6$

$\therefore \square = 18$

e) $\triangle + 1\frac{1}{2} = 2$

$\therefore \triangle = \frac{1}{2}$

f) $6 \times \hexagon = 30$

$\therefore \hexagon = 5$

g) $20 \div \square = 4$

$\therefore \square = 5$

h) $\hexagon - 2.5 = 4$

$\therefore \hexagon = 6.5$

i) $\square \times \square = 49$

$\therefore \square = 7$

j) $\dfrac{20}{\square} = 4$

$\therefore \square = 5$

k) $\triangle + \triangle + \triangle = 27$

$\therefore \triangle = 9$

l) $\hexagon \times 7 = 42$

$\therefore \hexagon = 6$

These are the **answers!**

Level 2

PATTERNS AND ALGEBRA

Average

Q1. **a)**

b)

Number of diamonds	1	2	3	4	5
Number of matches	4	8	12	16	20

c) Multiply the number of diamonds by 4 to get the number of matches.
OR Matches = diamonds shapes × 4

d) For 9 diamond shapes, we need 9 × 4 = 36 matches.

Q2. **a)**

b)

Number of pentagons	1	2	3	4	5
Number of matches	5	10	15	20	25

c) Multiply the number of pentagons by 5 to get the number of matches.
OR Matches = pentagon shapes × 5

d) For 12 pentagon shapes, we need 12 × 5 = 60 matches.

Q3. **a)**

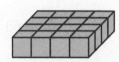

b)

Figure number	1	2	3	4	5	6
Number of blocks	1	4	9	16	25	36

Essential Exercises – Year 5 Maths
Warwick Marlin © Five Senses Education

c) Multiply the figure number by itself to get the number of blocks.
   OR blocks = (figure number) × (figure number)
   OR blocks = (figure number)^2
d) For figure 9, we will need 9 × 9 = 81 blocks.

Q4.
a) Subtract 3 from the previous number ⇒ next 2 numbers are 19 and 16.
b) Add 7 to the previous number ⇒ next numbers 2 are 49 and 56.
c) Double the previous number ⇒ next 2 numbers are 32 and 64.
d) Add $2\frac{1}{2}$ to the previous number ⇒ next 2 numbers are 17 and $19\frac{1}{2}$.
e) Subtract 2.5 from the previous number ⇒ next 2 numbers are 10.0 and 7.5.
f) Add 8 to the previous number ⇒ next 2 numbers are 72 and 80.

Q5.
i)   12 + 8 = 20
ii) 30 − 12 = 18
iii) 5 × 8 = 40
iv) 42 ÷ 6 = 7
v)   94 + 8 = 102
vi) 84 − 12 = 72
vii) 12 × 8 = 96
viii) 90 ÷ 6 = 15

Q6. Briefly write down the rule connecting the top numbers to the bottom numbers in each of the tables below. Also write down the 2 missing numbers in each table.

a)

Top number	5	6	7	8	9	10
Bottom number	12	13	14	15	16	17

Rule: add 7 to the top number to get the bottom number.

b)

Top number	4	5	6	7	8	9
Bottom number	12	15	18	21	24	27

Rule: multiply the top number by 3 to get the bottom number.

c)

Top number	25	24	23	22	21	20
Bottom number	19	18	17	16	15	14

Rule: subtract 6 from the top number to get the bottom number.

d)

Top number	30	27	24	21	18	15
Bottom number	10	9	8	7	6	5

Rule: divide the top number by 3 to get the bottom number.

Q7. Find the value of each symbol (□ , △ , ◐ , ⬡) in the number sentences below.

a) □ + 16 = 30
   ∴ □ = 14

b) △ − 12 = 28
   ∴ △ = 40

c) ◐ × 9 = 63
   ∴ ◐ = 7

d) □ ÷ 8 = 15
   ∴ □ = 120

e) △ + $2\frac{1}{4}$ = 6
   ∴ △ = $3\frac{3}{4}$

f) ⬡ × ⬡ = 64
   ∴ ⬡ = 8

g) 12 × ◐ = 72
   ∴ ◐ = 6

h) □ − 3.2 = 1.8
   ∴ □ = 5

i) $\frac{⬡}{4}$ = 15
   ∴ ⬡ = 60

Level 3

PATTERNS AND ALGEBRA

Average

PROBLEM SOLVING

Q1.
a) The number pattern is 5, 10, 15. (add 5)
The next two numbers in the pattern will be 20 and 25.
5, 10, 15, 20, 25, 30, 35, 40. Therefore the 8th number = 40.

b) The number pattern is 4, 8, 12. (add 4)
The next two numbers in the pattern will be 16 and 20.
4, 8, 12, 16, 20, 24, 28, 32. Therefore the 8th number = 32.

c) The number pattern is 5, 10, 15. (add 5)
The next two numbers in the pattern will be 20 and 25.
5, 10, 15, 20, 25, 30, 35, 40. Therefore the 8th number = 40.

d) The number pattern is 4, 7, 10. (add 3)
The next two numbers in the pattern will be 13 and 16.
4, 7, 10, 13, 16, 19, 22, 25. Therefore the 8th number = 25.

e) The number pattern is 3, 7, 11. (add 4)
The next two numbers in the pattern will be 15 and 19.
3, 7, 11, 15, 19, 23, 27, 31. Therefore the 8th number = 31.

f) The number pattern is 4, 6, 8. (add 2)
The next two numbers in the pattern will be 10 and 12.
4, 6, 8, 10, 12, 14, 16, 18. Therefore the 8th number = 18.

g) The number pattern is 5, 9, 13 (add 4)
The next two numbers in the pattern will be 17 and 21.
5, 9, 13, 17, 21, 25, 29, 33. Therefore the 8th number = 33

Q2. Find the value of each symbol in the number sentences below:
(Some answers maybe fractions).

a) $3 \times \square + 1 = 22$
$\therefore \ 3 \times \square = 21$
$\therefore \ \square = 7$

b) $5 \times \triangle - 3 = 27$
$\therefore \ 5 \times \triangle = 30$
$\therefore \ \triangle = 6$

c) $\oslash \times 7 = 22$
$\therefore \ \oslash = 22 \div 7$
$\therefore \ \oslash = 3\frac{1}{7}$

d) $4 \times \ominus + 5 = 7$
$\therefore \ 4 \times \ominus = 2$
$\therefore \ \ominus = \frac{1}{2}$

e) $\triangle + \triangle + \triangle = 13$
$\therefore \ \triangle = 4\frac{1}{3}$

f) $(\square \div 3) + 5 = 12$
$\therefore \ \square \div 3 = 7$
$\therefore \ \square = 21$

Q3.
a) 28, 25 (+ 8, − 3)
b) 41, 35 (+ 1, − 6)
c) 30, 31 (× 2, then + 1)
d) 26, 31 (+ 3, + 5)

Q4.
a) 12, 19, 26
b) 35, 32, 29
c) 6, 18, 54
d) 32, 16, 8
e) 3, 7, 23
f) 41, 21, 11

Essential Exercises – Year 5 Maths
Warwick Marlin © Five Senses Education

Q5.

a) $\square = \triangle + 1\frac{1}{2}$

△	3	4	$5\frac{1}{2}$	$10\frac{1}{2}$
□	$4\frac{1}{2}$	$5\frac{1}{2}$	7	12

b) $\ominus = \triangle + 2.5$

△	6	7	8.5	12.5
⊖	8.5	9.5	11.0	15.0

c) $\oslash = \square \div 3$

□	12	15	21	25
⊘	4	5	7	$8\frac{1}{3}$

d) $\hexagon = \ominus \times 10$

⊖	3.1	4.1	7.2	9.3
⬡	31	41	72	93

e) $\square = \triangle \times \triangle$

△	5	7	8	12
□	25	49	64	144

f) $\ominus = \oslash - \frac{1}{10}$

⊖	$\frac{3}{10}$	$\frac{5}{10}$	$\frac{7}{10}$	$1\frac{4}{10}$
⊘	$\frac{2}{10}$	$\frac{4}{10}$	$\frac{6}{10}$	$1\frac{3}{10}$

These are the **answers!**

Level 4

PATTERNS AND ALGEBRA

Difficult

Q1. a)

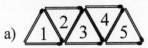

b)

Number of triangles	1	2	3	4	5	6
Number of matches	3	5	7	9	11	13

c) 31 matches will be required for 15 triangles.

d) Number of matches = (2 × number of triangles) + 1

Q2. a)

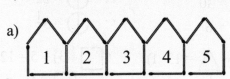

b)

Number of pentagons	1	2	3	4	5	6
Number of matches	5	9	13	17	21	25

c) 12 pentagons requires 49 matches.

d) Number of matches = (4 × number of pentagons) +1

Q3.

a) $\square + 12 = 37$

∴ $\square = 25$

∴ The number is 25.

b) $\triangle - 15 = 42$

∴ $\triangle = 57$

∴ The number is 57.

c) $\square \times 8 = 20$

∴ $\square = 2\frac{1}{2}$

∴ The number is $2\frac{1}{2}$.

d) $\triangle \div 2 = 6\frac{1}{2}$

∴ $\triangle = 13$

∴ The number is 13.

e) $(\ominus \times 4) - 5 = 47$

∴ $\ominus \times 4 = 52$

∴ $\ominus = 13$

∴ The number is 13.

f) $(\oslash \div 7) + 12 = 20$

∴ $\oslash \div 7 = 8$

∴ $\oslash = 56$

∴ The number is 56.

Q4. 5 people
10 hand shakes

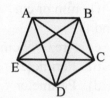

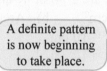

A definite pattern is now beginning to take place.

Number of people	2	3	4	5	6	7	8	9	10	11	12
Number of hand shakes	1	3	6	10	15	21	28	36	45	55	66

+2 +3 +4 +5 +6 +7 +8 +9 +10 +11

The pattern is +2, +3, +4, +5 etc. as shown above.
Therefore if there are 12 people, there will be 66 hand shakes.

Q5. A rule has been given connecting the bottom symbol or letter to the top symbol or letter. Write down the missing number in each table using the given rule.

a) $\square = (2 \times \triangle) + 5$

$\triangle$	3	4	7	9
$\square$	11	13	19	23

b) $\hexagon = (\oslash \times 4)\ 6$

$\oslash$	2	3	5	10
$\hexagon$	2	6	14	34

c) $B = (A \div 2) + 4$

A	6	10	12	20
B	7	9	10	14

d) $M = (N \times N) - 3$

N	4	5	8	9
M	13	22	61	78

e) $Q = (2 \times P) + 3$

P	1.5	2.5	4.5	7.5
Q	6	8	12	18

f) $Y = (X \div 2) + \frac{1}{2}$

X	6	9	12	21
Y	$3\frac{1}{2}$	5	$6\frac{1}{2}$	11

Essential Exercises – Year 5 Maths
Warwick Marlin © Five Senses Education

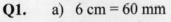

These are the **answers!**

Q1. a) 6 cm = 60 mm   b) 3 km = 3 000 m   c) 8 m = 800 cm
        d) 90 mm = 9 cm   e) 7 000 m = 7 km   f) 400 cm = 4 m

Q2. a) 7 mm   b) 3cm and 4 mm   c) 7 cm and 9 mm   d) 13 cm and 6 mm

Q3. a) 0. 7 cm   b) 3.4 cm   c) 7.9 cm   d) 13.6 cm

Q4. a) 2 cm   b) 3.4 cm   c) 1.6 cm   d) 4.8 cm

Q5. a) cm   b) m   c) mm
        d) km   e) cm or m   f) mm or cm
        Note: There are 2 possible answers for e) and f)

Q6. a) Area = 6 cm^2 b) Area = 8 cm^2 c) Area = 9 cm^2 d) Area = 5 cm^2

Q7. a) Perimeter = 10 cm   b) Perimeter = 14 cm
        c) Perimeter = 14 cm   d) Perimeter = 12 cm

Q8. a) 2 ha = 20 000 m^2 b) 30 000 m^2 = 3 ha c) 15 ha = 150 000 m^2

Q9. a) m^2 b) cm^2 c) cm^2
        d) m^2 e) ha   f) ha

Q10. a) Volume = 4 cm^2 b) Volume = 6 cm^3 c) Volume = 11 cm^3

Q11. a) 3L = 3 000 mL   b) 7 000 ml = 7L   c) $\frac{1}{2}$ a litre = 500 mL

Q12. a) mL   b) L   c) L   d) mL

Q13. a) 3 kg = 3 000 g   b) 5 000 g = 5 kg   c) $2\frac{1}{2}$ kg = 2 500 g

Q14. a) kg   b) g   c) g   d) kg

Q15. a) 8 am   b) 2 pm   c) 11:30 am   d) 7 pm
            or 8:00 am   or 2:00 pm   or 7:00 pm

Q16. a) 0900 or 09:00   b) 1500 or 15:00   c) 0500 or 05:00   d) 2000 or 20:00

These are the **answers!**

Q1. a) 4.5 cm = 45 mm   b) $2\frac{1}{2}$ km = 2500 m   c) $7\frac{1}{2}$ m = 750 cm
        d) 70 mm = 7 cm   e) 4 000 m = 4 km   f) 300 cm = 3 m

Q2. a) 8 mm   b) 39 mm   c) 71 mm   d) 96 mm

Q3. a) 0. 8 cm   b) 3.9 cm   c) 7.1 cm   d) 9.6 cm

Q4. a) Perimeter = 2 + 3 + 3.7 = 8.7 cm
        b) Perimeter = 3.5 + 1.6 + 3.5 + 1.6 = 10.2 cm
        c) Perimeter = 2 + 1.2 + 4 + 2.5 = 9.7 cm

Q5. a) m   b) cm   c) mm   d) km

Q6. a) Area = 6 cm^2 b) Area = 7 cm^2 c) Area = 5 cm^2

Q7. a) mm²   b) ha   c) m²   d) cm²

Q8. a) $3\frac{1}{2}$ ha = 35 000 m²   b) 40 000 m² = 4 ha   c) 1 cm² = 100 mm²

Q9. a) 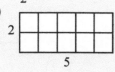   b) 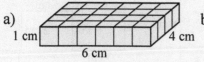   c) 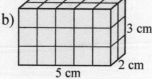   d)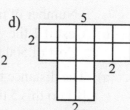

    Area = 10 units²   Area = 12 units²   Area = 16 units²   Area = 14 units²

Q10. a) Volume = 27 units³   b) Volume = 48 units³   c) Volume = 36 units³

Q11. a)  1 cm / 6 cm / 4 cm

Volume = 24 cm³

b) 3 cm / 5 cm / 2 cm

Volume = 30 cm³

c) 5 cm / 4 cm / 3 cm

Volume = 60 cm³

Q12. a) 2L = 2 000 mL   b) 5 000 mL = 5 L   c) $\frac{1}{4}$ of a litre = 250 mL

     d) 5 kg = 5 000 g   e) 3 000 g = 3 kg   f) $\frac{3}{4}$ of a kg = 750 g

Q13. a) L (litres)   b) g (grams)   c) kL (kilolitres)   d) t (tonnes)

Q14. a) 6:30 am   b) 4:15 pm   c) 10:25 am   d) 10:45 pm

Q15. a) 10:30 or 10 30   b) 19:30 or 19 30   c) 08:15 or 08 15   d) 18:35 or 18 45

These are the answers!

Level 3

USING UNITS OF MEASUREMENT

Difficult

PROBLEM SOLVING

Q1. 16 × 250 m = 4 000 m. Divide by 1 000 to get kilometres.

    ∴ I will run 4 000 ÷ 1 000 = 4 km

Q2. All 4 sides of a square are equal in length.

    ∴ Each side = 32 ÷ 4 = 8 m

    ∴ Area = length × length = 8 × 8 = 64 m²

Q3. 1. 72 m tall ⟹ multiply by 100 to change to cm.

    ∴ 1.72 × 100 = 172 cm

Q4. 2.4 m = 240 cm = 240 ÷ 30 = 8 pieces of material.

Must convert all lengths to the same units (cm) before dividing.

Essential Exercises – Year 5 Maths
Warwick Marlin © Five Senses Education

Q5. a) Area of the bathroom = 3 m × 5 m = 300 cm × 500 cm = 150 000 cm²
   Area of each tile   = 15 cm × 20 cm = 300 cm²
   ∴ Number of tiles   = 150 000 ÷ 300 = 500 tiles

   b) Cost if 1 tile = $ 2.50
   ∴ Cost of 500 tiles = 500 × $ 2.50 = $ 1250.00

Q6. a) The distance to Taree and back home = 2 × 13.5 km = 27 km
   If I do this 5 times per week, then distance = 5 × 27 km = 135 km

   b) The petrol used will be 135 ÷ 15 = 9 litres of petrol per week.

Q7. a)

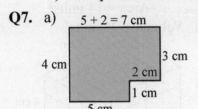

b)

c)

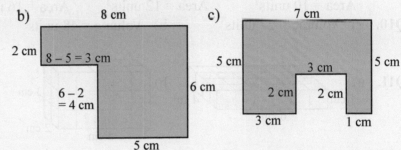

Perimeter = 4 + 7 + 3 + 2 + 1 + 5   Perimeter = 2 + 8 + 6 + 5 + 4 + 3   Perimeter = 5 + 7 + 5 + 1 + 2 + 3 + 2 + 3
   = 22 cm   = 28 cm   = 28 cm

Q8. a) 06:15 or 0615   b) 18:15 or 1815   c) 19:40 or 1940   d) 10:45 or 1045
   e) 11:27 or 1127   f) 14:35 or 1435   g) 22:35 or 2235   h) 06:07 or 0607

Q9. a) 1 hour & 40 minutes   b) 7 hours & 50 minutes   c) 13 hours & 24 minutes

Q10. Area of bedroom = 5 m × 4 m = 20 m²
   Cost of carpet   = 20 × $ 37.20
            = $ 744.00

Q11.

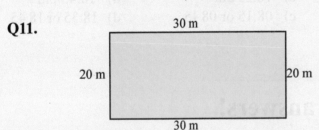

Length $= 1\frac{1}{2} \times$ width $= 1\frac{1}{2} \times 20 = 30$ m
Perimeter $= 30 + 20 + 30 + 20$
      $= 100$ m
Cost $= 100 \times \$ 14.35$
      $= \$1435.00$

Q12. a) Jug can hold 3 litres = 3 000 mL of water

   $3\,000 \div 400 = 7$ remainder 200 or $7\frac{1}{2}$ glasses.
   ∴ 7 glasses can be filled.

   b) 200 ml or $\frac{1}{2}$ a glass of water will be left in the jug.

Q13. Mass of carton = 24 × 500g or 24 × $\frac{1}{2}$ kg
            = 12 000 g   or 12 kg.

Q14. a) Number of shovels to fill wheel barrow = 40 ÷ 2.5 = 16
   b) 1 wheel barrow can move 40 kg of sand
   ∴ 60 wheel barrows can move 60 × 40 = 2 400 kg of sand.
   1 tonne = 1000 kg ⟹ therefore final answer = 2.4 t

Q15. Number of teaspoons of medicine (5 mL) = 480 ÷ 5 = 96
   I take 6 teaspoons each day ⟹ 96 ÷ 6 = 16 days
   ∴ The cough mixture will last for 16 days.

Q16. a)

7 cm
3 cm
5 cm A B 3 cm

Area = A + B
= (7 × 5) + (3 × 3)
= 35 + 9
= 44 cm²

b)

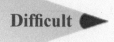

5 cm
3 cm D 6 cm
2 cm C

Area = C + D
= (3 × 2) + (5 × 6)
= 6 + 30
= 36 cm²

Q17. a) Volume = 60 cm³　　b) Volume = 30 cm³　　c) Volume = 56 cm³

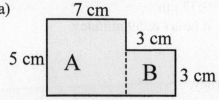

These are the **answers!**

Level 4

USING UNITS OF MEASUREMENT

Difficult

Q1.
a) 180 mm = 18 cm　　b) 1 400 m = 1.4 km　　c) 160 cm = 1.6 m
d) 5.3 cm = 53 mm　　e) 2.7 ha = 27 000 m²　　f) 7 500m² = 0.75 ha
g) 6.25 kg = 6 250 g　　h) 3 750 g = 3. 75 kg　　i) 4.7 t = 4 700 kg
j) 850 g = 0.85 kg　　k) 7.2 L = 7 200 mL　　l) 1 750 mL = 1.75 L

Q2. The figures in the quotations have exactly the same perimeters as the 3 figures shown below.

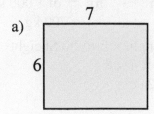

a)
7
6

b)
6
8

c)

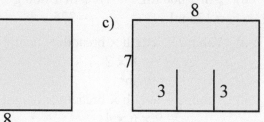

8
7
3 3

Perimeter = 7 + 6 + 7 + 6
= 26 m

Perimeter = 8 + 6 + 8 + 6
= 28 m

Perimeter = 8 + 7 + 8 +7 + 3 + 3
= 36 m

Q3. The area is 15 cm² at the start. If the sides are doubled, the new area is 6 × 10 = 60 cm².
Therefore the new rectangle will be 4 times larger.

Q4.
a) $\frac{1}{3}$ h = $\frac{1}{3}$ × 60
= 20 min

b) 5 min = 5 × 60
= 300 s

c) 3 days = 3 × 24
= 72 h

d) 15 s = $\frac{15}{60}$ min
= $\frac{1}{4}$ min

e) 8 h = $\frac{8}{24}$ day
= $\frac{1}{3}$ day

f) 4 h = 4 × 60 × 60 s
= 14 400 s

g) 210's = 210 ÷ 60
= 3$\frac{1}{2}$ minutes

h) $\frac{1}{10}$ min = $\frac{1}{10}$ × 60
= 6 s

i) $\frac{3}{4}$ day = $\frac{3}{4}$ × 24
= 18 h

Essential Exercises – Year 5 Maths
Warwick Marlin © Five Senses Education

Q5. a) (i) 11:14 am   (ii) 3:37 pm
  b) (i) 1 hour & 17 minutes   (ii) 4 hours & 59 minutes
  c) It arrived at 16:16 or 4:16 pm
  d) 7 hours & 11 minutes
  e) Dunning to Red Hill is the longest part of journey.
     The journey takes 1 hour & 39 minutes.

Q6. a) Area = length × breadth = 3.5 × 6.7 = 23.45 cm²
  b)

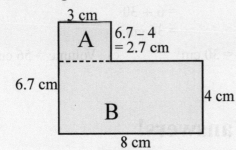

     Area = A + B
       = (3 × 2.7) + (8 × 4)
       = 8.1 + 32
       = 40.1 cm²

  c)

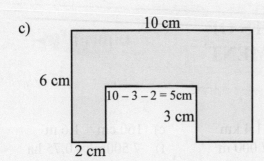

     Below is a clever way of doing this problem.
     Pretend there is one large rectangle
       = 10 × 6 = 60 cm²
     Now subtract the rectangle in white which
     is not shaded.
     ∴ Area = 60 – (5 × 3)
       = 45 cm²

Q7. a) $\frac{3}{4}$ of 1 000 mL   b) $\frac{1}{4}$ of 1 000 g   c) $\frac{3}{5}$ of 100 cm   d) $\frac{1}{5}$ of 10 000 m²
     = 750 mL   = 250 g   = 60 cm   = 2 000 m²
  e) $\frac{1}{8}$ of 1 000 mL   f) $\frac{3}{8}$ of 1 000 g   g) $\frac{4}{5}$ of 1 000 m   h) $\frac{7}{10}$ of 1 000 kg
     = 125 mL   = 375 g   = 800 m   = 700 kg

Q8. a) Volume = length × breadth × height   b) Volume = length × breadth Sheight
           = 5 × 8 × 2   = 7 × 4 × 8
           = 80 cm³   = 224 cm³
  c) Volume = length × breadth × height
           = 9 × 6 × 4
           = 216 cm³

Q9. a) 10 mL = 10 cm³   b) 60 cm³ = 60 mL   c) 1 L = 1 000 mL
  d) 1 L = 1 000 cm³   e) 10 mL = 10 g   f) 10 cm³ = 10 g
  g) 3 L = 3 kg   h) 120 mL = = 120 g   i) 2 000 cm³ = 2 000 g = 2 kg

Q10. a) Volume = length × breadth × height
             = 50 × 80 × 30
             = 120 000 cm³
  b) Capacity = 120 000 mL
  c) Capacity = 120 000 ÷ 1 000 = 120 L
  d) One litre of water weighs 1 kilogram.
     ∴ 120 L of water weighs 120 kg.

To change from mL to L
we have to divide by 1 000.
1 L = 1 000 mL
1 L weighs 1 kg

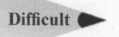

These are the **answers!**

USING UNITS OF MEASUREMENT

Difficult

PROBLEM SOLVING

Q1. a)

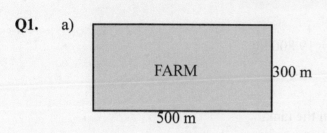

FARM 300 m

500 m

a) Perimeter = 500 + 300 + 500 + 300
   = 1 600 m = 1.6 km

b) Area = length × breadth
   = 500 m × 300 m
   = 150 000 m² = 15 ha

c) Each block = 50 m × 50 m
   = 2 500 m²
   ∴ Number of Subdivisions
   = 150 000 ÷ 2 500
   = 60 subdivisions

d) 1 subdivision costs $ 75 000
   ∴ 60 subdivisions cost 60 × $ 75 000
   = $ 4 500 000

Q2. a)

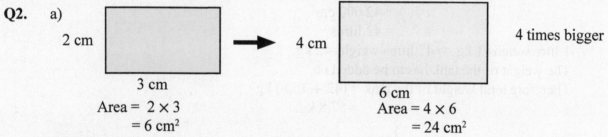

2 cm

3 cm

Area = 2 × 3
     = 6 cm²

4 cm

6 cm

Area = 4 × 6
     = 24 cm²

4 times bigger

Experiment with difficult sized rectangles, and double the length and breadth, and calculate the new area. You will find that IT IS ALWAYS 4 TIMES BIGGER!

Q3. a) Capacity = 160 mL   b) Capacity = 500 mL   c) Capacity = 1.75 L   d) Capacity = 40 mL
    Volume = 160 cm³   Volume = 500 cm³   Volume = 1 750 cm³   Volume = 40 cm³
    Mass = 160 g   Mass = 500 g   Mass   = 1.75 kg   Mass   = 40 g

Q4. Area = 64 cm² ⟹ therefore the length of each side = 8 cm
Therefore the volume = length × breadth × height
                     = 8 × 8 × 8
                     = 512 cm³

Q5. This is a difficult question, and it must be done by trial and error.

Trial 1: Let the length of the side of the small square be 1 cm.
         Therefore volume = 10 × 10 × 1 = 100 cm³

Trial 2: Let the length of the side of the small square be 2 cm.
         Therefore volume = 8 × 8 × 2 = 128 cm³

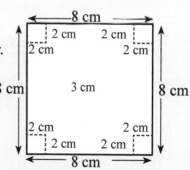

8 cm
2 cm   2 cm
2 cm   2 cm
8 cm   3 cm   8 cm
2 cm   2 cm
2 cm   2 cm
8 cm

Essential Exercises – Year 5 Maths
Warwick Marlin © Five Senses Education

Trial 3:   Let the length of the side of the small square be 3 cm.
Therefore volume = 6 × 6 × 3 = 108 cm³

Trial 4:   Let the length of the side of the small square be 4 cm.
Therefore volume = 4 × 4 × 4 = 64 cm³

1 t = 1 000 kg

It can be seen already that the side
of each small square has to be 2 cm
to give a maximum volume of 128 cm³.

Q6.   Volume of trench = length × breadth × height
= 8 × 4.5 × 0.5
= 18 cubic metres (m³)
∴ Weight of 1 cubic metres = 1 100 kg
∴ Weight of 18 cubic metres = 18 × 1 100 = 19 800 kg.
∴ Weight = 198 000 1 ÷ 1 000
= 19.8 tones

Q7.   a) In 5 minutes, 30 litres of water will be in the tank.
1 litre = 1 000 cm³ ⟹ 30 litres = 30 000 cm²
Volume = length × breadth × height
∴   30 000 = 40 × 30 × height
∴   Therefore height of water = 25 cm

b) Volume of water = 40 × 30 × 32 = 38 400 mL or 38.4 L
The water flows in at 6 litres per minute.
Therefore 38.4 ÷ 6 = 6.4 minutes = 6 minutes and 24 seconds.

c) Volume of water in the tank = 40 × 30 × 35
= 42 000 cm³
= 42 litres

1 litre weighs 1 kg ⇒ 42 litres weighs 42 kg.
The weight of the tank has to be added on.
Therefore total weight of the tank = (42 + 15.8) kg
= 57.8 kg

Q8.   a)

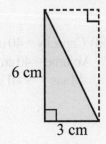

6 cm

3 cm

b)

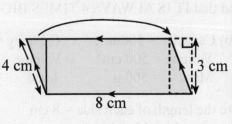

4 cm

8 cm

3 cm

c)

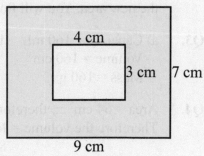

4 cm

3 cm   7 cm

9 cm

The right angled △
is half a rectangle.
∴ Area = ½ (6 × 3)
= 9 cm²

The triangle shown on
the left can be taken
over to the right to
form a rectangle.
∴   Area = 8 × 3
= 24 cm²

Find the area of the large
rectangle, and subtract the
unshaded rectangle in the centre.
∴ Shaded are = (9 × 7) – (4 × 3)
= 63 – 12
= 51 cm²

Q9. Volume of cube = 343 cm³

$\therefore$ length $\times$ length $\times$ length = 343

$\therefore 7 \times 7 \times 7 = 343$ ($\sqrt[3]{216}$)

$\therefore$ length of each side of cube = 7 cm

$\therefore$ Area of one face = $7 \times 7 = 49$ cm²

$\therefore$ Area of 6 faces = 6×49

$= 294$ cm²

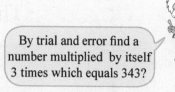

By trial and error find a number multiplied by itself 3 times which equals 343?

Q10. a) Area of bedroom A = 3.2 m $\times$ 4.2 m

$= 13.44$ m²

b) Split it up into 2 rectangles.

$\therefore$ Total area = $(3.8 \times 4.0) + (1.4 \times 3.2)$

$= 19.68$ m²

c) Area of complete extension = $19.68 + 13.44 + 13.44$

$= 46.56$ m²

Q11. a) In 1 hour the car will travel 60 km.

In $\frac{1}{5}$ hour the car will travel 12 km.

$\therefore$ In $2\frac{1}{5}$ hours the car will travel $60 + 60 + 12 = 132$ km

b) It will take 3 hours to travel 180 km.

The extra 15 km will take $\frac{1}{4}$ of an hour.

$\therefore$ Time to travel 195 km = $3\frac{1}{4}$ hours or 3 hours and 15 minutes

Q12. It takes 7 men 40 hours to paint the walls.

$\therefore$ It takes 1 man $40 \times 7 = 280$ hours to paint the walls.

$\therefore$ It takes 5 men $\frac{280}{5} = 56$ hours to paint the walls.

Essential Exercises – Year 5 Maths
Warwick Marlin © Five Senses Education

These are the **answers!**

Q1. a) cube   b) sphere   c) triangular pyramid   d) triangular prism

      a) cylinder   b) rectangular prism   c) cone   d) square pyramid

Q2. a) 6 faces   b) 5 faces   c) 7 faces

Q3. a) 12 edges   b) 8 edges   c) 15 edges

Q4. a) 8 vertices   b) 5 vertices   c) 10 vertices

Q5. a) rectangular prism   b) square pyramid   c) hexagonal prism

      d) triangular prism   e) triangular pyramid

Q6. a)   b)

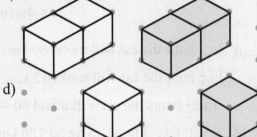

c)   d)

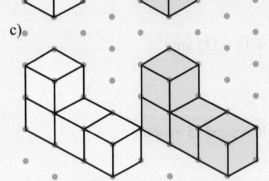 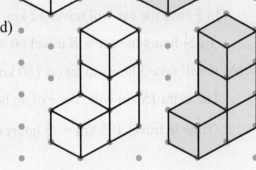

Q7. a) rectangular prism

b)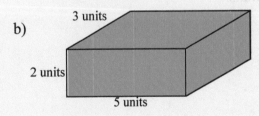

c) volume = length × breadth × height

$$= 5 \times 3 \times 2$$
$$= 30 \text{ units}^3$$

d) Look at the net and count the squares.
Area = 10 + 15 + 6 + 6 + 10 + 15
      = 62 units²

Q8. a) Front view: b) Side view: c) Top view:

09. a) 12 tetracubes   b) 15 tetracubes

Level 2

SHAPE

Average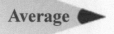

Q1. (i) a) triangle   b) rectangle or square c) hexagon   d) circle
(ii) The solids in a, c and d all have the same cross section.
(iii) The solids in a and c are prisms.
(iv) The solid in d (cylinder) is neither a prism nor a pyramid.

Q2. a) cylinder   b) cone   c) cylinder   d) cylinder
e) cone   f) sphere   g) rectangular prism   h) cubes
i) triangular prism   j) rectangular prism   k) sphere   l) triangular prism

Q3. a) triangular prism   b) pentagonal pyramid   c) hexagonal prism

Q4. a) 5 faces   b) 6 faces   c) 8 faces

Q5. a) 9 edges   b) 10 edges   c) 18 edges

Q6. a) 6 vertices   b) 6 vertices   c) 12 vertices

Q7.

			Back			
Side		Bottom		Side
		Front		
		Top		

Q8. w → d   x → c   y → b   z → a

Q9. ⌐You simply have to redraw the shapes and compare them to the

Q10. ⌐shapes given in the question.

Q11. a) Front view: b) Side view: c) Top view:

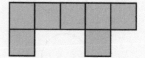

Essential Exercises – Year 5 Maths
Warwick Marlin © Five Senses Education

These are the **answers!**

PROBLEM SOLVING

Q1.   A → 3   B → 5   C → 4
         D → 6   E → 1   F → 2

Q2.   1. Name: square prism or cube   2. Name: pentagonal prism
         3. Name: rectangular prism   4. Name: rectangular or square pyramid
         5. Name: triangular prism   6. Name: cylinder

Q3.   a) prism
         b) It has a constant or uniform cross section of a hexagon.
         c) 8 faces
         d) 18 edges
         e) 12 vertices
         f) hexagonal prism

Q4.   Draw the net on ordinary square
         grid paper shown on the right,
         for the rectangular prism below.

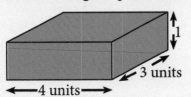

Q5.   Redraw the solids below on
         isometric dot paper.

   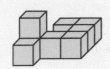   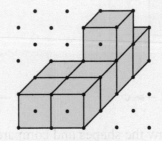   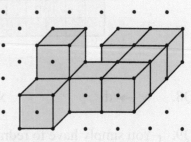

	Top View	Front view	Side view

Q6.   a)   Cone

         b)   Triangle prism

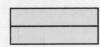

         c)   Sphere

Q7. a) Solid X = 18 cubes   Solid Y = 7 cubes

∴ 11 cubes must be subtracted from solid X to get solid Y.

b) Solid 3 × 3 × 3 cube = 27 cubes

∴ 9 more cubes have to be added to solid X to make it a perfect cuboid.

c) Solid Y = 7 cubes

∴ 20 cubes have to be added to solid Y to make it a perfect cuboid.

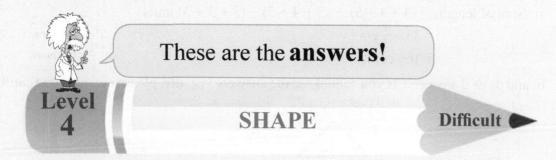

These are the **answers!**

Level 4

SHAPE

Difficult

Q1. a) Rectangular prism (cube) on the bottom. Rectangular pyramid on the top.

b) Cylinder on the bottom. Cone on the top.

Q2. Number of faces = 9

Number of edges = 16

Number of vertices = 9

Q3. a) pentagonal prism

b) hexagonal pyramid

c) cylinder

d) cone

Q4. a) The number of sides on the perimeter = 14 (by counting)

∴ Length of 14 sides = 98 cm

∴ Length of 1 side = 98 ÷ 14 = 7 cm

∴ Volume of cube = length × length × length = 7 × 7 × 7 = 343 cm³

b) Area of 1 face = 7 × 7 = 49 cm³

∴ Area of 6 faces = 6 × 49 = 294 cm²

c) A cube has 12 edges in total.

∴ Sum of the edges = 12 × 7 = 84 cm²

Q5. a) Length of the side of the square base = 10 cm – 3 cm = 7 cm

∴ Volume of rectangular prism = 7 × 7 × 3

                = 147 cm³

b) Area of square base + square top = 49 + 49 = 98 cm²

Area of 4 rectangular sides = 4 × (3 × 7) = 84 cm²

∴ Total area of 6 faces = 98 + 84

                = 182 cm²

c) There are 12 edges in total.

8 edges are 7 cm in length.

4 edges are 3 cm in length.

Sum of all edges = 8 × 7 + 4 × 3

                = 68 cm

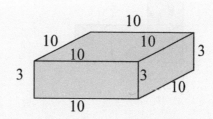

Essential Exercises – Year 5 Maths
Warwick Marlin © Five Senses Education

Q6. a) A triangular prism is formed.

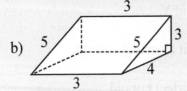

b)

Let the length of 1 square on the grid paper = 1 unit.

c) There are 9 edges altogether.
   Sum of lengths = $(3 + 4 + 5) + (3 + 4 + 5) + (3 + 3 + 3)$ units
   $$= 33 \times \frac{1}{2} \text{ cm}$$
   $$= 16\frac{1}{2} \text{ cm}$$

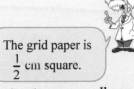

The grid paper is $\frac{1}{2}$ cm square.

Q7. b) and d) $\Rightarrow$ 2 answers: If you cannot see the answers visually, please cut out some cardboard and make up a die with dots as shown.

Q8.

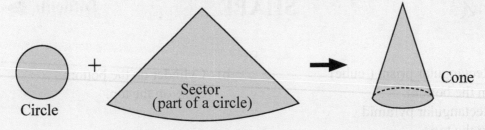

Circle + Sector (part of a circle) → Cone

Q9. a)

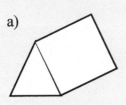

triangular prism

b)

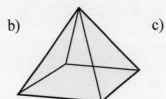

square pyramid

c)

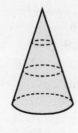

cone

d)

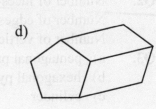

pentagonal prism

Q10.   Front View   Top View   Side View

a)

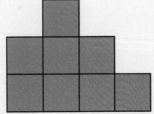

b)

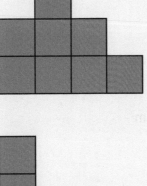

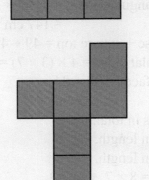

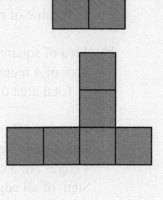

c)

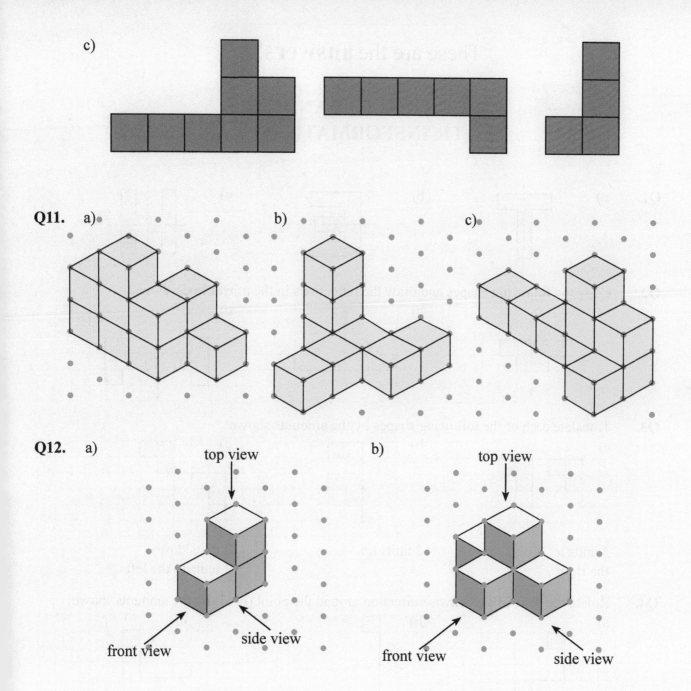

Q11. a)

b)

c)

Q12. a)

top view

front view

side view

b)

top view

front view

side view

Level 1

LOCATION AND TRANSFORMATION

Easier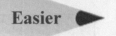

Q1. a)   b)   c)

Q2. Copy the following shapes and draw the reflections in the mirror lines shown:

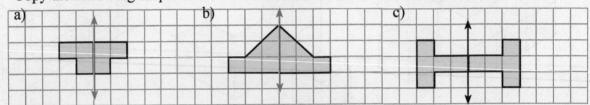

a)   b)   c)

Q3. Translate each of the following shapes by the amounts shown:

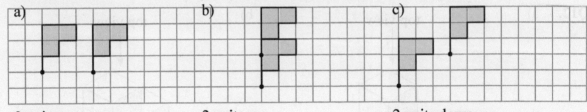

a)   b)   c)

3 units to
the right

2 units up

2 units down
3 units to the left

Q4. Rotate the flags in a clockwise direction around the point (bold) by the amounts shown:

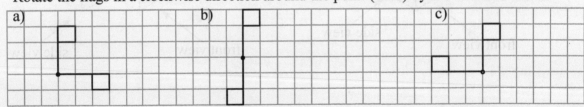

a)   b)   c)

Rotate 90°
($\frac{1}{4}$ turn)

rotate 180°
($\frac{1}{2}$ turn)

rotate 270°
($\frac{3}{4}$ turn)

Q5. a) △ = (D, 5)   b) ✗ = (D, 3)   c) ✚ = (F, 2)
d) ◓ = (B, 1)   e) ◯ = (A, 4)

Q6. The deer are <u>South</u> of the camping site.
The lake is <u>West</u> of the camping site.
The forest is <u>East</u> of the camping site.
The mountains are <u>North</u> of the camping site.

Q7. a) yes   b) no   c) yes   d) no (tricky!)
e) no   f) yes   g) yes   h) yes

Q8. (i) The square can rotate and fit onto itself 4 times.
Therefore it has rotational symmetry of order 4.

(ii) The letter Z can rotate and fit onto itself 2 times.
Therefore it has rotational symmetry of order 2.

These are the **answers!**

LOCATION AND TRANSFORMATION

Average

Q1. a) 1 cm □ 50 m on land and ⇒ 3 cm □ 150 m on land

b) 8 cm □ 400 m on land

c) 50 m on land is 1 cm on the map.
∴ 350 m on land is 7 cm on the map.

d) $\frac{1}{4}$ of a kilometre = 250 m. On this map, this will be 5 cm.

e) 1 cm = 10 mm and 1 cm □ 50 m
∴ 1 mm = 5 m on land

Q2. Using grid paper similar to that shown on the right, mark in the following grid references with a solid bold dot.

i) (C, 1)   ii) (D, 4)   iii) (F, 2)

iv) (A, 5) v) (B, 3) vi) (E, 0)

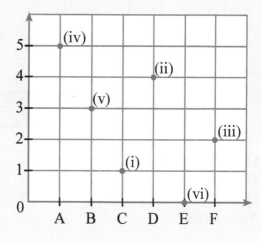

Q3. Draw in the line(s) of symmetry for the following shapes:

a)   b)   c)   d)

      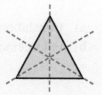

Q4. Copy the following shapes and draw the reflections in the mirror lines shown.

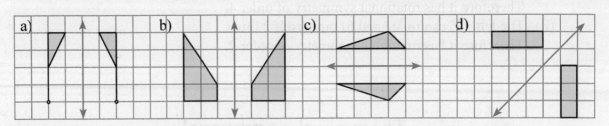

a)   b)   c)   d)

Q5. Translate each of the shapes below by the amounts shown:

a)

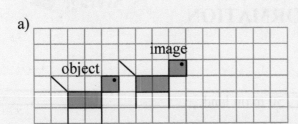

b)

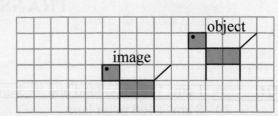

4 units to the right and
1 unit up

5 units to the left
and 2 units down

Q6. a)   b)   c)

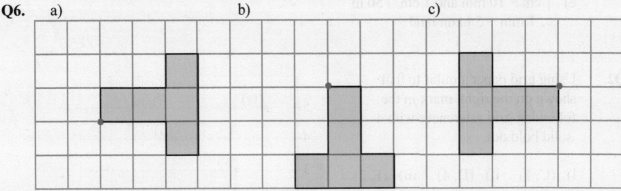

Q7. a) OA = 1.7 cm and OA^1 = 5.1 cm
   b) OA^1 is 3 times longer that OA.
   c) OB^1 is 3 times longer than AB.
   d) Scale factor = 3

Q8. i) West or W   ii) South or S   iv) North West or NW
   iv) East or E   v) North East or NE   vi) North or N
   vii) South East or SE   viii) South West or SW

Q9. a) translation, reflection, rotation, enlargement
   b) enlargement

These are the **answers!**

PROBLEM SOLVING

Q1. a) North West or NW b) They saw a lake.
c) (3, J) d) They saw a church.
e) 7 cm on the map = 7 × 10 km = 70 km
f) 30 km ÷ 2 hours ⟹ average speed = 15 km/h
g) West or W h) 8.5 cm on the map = 8.5 × 10 km = 85 km
i) South West or SW j) They saw a forest.
k) They passed over a bridge. l) (13, D)
m) 40 km ÷ $1\frac{1}{4}$ hours ⟹ average speed = 32 km/h
n) 85 km + 70km + 30 km + 20 km + 85 km + 110 km + 30 km + 40 km = 470 km

Q2. a) rotation b) translation c) reflection d) enlargement

Q3.

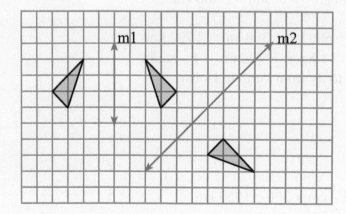

Q4. 2 figures are CONGRUENT if they have both the same size and shape c).

Essential Exercises – Year 5 Maths
Warwick Marlin © Five Senses Education

Q1. a) Sydney = (22, F)   b) Melbourne = (18, D)
         c) Perth = (3, G)   d) Brisbane = (24, J)

Q2. a) Katherine   b) Mount Isa   c) Mackay   d) Adelaide

Q3. a) Alice Springs   b) (12, M)

Q4. Port Macquarie

Q5. Broken Hill

Q6. The actual ruler measures approximately 9 cm.
         But 1 cm = 300 km
         ∴ Distance from Perth to Hobart = 9 × 300 = 2 700 km

Q7. 600 km + 600 km + 600 km + 600 km + 300 km = 2 700 km
         1 hour   1 hour   1 hour   1 hour $\frac{1}{2}$ hour $4\frac{1}{2}$ hours
         The plane will take $4\frac{1}{2}$ hours to fly from Perth to Hobart.

Q8. Darwin = (11, T)

Q9. The ruler measures $3\frac{1}{2}$ cm.
         But 1 cm = 300 km
         ∴ Distance from Darwin = $3\frac{1}{2}$ cm × 300 = 1050 km

Q10. Kalgoorlie or Esperance lies almost directly south of Derby.

Q11. The coordinates where the 3 states meet are at approximately (15, K).

Q12. Reflect each of the following shapes in the lines shown:

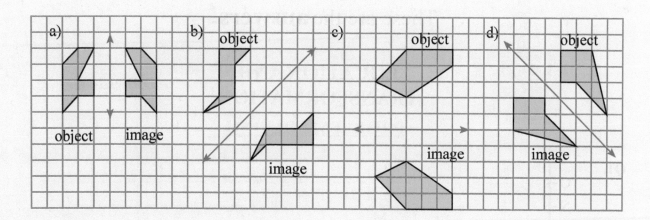

Q13. Translate each of the following shapes by the amounts shown:

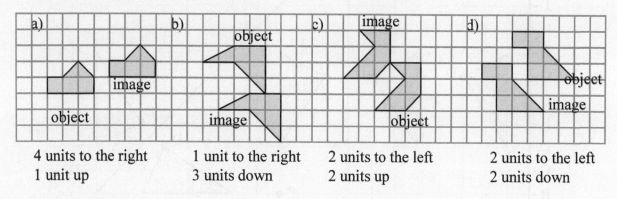

a) 4 units to the right
1 unit up

b) 1 unit to the right
3 units down

c) 2 units to the left
2 units up

d) 2 units to the left
2 units down

Q14. Rotate each flag below through 90° ($\frac{1}{2}$ turn) in a clockwise direction around the solid dot shown:

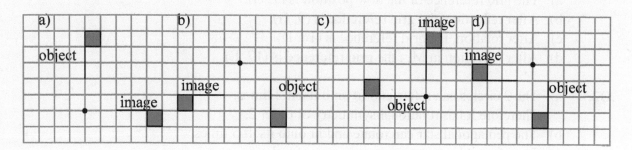

Essential Exercises – Year 5 Maths
Warwick Marlin © Five Senses Education

Level 5

LOCATION AND TRANSFORMATION

PROBLEM SOLVING

Difficult

Q1.

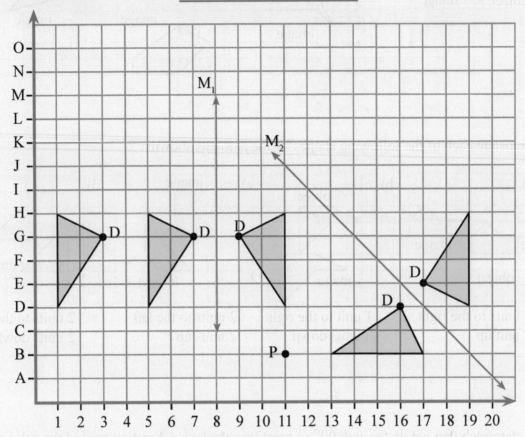

a) The grid reference of the new position is (7, G).

b) After reflection, the grid reference is (9, G).

c) After rotation, the grid reference is (16, D).

d) After reflection in M_2 , the grid reference is (17, E).

Q2. a) The 2 circles can rotate and fit onto itself 2 times.
Therefore it has rotational symmetry of order 2.

b) The pentagonal star can rotate and fit onto itself 5 times.
Therefore it has rotational symmetry of order 5.

c) The 3 flagged figure can rotate and fit onto itself 3 times.
Therefore it has rotational symmetry of order 3.

d) The cross can rotate and fit onto itself 4 times.
Therefore it has rotational symmetry of order 4.

Q3. a) OB = 3 units

b) OB^1 = 12 units

c) OB^1 is 4 times longer than OB.

d) The scale factor = 4, because the original object has been enlarged or magnified 4 times.

Q4.

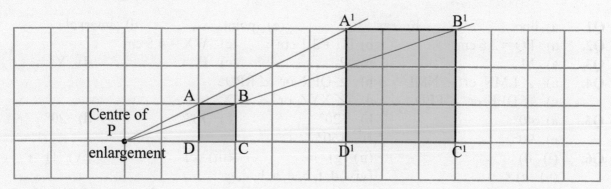

a) PD = 2 units

b) PD^1 = 6 units

c) Area of ABCD = 1 square centimetre or 1 cm^2

d) Area of A^{1}B^{1}C^{1}D^1 = 9 square centimetre or 9 cm^2

e) Area of A^{1}B^{1}C^{1}D^1 is 9 times bigger than the area of ABCD.

Essential Exercises – Year 5 Maths
Warwick Marlin © Five Senses Education

These are the answers!

Level 1 — GEOMETRIC REASONING — Easier

Q1. a) line   b) ray   c) point   d) interval

Q2. a) PQ = 2.6 cm   b) TU = 3.1 cm   c) WX = 4.5 cm

Q3. a) M   b) P   c) E   d) Y

Q4. a) ∠LMN or ∠NML   b) ∠QPR or ∠RPQ
    c) ∠DEF or ∠FED   d) ∠XYZ or ∠ZYX

Q5. a) 40°   b) 120°   c) 70°   d) 20°
    e) 90°   f) 160°

Q6. (i) d   (ii) g   (iii) c   (iv) f
    (v) a   (vi) d, f, b, e, a, h, c, g.

Q7. a) rectangle   b) octagon   c) pentagon   d) hexagon
    4 sides   8 sides   5 sides   6 sides
    4 angles   8 angles   5 angles   6 angles

Q8. a) obtuse angle   b) right angle   c) acute angle   d) acute angle
    e) right angle   f) obtuse angle   g) acute angle   d) obtuse angle

Q9. a) I cannot call it ∠D because there would be confusion with the angle right next to it.
    b) Any of the following: ∠BDC or ∠CDB or ∠BD̂C or ∠CD̂B.

These are the answers!

Level 2 — GEOMETRIC REASONING — Average

Q1. a) interval   b) ray   c) line   d) interval

Q2. a) QP̂R or RP̂Q   b) LN̂M or MN̂L   c) RT̂S or ST̂R   d) KT̂V or VT̂K

Q3. a) 25°   b) 65°   c) 45°   d) 155°

Q4. a) 40°   b) 60°   c) 130°   d) 100°

    Note: If you got any answers 2 degrees either side of the above answers, then mark your answer as correct.

Q5. a) 50° angle   b) 80° angle

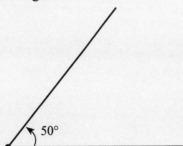

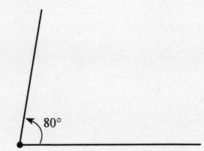

c) 70° angle

70°

d) 120° angle

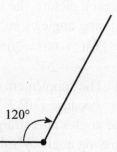

120°

Q6.
a) 70° = acute angle
c) 90° = right angle
e) 142° = obtuse angle
g) 360° = revolution

b) 180° = straight angle
d) 39° = acute angle
f) 200° = reflex angle
h) 100° = obtuse angle

These are the **answers!**

Level **3**

GEOMETRIC REASONING

Average

Q1.
a) RQ, RP, and PQ   or $\overline{RQ}, \overline{RP}$ and $\overline{PQ}$
b) PQ and QP   or $\overrightarrow{PQ}$ and $\overrightarrow{QP}$
c) PQ or $\overleftrightarrow{PQ}$
d) $\overline{RP}$ or $\overline{PR}$
e) $\overline{RQ}$ or $\overline{QR}$
f) $\overline{PQ}$ or $\overline{QP}$
g) ∠RPQ or ∠QPR or $R\hat{P}Q$ or $Q\hat{P}R$

Q2.
a) reflex angle
d) revolution

b) right angle
e) obtuse angle

c) acute angle
f) straight angle

Q3.
a) 170°
d) 100°

b) 80°
e) 20°

c) 45°
f) 135°

Q4.
a) 90°

b) 20 units is
$\frac{1}{3}$ of a revolution.
$\frac{1}{3}$ of 360°
= 120°

c) 5 units
is $\frac{1}{12}$ of a revolution.
$\frac{1}{12}$ of 360°
= 30°

d) From the 4 to the 6, the angle is $\frac{2}{12}$ of a revolution = 60°. The hour hand is halfway between the 3 and the 4 = $\frac{1}{2}$ of 30° = 15°.
Therefore total angle size is 60° + 15° = 75°.

Q5.
a) ∠KTM or ∠MTK
b) ∠ECA or ∠ACE
c) ∠YWZ or ∠ZWY

Q6.
a) Complement of 65° is 25°,
because 65° + 25° = 90°

b) Complement of 31° is 59°,
because 31° and 59° = 90°

Q7. In each picture, the whole angle is a right angle or 90°. Therefore we can find the other missing angle by subtracting the known angle from 90°.

   a) D$\hat{B}$C = 90° − 70°
      = 20°
   b) A$\hat{B}$E = 90° − 28°
      = 62°
   c) C$\hat{B}$F = 90° − 53°
      = 37°

Q8. a) The supplement of 110° is 70°, because 110° + 70° = 180°.
   b) The supplement of 39° is 141°, because 39° + 141° = 180°.

Q9. The angles on a straight angle always add upto 180°. Therefore we can find the size of the missing angle by subtracting the known angle from 180°.

   a) ∠ SQR − 180° − 158°
      =22°
   b) ∠ TQV = 180° − 42° - 34°
      = 104°
   c) ∠ WQP = 180° − 67°
      = 113°

Q10. a) Triangle C has 3 acute angles.
   b) Triangle A has 1 obtuse angle.
   c) Triangle B has 1 right angle and 2 acute angles.

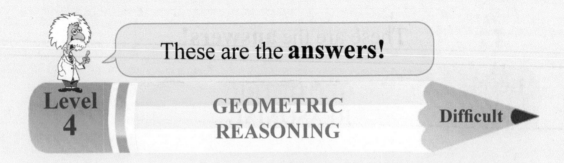

These are the **answers!**

Level 4

GEOMETRIC REASONING

Difficult

Q1. **Note:** Mark your answer correct if it is 2° either way of the answers given below.
   a) 38°
   b) 75°
   c) 40°
   d) 48°
   e) 60°
   f) 128°

Q2. a)

   b)

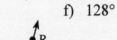

   c)

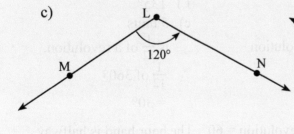

   d)

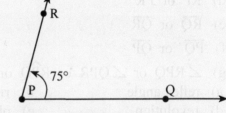

   e)

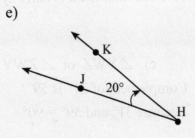

   f)

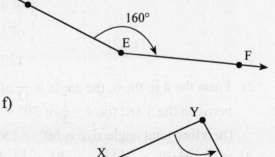

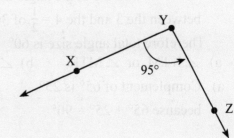

Q3. a) B$\hat{A}$C and C$\hat{A}$D are adjacent angles because they lie on opposite sides of a common arm AC.

b) B$\hat{A}$D = 40° + 20° = 60°

Q4. a) Q$\hat{P}$R and R$\hat{P}$S are adjacent angles.

b) Q$\hat{P}$S is a right angle, because 60° + 30° = 90° (= right angle)

Q5. a) N$\hat{M}$L and L$\hat{M}$P are adjacent angles.

b) N$\hat{M}$P is a straight angle because 35° + 145° = 180° (= straight angle)

Q6. a) T$\hat{Q}$R = 90° (right angle) ∴ P$\hat{Q}$R = 90° – 48° = 42°

b) T$\hat{Q}$P = 105° ∴ P$\hat{Q}$R = 105° – 37° = 68°

c) T$\hat{Q}$R = 180° ∴ P$\hat{Q}$R = 180° – 142° = 38°

Q7. a) right angle   b) revolution   c) acute angle

d) right angle   e) reflex angle   f) straight angle

These are the **answers!**

GEOMETRIC REASONING

Level 5   Difficult

PROBLEM SOLVING

Q1. There are 360° in a complete revolution.

∴ 360 ÷ 24 = 15

∴ The angle between each spoke is 15°.

Q2. a) There are 360° in a complete revolution or full turn.

∴ Angle between N and E is $\frac{1}{4}$ of a revolution = 90°

b) Angle between N and S is $\frac{1}{2}$ of a full turn = 180°

c) Reflex angle between N and w is $\frac{3}{4}$ of a full turn = 270°

d) Angle between S and NW is $\frac{1}{8}$ of a full turn = 45°

e) Angle between S and SE is $\frac{7}{8}$ of a full turn = 315°

OR Angle = $\frac{1}{4}$ turn + $\frac{1}{4}$ turn + $\frac{1}{4}$ turn + $\frac{1}{8}$ turn

= 90° + 90° + 90° + 45°

= 315°

Q3. a) 5 minutes is $\frac{5}{60}$ or $\frac{1}{12}$ of a complete revolution or full turn.

∴ Angle = $\frac{1}{12}$ of 360° = 30°

b) In 5 minutes the hand will turn through 30°.

∴ In 1 minute the hand will turn through 6°.

c) The number of minute divisions on the clock between the minute hand and the hour hand at 5:12 is exactly 14.

1 minute division represents an angle of 6°.

∴ 14 minute divisions represents an angle of 14 × 6° = 84°

Essential Exercises – Year 5 Maths
Warwick Marlin © Five Senses Education

d) The number of minute divisions on the clock face between the minute hand and the hour hand at 2:36 is exactly 23.

1 minute division represents an angle of $6°$.

∴ 23 minute divisions represents an angle of $23 \times 6° = 138°$

e) When the minute hand turns through an angle of 15 minutes, the hour hand turns through an angle of $\frac{1}{4}$ of $30°$.

∴ hour hand turns through an angle of $7\frac{1}{2}°$.

Q4. 1 click = 1 revolution of the wheel = 1 metre

∴ 500 clicks = 500 m

This happens 4 times $\Rightarrow$ 500 + 500 + 500 + 500 + 278 = 2 278 m

Distance from her house to school = 2. 278 km

Q5. There is a total of 14 triangles.

Q6. Measure the acute angle = $60°$

There are $360°$ in full turn or 1 revolution.

∴ Reflex angle = $360° - 60°$
$= 300°$

Q7.
a) $Z\hat{Y}Z = 60°$
b) $X\hat{Z}Y = 40°$
c) $Y\hat{X}Z = 80°$

d) Sum of the 3 angles = $60° + 40° + 80° = 180°$

Q8. The 3 angles will always form a straight angle (or straight line) at the base. This means that the 3 angles of any shaped triangle always add upto exactly $180°$.

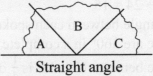

Straight angle

Q9.

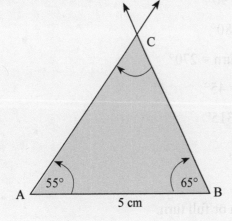

If we measure the size of $A\hat{C}B$ we get exactly $60°$.

From Q8. we know that the 3 angles of any shaped triangle should add upto $180°$.

$\hat{A} = 55°$ and $\hat{B} = 65° \Rightarrow$ this leaves $60°$ for $\hat{C}$.

OR: $55° + 65° + \hat{C} = 180°$

Q10.
a) $X = 90° - 62°$
∴ $X = 28°$

b) $Y = 180° - 134°$
∴ $Y = 46°$

c) $W = 180° - 83° - 32°$
$= 65°$

d) $V = 43° - 21°$
$= 22°$

e) 3 angles of a
△ $= 180°$
∴ $u = 180° - 90° - 37°$
$= 53°$

f) $Z = 360° - 127° - 141°$
$= 92°$

These are the **answers!**

Q1. Answers to these questions may vary slightly.

a) Likely
b) Highly unlikely
c) Impossible
d) Highly unlikely
e) Answers will vary
f) Certain
g) Unlikely
h) Even chance
i) Highly likely
j) Even chance
k) Highly likely

Q2. a) There are 100 jelly beans altogether, and 50 are blue.

∴ Chance of taking out a blue jelly bean $= \frac{50}{100} = \frac{1}{2}$

b) Chance of taking out a yellow jelly bean $= \frac{50}{100} = \frac{1}{2}$

c) Chance of taking out a blue or yellow jelly bean $= \frac{100}{100} = 1$.
Taking out either a blue or yellow jelly bean is CERTAIN.

d) Chance of taking out a green jelly bean $= \frac{0}{100} = 0$.
There are no green jelly beans, therefore the chance is IMPOSSIBLE.

> Fractions can be simplified.

Q3. a) Red is one part out of 4 equal parts.

∴ Chance of landing on red = 1 chance in 4 or $\frac{1}{4}$.

b) Red is one part out of 3 equal parts.

∴ Chance of landing on red = 1 chance in 3 or $\frac{1}{3}$.

c) Red is one part out of 6 equal parts.

∴ Chance of landing on red = 1 chance in 6 or $\frac{1}{6}$.

d) No parts are shaded red out of the 3 equal parts.

∴ Chance of landing on red = 0 chance in 3 or $\frac{0}{3}$ or 0.

In other words, it is impossible for the pointer to land on red.

Q4. a) 3 are yellow   b) 6 are blue   c) 10 are red   d) 1 is green

e) There are more red marbles than any other colour, so red is the most likely colour.

f) Lei is more likely to take out a blue marble, because there are 6 blue marbles and only 1 green marble.

g) Green is the least likely marble to be picked.

h) red, blue, yellow, green are in order from most likely to least likely.

Q5. a) Chance of picking a yellow marble = 3 chances in 20 $= \frac{3}{20}$.

b) Chance of picking a blue marble = 6 chances in 20 $= \frac{6}{20}$ or $\frac{3}{10}$.

c) Chance of picking a red marble = 10 chances in 20 $= \frac{10}{20}$ or $\frac{1}{2}$.

d) Chance of picking a green marble = 1 chances in 20 $= \frac{1}{20}$.

Essential Exercises – Year 5 Maths
Warwick Marlin © Five Senses Education

Q6. There are 6 different spinners shown below. Colour each spinner to show the given outcome. If you do not have coloured crayons then simply label the triangle(s) with the first letter of the colour eg. red (R), blue (B) etc.

a)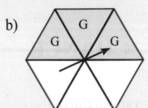

a $\frac{1}{6}$ chance of spinning blue

⇨ Any 1 of the triangles must be blue.

b)

a $\frac{1}{2}$ chance of spinning green

⇨ Any 3 of the triangles must be green.

c)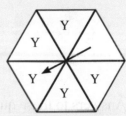

a $\frac{5}{6}$ chance of spinning yellow

⇨ Any 5 of the triangles must be yellow.

d)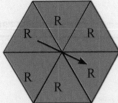

a certain chance of spinning red

⇨ All of the triangles must be red.

e)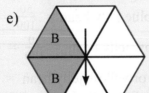

a $\frac{1}{3}$ chance of spinning black

⇨ Any 2 of the triangles must be black.

f)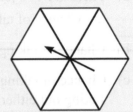

no chance of spinning purple

⇨ No triangles must be shaded.

These are the **answers!**

Level 2

CHANCE

Average

Q1. a) Fraction of red = $\frac{1}{8}$ b) Fraction of green = $\frac{3}{8}$ c) Fraction of blue = $\frac{4}{8}$
d) Unlikely   e) Even chance   f) Very unlikely
g) Very likely   h) Impossible

Q2. a) The cricket card with Ricky Ponting has the highest chance.
b) The swimming card with Ian Thorpe has the least chance.
c) 1 chance in 10 = $\frac{1}{10}$ (because there is only 1 swimming card)
d) 6 chances in 10 = $\frac{6}{10}$ (because there are 6 cricket cards)
e) 3 chances in 10 = $\frac{3}{10}$ (because there are 3 tennis cards)
f) 0 chances in 10 = $\frac{0}{10}$ = 0 (impossible because there are no hockey cards)

Q3. When a single die is tossed, there are 6 different possible numbers that can show.

a) The number 3 → 1 chance in 6 = $\frac{1}{6}$ (because there is only one number 3).

b) Any odd number → 3 chances in 6 = $\frac{3}{6}$ or $\frac{1}{2}$ (because there are 3 odd numbers).

c) A number greater than 2 → 4 chances in 6 = $\frac{4}{6}$ or $\frac{2}{3}$ (because there are 4 numbers greater than 2).

d) Any number which is not 4 → 5 chances in 6 = $\frac{5}{6}$ (because 5 of the other numbers are not 4).

e) A number equal to or greater than 3 → 4 chances in 6 = $\frac{4}{6}$ = $\frac{2}{3}$ (because there are 4 numbers greater than or equal to 3 → 3, 4, 5 or 6)

f) A number greater than 6 → 0 chances in 6 = 0 (impossible because there are no numbers greater than 6).

Q4.
a) 10 even numbers
b) 8 multiples of 3 (3, 21, 18, 6, 15, 12, 24, 9)
c) 3 prime numbers (3, 13, 17)
d) 6 numbers greater than 20 (21, 26, 32, 40, 24, 28)
e) Highly unlikely
f) Unlikely
g) Likely
h) Unlikely
i) Impossible
j) Highly unlikely
k) Certain

Q5.
a) When a single coin tossed, there are only 2 possible results, either a head shows or a tail shows.

Chance of a head showing = 1 chance in 2 = $\frac{1}{2}$

b) Chance of a tail showing = 1 chance in 2 = $\frac{1}{2}$

c) Jenny would expect a head to show in about half the number of tosses, because head has an even chance of showing.
Therefore she would expect a head to show about 100 times.

d) Yes, this could happen, but it is very, very unlikely.
Maybe it could land on its thin edge 1 in a 1000 tosses.

Q6.
a) A girl has a higher chance of being picked, because there are 16 girls and ONLY 4 boys.
b) There are 20 students in the class altogether.

∴ Probability of picking a girl = 16 chances in 20 = $\frac{16}{20}$ or $\frac{4}{5}$

c) There are 20 students in the class altogether.

∴ Probability of picking a boy = 4 chances in 20 = $\frac{4}{20}$ or $\frac{1}{5}$

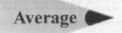
These are the **answers!**

PROBLEM SOLVING

Q1. a) Highly unlikely $\Rightarrow$ Probability = 1 chance out of 10 = $\frac{1}{10}$ or 0.1

b) Even chance $\Rightarrow$ Probability = 5 chances out of 10 = $\frac{5}{10}$ or 0.5

c) Highly likely $\Rightarrow$ Probability = 8 chances out of 10 = $\frac{8}{10}$ or 0.8

d) Unlikely $\Rightarrow$ Probability = 4 chances out of 10 = $\frac{4}{10}$ or 0.4

e) Impossible $\Rightarrow$ Probability = 0 chances out of 10 = 0 or 0.0

Q2. Answers to these questions may vary slightly.

a) Highly likely
b) Highly unlikely
c) Highly likely
d) Unlikely
e) Even chance
f) Unlikely
g) Highly unlikely
h) Likely
i) Even chance

Q3. There are 4 different five sided spinners shown below. Shade each spinner to show the given outcome.

a) 60% chance

$60\% = \frac{60}{100} = \frac{3}{5}$

$\Rightarrow$ 3 out of 5

b) 20% chance

$20\% = \frac{20}{100} = \frac{1}{5}$

$\Rightarrow$ 1 out of 5

c) 40% chance

$40\% = \frac{40}{100} = \frac{2}{5}$

$\Rightarrow$ 2 out of 5

d 80% chance

$80\% = \frac{80}{100} = \frac{4}{5}$

$\Rightarrow$ 4 out of 5

Shade any 3 out of 5 △'s

Shade any 1 out of 5 △'s

Shade any 2 out of 5 △'s

Shade any 4 out of 5 △'s

Q4. a) There is only 1 ace of spades, and there are 52 cards in the pack.

$\therefore$ Probability = 1 chance out of 52 = $\frac{1}{52}$

b) There are 4 different aces, and there are 52 cards in the pack.

$\therefore$ Probability = 4 chances out of 52 = $\frac{4}{52} = \frac{1}{13}$ (Simplified)

c) There are 13 diamond cards, and there are 52 cards in the pack.

$\therefore$ Probability = 13 chances out of 52 = $\frac{13}{52} = \frac{1}{4}$ (Simplified)

or There are 4 equal suits, and diamonds is one of the four suits.

$\therefore$ Probability = 1 chance out of 4 = $\frac{1}{4}$

d) There are 26 red cards (diamonds and hearts), and there are 52 cards in the pack.

∴ Probability = 26 chances out of 52 = $\frac{26}{52}$ = $\frac{1}{2}$ (Simplified)

<u>or</u> Half the pack are red cards, and half the pack are black cards.

∴ Probability = 1 chance in 2 = $\frac{1}{2}$

e) There are 20 honour cards, and there are 52 cards in the pack.

∴ Probability = 20 chances out of 52 = $\frac{20}{52}$ = $\frac{4}{13}$ (Simplified)

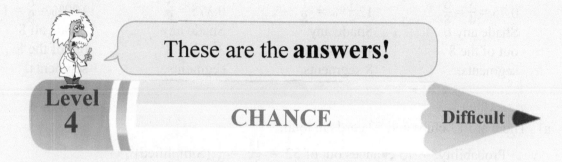

These are the **answers!**

Level 4   **CHANCE**   **Difficult**

Q1. blue = 5,   red = 10,   green = 1,   yellow = 4

a) chance of picking a yellow ball = $\frac{4}{20}$ = $\frac{20}{100}$ = 20%

b) chance of picking a blue ball = $\frac{5}{20}$ = $\frac{25}{100}$ = 25%

c) chance of picking a red ball = $\frac{10}{20}$ = $\frac{50}{100}$ = 50%

d) chance of picking a green ball = $\frac{1}{20}$ = $\frac{5}{100}$ = 5%

e) The red ball has an EVEN chance of being picked.

f) The green ball is MOST UNLIKELY to be picked.

Q2. There are 8 different spinners shown below. Using a pencil, shade each spinner grey to show the given outcome.

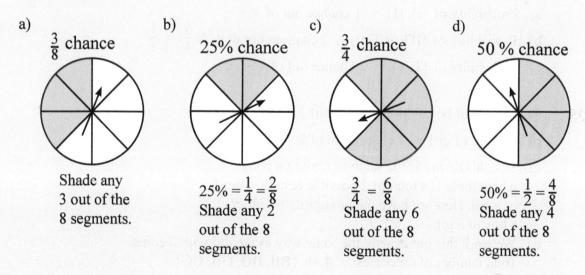

a)
$\frac{3}{8}$ chance

Shade any 3 out of the 8 segments.

b)
25% chance

25% = $\frac{1}{4}$ = $\frac{2}{8}$
Shade any 2 out of the 8 segments.

c)
$\frac{3}{4}$ chance

$\frac{3}{4}$ = $\frac{6}{8}$
Shade any 6 out of the 8 segments.

d)
50 % chance

50% = $\frac{1}{2}$ = $\frac{4}{8}$
Shade any 4 out of the 8 segments.

Essential Exercises – Year 5 Maths
Warwick Marlin © Five Senses Education

e)   0.75 chance   f) $12\frac{1}{2}$ % chance   g)   0.375 chance   h)   100% chance

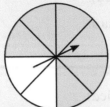 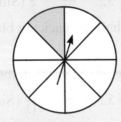 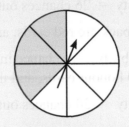 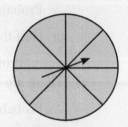

$0.75 = \frac{3}{4} = \frac{6}{8}$
Shade any 6
out of the 8
segments.

$12\frac{1}{2}\% = \frac{1}{8}$
Shade any
1 out of the
8 segments.

$0.375 = \frac{3}{8}$
Shade any
3 of the 8
segments.

$100\% = \frac{8}{8} = 1$
Shade all 8
out of the 8
segments.

Q3.   a)   There are 13 clubs and 52 cards in total.

∴   Probability = 13 chances out of 52 = $\frac{13}{52}$ = $\frac{1}{4}$ (Simplified)

b)   There is only one 7 of diamonds and 52 cards in total.

∴   Probability = 1 chance out of 52 = $\frac{1}{52}$

c)   There are four 7's and 52 cards in total.

∴   Probability = 4 chances out of 52 = $\frac{4}{52}$ = $\frac{1}{13}$ (Simplified)

d)   There are 26 black cards (clubs or spades) = 26 chances out of 52 = $\frac{26}{52}$ = $\frac{1}{2}$ (Simplified)

e)   There are 12 cards (2 or 3 or 4 from any suit) and 52 cards in total.

∴   Probability = 12 chances out of 52 = $\frac{12}{52}$ = $\frac{3}{13}$ (Simplified)

f)   There are 16 cards (A, K, Q, or J from any suit) and 52 cards in total.

∴   Probability = 16 chances out of 52 = $\frac{16}{52}$ = $\frac{4}{13}$ (Simplified)

Q4.   There is a total of 4 different outcome or possibilities.

a)   Probability of {H, H} = 1 chance out of 4 = $\frac{1}{4}$

b)   Probability of {HT or TH} = 2 chances out of 4 = $\frac{2}{4}$ = $\frac{1}{2}$

c)   Probability of {T, T} = 1 chance out of 4 = $\frac{1}{4}$

Q5.   a)   Chance of boy = 1 chance out of 2 = $\frac{1}{2}$

b)   Chance of girl = 1 chance out of 2 = $\frac{1}{2}$

c)   Yes, this theory is the same as tossing a coin,
where these is a total of 2 possible results, a head
or a tail. Here we have the possibility of either
a boy or a girl.

d)   We work this out exactly the same way as we did with 2 coins.
Total number of outcomes = 4 ⇒ {BB, BG, GB, GG}

Chance of {B, B} = 1 chance out of 4 = $\frac{1}{4}$

e) Chance of {BG or GB} = 2 chances out of 4 = $\frac{2}{4}$ = $\frac{1}{2}$

f) Chance of {G, G} = 1 chance out of 4 = $\frac{1}{4}$

g) Yes, this theory is identical to tossing 2 coins into the air.

h) We have worked out in f) that the chance of {G G} = $\frac{1}{4}$

Therefore we would expect {G G} to turn up about $\frac{1}{4}$ of the times.

One quarter out of 1000 families = $\frac{1}{4}$ × 1000 = 250 times.

Out of 1000 families, we would expect about 250 of them to have 2 daughters.

Q6. These is a total of 36 different outcomes when we toss 2 dice.

a) The total of 4 comes up 3 times ⟹ , ,

b) The total of 12 comes up 1 time ⟹

c) There are 6 different ways of throwing a total of 7.

∴ Chance of throwing a total of 7 = 6 chances out of 36 = $\frac{6}{36}$ = $\frac{1}{6}$

In 36 throws, we would expect a 7 to occur $\frac{1}{6}$ of the time.

$\frac{1}{6}$ × 36 = 6 times

d) There are 4 different ways of throwing a total of 5.

∴ Chance of throwing a total of 5 = 4 chances out of 36 = $\frac{4}{36}$ = $\frac{1}{9}$

In 36 throws, we would expect a 5 to occur $\frac{1}{9}$ of the time.

$\frac{1}{9}$ × 36 = 4 times

e) The total of 7 has the highest chance of happening.

f) The total of 2 and 12 have the least chance of happening. The reason is that there is only 1 way to get 2 and 1 way to get 12.

Essential Exercises – Year 5 Maths
Warwick Marlin © Five Senses Education

These are the **answers!**

Q1. a) The data is CATEGORICAL.

b)

Bicycle	

$2 \times 30 = 60$ students travel by bicycle.

c) Number of students who walk $= 5 \times 30 = 150$ students.
   Number of students coming by car $= 4 \times 30 = 120$ students.
   $\therefore$ 30 more students walk rather than come by car.

d) Half a face $= 15$ students
   $\therefore$ Students who catch the bus $= 30 + 15 = 45$ students.

e) $15\frac{1}{2}$ faces $= 15\frac{1}{2} \times 30 = 465$ students were involved in the survey.

Q2. a) 4 students went to bed at 11 p.m.
b) 7 students went to bed at 9:30 p.m.
c) The most popular bed time was 10 p.m.
d) $8 + 4 + 3 = 15$ students went to bed after 10 p.m.
e) $7 + 12 + 8 + 4 + 3 = 34$ students were involved in the survey.
f) The information was collected by SURVEY.

Q3. a) The data is NUMERICAL because it involves marks out of 10.
b) A mark of 8 (out of 10) was obtained by most students.
c) $1 + 3 + 2 + 3 + 7 + 4 + 2 = 22$ students sat for the test.
d) $3 + 7 + 4 + 2 = 16$ students passed the spelling test.
e) Average $= \dfrac{\text{total marks}}{\text{total of students}} = \dfrac{164}{22} = 7.45$

$\therefore$ Class Average $= 7.5$ (correct to 1 d.p.)

Note:

total marks $= 1 \times 4 + 3 \times 5 + 2 \times 6 + 3 \times 7$
$+ 7 \times 8 + 4 \times 9 + 2 \times 10$
$= 164$

Score mark	Tally	Total
4	I	1
5	III	3
6	II	2
7	III	3
8	HHH II	7
9	IIII	4
10	II	2

Q4. a)

Favourite Pet	Tally	Total
Dog	~~HHH~~ ~~HHH~~	10
Cat	~~HHH~~ III	8
Fish	II	2
Bird	~~HHH~~ I	6
Hamster	IIII	4

b)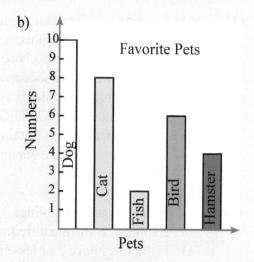

c) The data is categorical, because it involves categories (and not numbers).

d) The third most popular pet was the bird.

e) 6 more students preferred dogs to hamsters.

Q5. a) 25 books were sold on Friday.

b) The second highest number of books were sold on Tuesday.

c) 50 books were sold on Saturday, and 35 books were sold on Thursday.
∴ 15 more books were sold on the Saturday.

d) The most books were sold on Saturday, because it is the weekend, and many people do not go to work and therefore have more time to browse around bookshops.

e) Average books sold each day $= \dfrac{\text{total number of books}}{\text{total number of days}} = \dfrac{20 + 40 + 30 + 35 + 25 + 50}{6}$

∴ Average $= \dfrac{200}{6} = 33.3$ or rounded down $= 33$ books per day

f) The data is numerical because it involves numbers, and we can find the average number of books sold each day.

These are the **answers!**

Level **2** DATA REPRESENTATION AND INTERPRETATION Average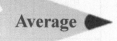

Q1. a) 5 cupcake pictures represents 60 muffins.
∴ 1 cupcake picture represents $60 \div 5 = 12$ muffins.

b) 1 cupcake picture represents 12 items of food.
∴ 6 cupcake picture represents 72 cakes.

c) 1 cupcake picture represents 12 items of food.
∴ $2\frac{1}{2}$ cupcake picture represents $2\frac{1}{2} \times 12 = 30$ loaves of bread.

d) Number of pies sold $= 7\frac{1}{2} \times 12 = 90$
Number of cakes sold $= 6 \times 12 = 72$
∴ 18 more pies were sold than cakes.

e) Answers may vary, but we think he should NOT continue making pizzas, because he doesn't seem to sell many of them. Pizzas are not very popular in the bakery.

Essential Exercises – Year 5 Maths
Warwick Marlin © Five Senses Education

Q2. a) Bowling was the least popular sport.

b) 90 students chose tennis, and 60 students chose basketball.

∴ 30 more students chose tennis rather than basketball.

c) 145 students chose soccer.

d) Total number of students = 30 + 60 + 70 + 90 + 145 = 395

e) The information is CATEGORICAL, because the sports represent different categories.

f) The information was obtained by "SURVEY".

g) No, it is not accurate enough. In this graph we can only show accuracy to the nearest 5 students.

Q3. a) 5 families have 3 siblings.

b) 2 siblings is the most frequent number in each family.

c) 17 families have 2 or less siblings.

d) 29 students were involve in the survey.

e) NO families have 8 siblings.

f) 7 families have 4 or more siblings.

g) The data is NUMERICAL because it involves numbers.

Q4. a) The temperature at 8 p.m. was 14^0C.

b) Difficult to tell exactly, but approximately at 10 a.m.

c) The lowest temperature was 6^0C, and it occurred at 4 a.m.

d) 12 p.m. = 25^0C and 4 p.m. = 16^0C ⟹ the temperature fell 9^0C.

e) The temperature range is the difference between the highest temperature and the lowest temperature.

∴ Temperature range = 25^0C – 6^0C = 19^0C

f) The temperature difference is = 25^0C – 12^0C = 13^0C

Q5. a)

COLOUR	TALLY	FREQUENCY
Blue	卌 卌 I	11
Red	卌 III	8
Black	卌 II	7
White	卌 卌 卌	15
Gold	卌 IIII	9
Green	III	3

b)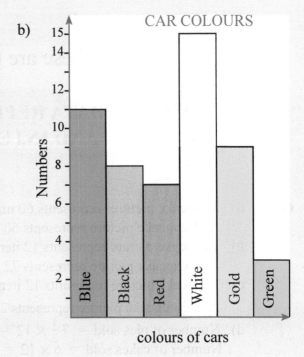

b) Total number of cars
= 11 + 8 + 7 + 15 + 9 + 3
= 53

c) Blue cars = 11 and green cars = 3

∴ 8 more blue cars went past her.

d) White is a good reflector of heat, and in a hot country like Australia (where the sun shines a lot), this is an important factor.

These are the **answers!**

PROBLEM SOLVING

Q1. a)

Year	New houses
2007	🏠🏠🏠🏠🏠🏠
2008	🏠🏠🏠🏠🏠
2009	🏠🏠🏠🏠
2010	🏠🏠🏠
2011	🏠🏠

🏠 represents 4 000 new houses

b) 2 000 new houses are shown by HALF a house ⟹ 🏠

c) We would have to somehow draw $1\frac{1}{4}$ houses. To draw $\frac{1}{4}$ of a house would be too difficult.

d) The number of new houses are getting less and less each year, from 2007 until 2011.

e) Maybe more people are out of work, and therefore they cannot afford a new house.

f) This question is linked to e). Yes, the world wide recession in 2008 would have definitely contributed to the decline in new houses. People have less money, more people are out of work, and people are less confident of the economy.

Q2. a)

Result	Tally	Total
Head, Head (HH)	卌 IIII	9
Tail, Tail (TT)	卌 卌	10
Head or Tail (HT)	卌 卌 卌 卌 I	21

c) Jenny tossed the 2 coins 40 times.

d) A head and tail combination occured 21 times.

e) There is only one way of getting a head, head or a tail tail.
But there are 2 ways of getting a head or tail combination.
We can get a head on the first coin, and a tail on the second coin, or we get a tail on the first coin and head on the second coin. So there are twice as many chances for the coin to show a head or tail result.

b)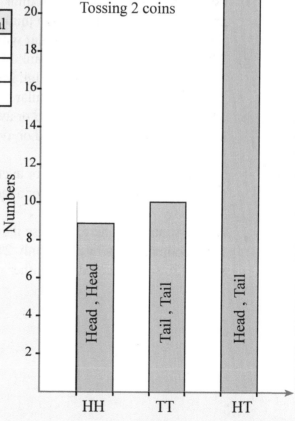

Essential Exercises – Year 5 Maths
Warwick Marlin © Five Senses Education

Q3. a)

Fruit	Tally	Total
banana	IIII	5
orange	IIIII	6
mango	IIIII IIIII	10
peach	IIIII II	7
apple	II	2

b)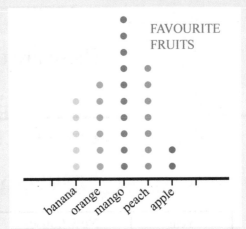

FAVOURITE FRUITS

banana orange mango peach apple

c) The data is CATEGORICAL.

d) It is not mango or peach season, so these 2 fruits will be very expensive and difficult to find. They will probably decide to stock oranges, because this is the third most popular fruit.

e) 30 students were involved in the survey.

f) The data was collected by "SURVEY".

Q4. a) 31 women thought that Mr. Goodman was average.

b) 28 men thought that Mr. Trusting was poor.

c) 28 women compared to 18 women.

∴ 10 more women thought that Mr. Trusting was excellent compared to Mr. Goodman.

d) 18% of men and 26% of women are still unsure of Mr. Goodman.

∴ A total of 44% of women and men are still unsure of him.

e) 10% of men and 6% of women are still unsure of Mr. Trusting.

∴ A total of 16% of women and men are still unsure of him.

f) 18% + 16% = 34% of women think Mr. Goodman is either good or excellent.

28% + 19% = 47% of women think Mr. Trusting is either good or excellent.

∴ Mr. Trusting is more popular with women votes by a margin of 13%.

g) 23% + 27% = 50% of men think Mr. Goodman is either good or excellent.

13% + 16% = 29% of men think Mr. Trusting is either good or excellent.

∴ Mr. Goodman is more popular with men voters by a margin of 21%.

h) Mr. Goodman : excellent, good or average → men = 23% + 27% + 22% = 72% } 137
   Mr. Goodman : excellent, good or average → women = 18% + 16% + 31% = 65% }

   Mr. Trusting : excellent, good or average → men = 13% + 16% + 33% = 49% } 135
   Mr. Trusting : excellent, good or average → women = 28% + 19% + 39% = 86% }

Answers may vary here, because the votes at this stage are very, very close.
Mr. Goodman leads by about only 2%, but there are many unsure women
voters (26%) who could vote either way on election day.

These are the **answers!**

Q1. a) | Wed | [books pictograph] | $3\frac{1}{2}$ pictures represents 14 books.

∴ 1 picture represents 4 books.

b) The least number of books were borrowed on Monday ⟹ 8 books.

c) Total number of books borrowed = 8 + 16 + 14 + 12 + 22
= 72

d) More books would be borrowed on Friday, because the weekend gives the students more time to read and complete school projects.

Q2.

Day	Tally of books borrowed	Total
Mon	ℍℍ ⦀⦀	8
Tue	ℍℍ ℍℍ ℍℍ ⦀	16
Wed	ℍℍ ℍℍ ⦀⦀⦀⦀	14
Thur	ℍℍ ℍℍ ⦀⦀	12
Fri	ℍℍ ℍℍ ℍℍ ℍℍ ⦀⦀	22

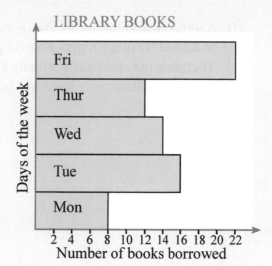

LIBRARY BOOKS

Days of the week

Number of books borrowed

Q3. a) Her temperature at the start is 38.8°C.

b) It is 1.8°C higher than normal body temperature.

c) Her highest temperature is 40.2°C.

d) Her temperature remained steady between 4 a.m. and 8 a.m.

e) After 8 a.m. she began to dramatically improve, because her temperature started dropping down towards normal.

f) Her temperature was 38.4°C at approximately 10 a.m.

g) At 8 a.m. her temperature was 39.6°C.
At 12 p.m. her temperature was 37.6°C.
Therefore, her temperature dropped 2°C.

Q4. a)

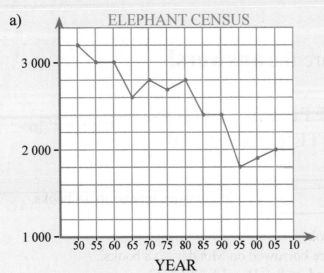

ELEPHANT CENSUS

YEAR

b) In 1993, there were approximately 2 000 elephants in the park.

c) The overall picture shows that the elephant population is declining or becoming smaller between 1950 and 1995.

d) From the graph, it looks like the advertising campaign started in 1995, because the elephant population started increasing again after that year.

e) There is simply not enough forest and food for the elephants.
They are competing with the rapidly increasing African population for food, and it is sadly obvious who is going win the battle with guns and rifles and other deadly weapons.

f) Another reason for the decline of the elephants and rhinoceroses is that their tusks and horns are highly prized by certain Eastern nations in the world.
Therefore they are usually cruelly killed simply because money can be earned for the value of their ivory tusks and horns.

ABOUT THE AUTHOR

Warwick went to St Bees school in the North of England where he completed 'A' levels in Maths, Physics and Chemistry. He obtained his Bachelor of Science (B.Sc.) at the University of Natal (South Africa) in 1970, majoring in Pure Maths and Physics.

He completed his Diploma in Education (Dip.Ed.) at Christchurch (NZ). He has had over 30 years of teaching experience mainly in Australia, but also in South Africa and New Zealand.

He was the Author, Editor and Publisher of all the books in the original Understanding Maths Series, which were first published in 1988.

In 1986 he was also the Founder and Senior Director of Australian Youth Challenge – a program designed to help teenagers in the key areas of self esteem, motivation, goal setting, communication and study skills.

He was the Coordinator and Principal for the July Holiday Maths courses which ran successfully for 15 years at St Andrews Cathedral School in Sydney.

In the latest series of *Understanding Maths*, he is the author of the Year 5, 6, 7, 8, 9 and 10 books. He is also the author of all 8 books in the *Important Facts and Formulas* series.

He is the co-author of the 6 elementary books in the '*Essential Exercises Series*'.

He is the editor of the 6 books in the '*Understanding Comprehension Series*'.

In 2010, he moved and relocated to the Philippines full time, and he transferred the publishing and distribution of his books in Australia to *Five Senses Education Pty. Ltd.* He is still very active in writing and updating books on behalf of *Five Senses Education*.

During the last two years he has developed and written new ADVANCED versions of the 'Understanding Maths Series' (for books Year 3, 4, 5 and 6). Compared to the standard versions, these new books contain:

i) additional exercises
ii) more challenging exercises
iii) extra 'problem solving' or 'word problem' exercises

> These 4 new ADVANCED books are aimed primarily at the more capable and gifted students.

'*The best teacher is not the one who knows the most, but the one who is most capable of reducing knowledge to that simple compound of the obvious and wonderful...*'

H.L. Menken

Essential Exercises – Year 5 Maths
Warwick Marlin © Five Senses Education